W9-BEN-594

How to Make Your Advertising TWICE as Effective at HALF the Cost

Also by Herschell Gordon Lewis:

Direct Mail Copy that Sells

How to Handle Your Own Public Relations

The Businessman's Guide to Advertising and Sales Promotion

More Than You Ever Wanted to Know About Mail Order Advertising

(as coauthor)
Symbol of America: Norman Rockwell

How to Make Your Advertising TWICE as Effective at HALF the Cost

Herschell Gordon Lewis

Prentice-Hall, Inc.
Englewood Cliffs, New Jersey

Prentice-Hall International, Inc., *London*
Prentice-Hall of Australia, Pty. Ltd., *Sydney*
Prentice-Hall Canada Inc., *Toronto*
Prentice-Hall of India Private Ltd., *New Delhi*
Prentice-Hall of Japan, Inc., *Tokyo*
Prentice-Hall of Southeast Asia Pte. Ltd., *Singapore*
Whitehall Books, Ltd., *Wellington, New Zealand*
Editora Prentice-Hall do Brasil, Ltda., *Rio de Janeiro*
Prentice-Hall Hispanoamericana, S. A., *Mexico*

© 1986 by
Prentice-Hall, Inc.
Englewood Cliffs, N.J.

*All rights reserved. No part of this
book may be reproduced in any form or
by any means, without permission in
writing from the publisher.*

Library of Congress Cataloging in Publication Data

Lewis, Herschell Gordon
  How to make your advertising twice as effective
at half the cost

  Originally published: Chicago : Nelson-Hall, c1979.
  Includes index.
  1. Advertising.   2. Advertising—Costs.   I. Title.
HF5823.L53   1986   659.1′068′1   85-9573

ISBN 0-13-417882-3

ISBN 0-13-417874-2 (PBK)

Printed in the United States of America

Preface

Is it really possible to make your advertising twice as effective at half the cost?

I think it is.

It's possible because so much advertising is the complacent employment of stale ideas. It's possible because so much advertising is an extension of the ego of the person paying for it. It's possible because the giant advertisers have trained us to expect and accept costly failures.

You bought this book because you *don't* expect or accept costly failures.

As you'll quickly see, the magic formula for making your advertising more effective, and saving money as you do it, has two components:

1. Always put yourself in the position of the person *receiving* your message. Designing ads that show off your personal brilliance is the kind of expensive luxury we'd expect from people who don't care about the principles this book describes.
2. Aim every advertising message at the most people who can and will buy what you have to sell. Don't waste money on those who aren't part of that group.

If you're looking for another typical book on advertising—a salty reminiscence of the great old days, with lots of name-droppings and in-talk—this isn't it. If you're looking for a typical marketing textbook, full of descriptions of famous advertising campaigns by corporate giants whose decisions are made in committee (there's safety for the individual in that) and whose quarterly budget is ten times your lifetime budget, this isn't it. If you're looking for a doctoral thesis tracing the history of advertising, this isn't it.

As curmudgeon-in-residence within the world of advertising, I've come to the ultimate conclusion that those who make a mystery out of what we do are too insecure for you to hire.

The principles of advertising *can* be codified into a set of easy-to-apply rules, and the old-time "We always did it this way" approach, glorifying seat-of-the-pants decisions, not only doesn't make sense now; it didn't make sense then, but we were in too primitive an analytical position to know it.

This book is a "how-to" manual, peppered with rules. Like you, I know the danger of following rules slavishly: You can build a static pattern in which creativity slowly disappears, something like the brightness of a kitchen floor disappearing under a daily coating of wax.

I suggest you make a regular practice of removing some of the old wax before adding new wax. Staleness is the cellmate of complacency, as advertising instructors whose lectures are based on last year's notes should know.

The purpose of this book isn't to entertain you. I assume you want to know how to get the most action out of a Yellow Pages ad, or how to produce a television commercial without going broke, or how to make your advertising as risk-free as possible.

To insure success, I ask two favors, please:

1. Read the Three Laws in Chapter 1 at least twice.
2. Throw out or donate to a museum any books on advertising procedure printed before 1980.

Undoubtedly, in writing this Advertising Survival Kit for the waning years of the 20th century, my own prejudices have seeped through the keys of the word processor. I defend this seepage justifiably: Prejudices are themselves nurtured by experience. I'm prejudiced against any advertising that wastes money and doesn't communicate, and if you share that prejudice I'll be waiting for you at the summit of Mount Olympus.

Acknowledgments

I'm grateful to the pleasantly literate folks at Prentice-Hall, Inc., especially Mr. Ron Ledwith, Ms. Evan Holstrom, and Ms. Bette Schwartzberg, for their encouragement, unflagging good nature, and their professionalism.

My thanks to Bob Bly for permission to reprint his article, "Ten Ways to Stretch Your Advertising Budget," which appears as Appendix 4.

Principal credit for the book's appearing at all goes to my wife and business partner Margo, without whose wisdom and help the original manuscript might still be lying unfinished on my desk.

Contents

Chapter 4: How to Deal with Suppliers 32

Chapter 5: How to Make Selling by Mail Pay 46

Chapter 6: Caution: TV Advertising Can Be Hazardous to Your Wealth 68

Chapter 7: Radio: Sometimes Your Best Buy 88

Chapter 12: How to Write Advertising Copy that Sells   149

Chapter 13: A Look toward the Future   184

Chapter 14: Problem-Solving: Try It for Yourself   200

Chapter 15: Examples of Good and Bad Advertising   213

1

The Premise

Most of the "how-to" aspects of this book are based on Lewis's Three Laws of Mass Communications. Depending on the sophistication of your own background, you might regard one or another of these laws as a truism or you might think it simplistic. I doubt that anyone would disagree with them.

Several "sublaws" also exist, but they pertain only to one facet of mass communications, such as direct response or television. These three laws pertain to every ad you create, for any medium.

Anyone who is serious about communicating with prospective buyers would do well to memorize these three laws in order to check every ad produced against them.

LEWIS'S FIRST LAW OF MASS COMMUNICATIONS

Effective advertising is that which reaches, at the lowest possible cost, the most people who can and will buy what you have to sell.

Note the restrictions. You don't succeed merely by reaching "the most people." It's a more complex marketing mix than that. You must reach the most people *who can and will buy what you have to sell.* You must go for class, not mass; selectivity, not scattershot.

You must reach the audience or readership at the lowest possible cost. Sure, there are all kinds of other ways, and the easiest is to lapse into a technique that adds expense by diluting the mix—that is, to spend more to reach them by paying for wastage, which means you've bought advertising that reaches too high a percentage of nonbuyers along with any legitimate prospects.

While logical and thoughtful media buying is very much a part of this law, the key lies in the word "reach." You can't just find these potential buyers and then leave them untouched. You have to nail your message into their skulls. Reaching your buyers is what at least half this book is about.

LEWIS'S SECOND LAW OF MASS COMMUNICATIONS

In this Age of Skepticism, cleverness for the sake of cleverness may well be a liability rather than an asset.

This is the law that offends novices. Tyros who haven't had the experience of running a clever ad that results in phone calls from friends telling them how clever they are, but no business from buyers, may still feel that cleverness can be equated with good salesmanship. Don't you believe it. A good salesman is clever enough to make the *buyer* feel clever.

On the other hand, don't withdraw into a sullen statement of facts at the expense of a sense of humor. This law refers to cleverness for the sake of cleverness, not cleverness for the sake of salesmanship. If cleverness relates to a product, enhances it, glorifies its image, or forces the reader, listener, or viewer to remember it fondly, then cleverness works.

What is the "Age of Skepticism"? Chapter 3 discusses this evolution of the 1980s in detail. Don't ask someone who wrote ads in the 1960s: He never heard of it.

LEWIS'S THIRD LAW OF MASS COMMUNICATIONS

$$E^2 = 0$$

Huh?

It's a simpler equation than you might think. It means that when you emphasize everything, you emphasize nothing.

Perhaps you know someone who shouts every word. You

never can tell what is important. But what if he whispered, whispered, whispered, and then, wham! A shouted word. The emphasis would be clear.

Many ads are written on a flat plane. The advertiser has a lot to say, so the ad says everything in the same type size, speaks all the words with the same emphasis in a radio spot, shows each scene with equal emphasis in a television commercial, or displays every line with equal position in a business letter or circular. That advertiser either believes everything is equally important or is afraid to miss your "hot-button" by leaving anything out. What happens is that the ad fails to motivate you because it hasn't connected with you. The message is there, but it's watery and thinned below the impact level.

A Fourth Law applies mainly to mail order advertising, but in the Age of Skepticism it's worth mentioning because so much advertising doesn't bother to motivate us!

Tell the reader what to do.

With the amount of waste in advertising, this extra Law isn't a bad idea for *all* media.

If you read no further, you have Lewis's Laws of Mass Communications—but if you want to know how to turn them into dynamic, force-communicating ads, it might be a good idea to read on.

2

The Tempo of the Times

If there is any correlation between the raw expenditure of advertising dollars and results, I'm unaware of it. In today's brutal, competitive atmosphere, the gloves are off and some complacent, king-of-the-hill advertisers have been knocked off their perches by irreverent newcomers too naive to realize that they "just couldn't do that."

I know, as I hope you do, that while brains are a wonderful and powerful substitute for dollars, dollars are a weak and ineffective substitute for brains.

An old, creaky theory of advertising was called "Watsonian behaviorism" after the psychologist John Watson, who espoused the concept in the 1930s. Stripped of its pedagogical jargon, Watsonian behaviorism comes down to this:

> A human being's mind is a blank slate at birth. Whoever uses the most chalk to write on this slate makes the most impressions.

To advertisers this concept would mean that whoever spent the most money to reach the buyer should get the most sales. A dangerous theory! It's like the old New York Yankees, who bought every big hitter and thereby dominated the American League for years. The implication is that whoever spends the most money becomes the most powerful, at the expense of the little advertiser; he has more chalk, writes more lines, and makes more impressions.

What's lacking in this theory, which is still espoused by those who think in terms of dollars, not brains, is one key word: *impact*.

For example, consider a big ballroom lit by a thousand

light bulbs. These light bulbs provide ample illumination for six hours, and then, pow! Someone shoots off a strobe light while taking a photograph. The interval of that strobe is substantially less than $\frac{1}{50}$ of a second, yet every head in the room turns to find its source. One bulb, for $\frac{1}{50}$ second, versus 1,000 bulbs for six hours. Hardly a fair fight, is it?

No, it isn't. That single bulb had impact, just as one blinking light in a row of unblinking ones has impact, and just as the lead dancer's red suit stands out from the white suits of the chorus. A spotlight focuses attention in the midst of sameness, and if you don't believe that, don't worry: You'll see enough examples in this book to convince you . . . I hope.

How the Giants Stumble

In mid-1977 Kentucky Fried Chicken decided to replace its advertising agency, Leo Burnett. Burnett had held the account for nine years, doing a pretty good job, according to both agency and client. About $16 million a year in advertising dollars was involved.

Even within the advertising profession, at the time of the severance, if the average knowledgeable person were asked what KFC's advertising campaign was, he would reply, "Finger-lickin' good."

He would be wrong. More than two years earlier, tonguing the grease off the fingers was abandoned for a no-impact campaign called, "Hey, it's a Kentucky Fried Chicken Day." Six months later this was replaced by another bunch of words masquerading as a campaign: "Real Goodness." This slogan ran for two years, as sales steadily declined. Just before the ax fell, another campaign was started: "America's Country Good Meal." (At this writing, the campaign is "America loves what the Colonel Cooks.")

The first campaign was hardly more memorable or unique than any of the others; rather, the problem was that it was abandoned without any real reason.

Ad pros will tell you that a campaign grows old. It no longer has any impact. To some extent this is true; it's far more true of novelty campaigns than of straightforward factual advertising. But if you're going to replace an idea, replace it with something at least as powerful; and if the previous campaign worked, tie the new one into the old one. Otherwise you're in the position of a radio station that suddenly switches from classical music to hard rock, a theater that switches from Disney to X-rated films, a manufacturer of luxury cars that suddenly brings out a subcompact as its only model. You abandon your old customers without developing new ones, dangerous unless you have the money to ride your actions out. Here, perhaps, is where behaviorism might help, because this part of Watson's approach does hold up: You *can* buy awareness, even if you can't buy brand loyalty.

Ultimately, the sale of any product or service depends on consumer acceptance. Brands aren't out-advertised into oblivion. They just don't keep pace as products, and when a product is obsolete or ineffective, advertising ultimately must fail. Dr. West's Tooth Powder, Sal Hepatica, Ipana—where are the joys of yesteryear? Peak wasn't on the shelves when these products were in their heyday. Tide didn't out-advertise Rinso; it was simply a better product. Tylenol did indeed advertise itself into the number one position in analgesics, but it did so by claiming a benefit—no stomach bleeding—that Bayer and Anacin could not match. Now the ibuprofen products such as Advil are eating into the marketplace.

In Chapters 3 and 12 we talk about persuasive techniques, but even before you read that far, consider the advantage of attacking another advertiser bigger than you are. If you're successful and attack him factually, based on his weaknesses, before long you may find you've switched roles; defensively, he'll have to attack you back.

That's exactly what Bayer did. In addition to big-space ads headed "Makers of Tylenol: Shame on you!" Bayer brought out its own nonaspirin pain reliever to compete in the new market it never made.

The embattled sugar industry, stung by inroads made by aspartame ("NutraSweet"), the low-calorie sweetener made by G. D. Searle & Co., let loose a counterattack in late 1984.

First, the Sugar Association (look in the Washington, D.C.

phone book and you'll see an association for just about everything) asked the Federal Trade Commission to declare NutraSweet advertising "deceptive" because, according to the Association, NutraSweet isn't "low-calorie" but rather a "high-intensity sweetener."

Next, the Association planned an advertising campaign touting the good things about sugar.

(Meanwhile, the NutraSweet snowball gathered momentum as soft drink bottlers and food processors, switching from saccharine to aspartame, spent about $250 million in 1984 on advertising and sales promotion.)

How to Drown in Bureaucracy

A lot of advertisers are blissfully unaware of the regulations that can strangle their marketing programs. Some advertisers offer "deals" and special advertising allowances to various customers, not knowing that the Robinson-Patman Act forbids such unequal treatment among retailers who buy from them. Some advertisers claim their product is "the best," not knowing that a mailing addressed to the wrong name on a list—a name representing a Federal Trade Commission decoy—could bring agents demanding proof, with penalties if they're unable to prove their claim. Many advertisers never heard of the Moss-Magnusson Bill, which enables the Federal Trade Commission to haul them into court without prior hearings, and which binds all competitors to a consent order signed by any of them, thereby making all guilty if one admits guilt.

They do know that sometimes a newspaper will reject, censor, or change an ad arbitrarily, that the Better Business Bureau actually has the power to keep their ads out of the newspapers and off the air, and that the local consumer fraud unit is gunning for them the minute they make any claim of superiority.

If you use the mails, a host of other policemen are lying in the bushes, waiting to shovel penalties all over you (see Chapter 5).

Oddly, no one regulates any sign a person may hang in a

window. The same outrageous claims the media reject from advertisers are okay on your own premises; you haven't used the public airways, the mails, or the newspapers. But don't try fake claims on the phone, because wire fraud statutes cover those too.

These laws aren't all bad. Consumers need protection against phony claims. The questions is: Who decides which claims are phony? And who protects the advertiser against unjust demands by bureaucrats?

But does this mean advertisers can't sell merchandise? Does it mean they can't persuade someone to use their services? Not at all. All advertisers are bound by the same restrictions, although inevitably there is a competitor who uses unethical methods. What it all means is that every advertiser should become a student of the bureaucratic waters, so he'll know where he can swim and where the current is just too strong to survive.

The Value of Knowing Your Competition

What advertising costs—or should cost—is an area of mystery to many, including a lot of people who are charged with the responsibility for how much money will be spent. Inevitably, every advertising consultant or manager is asked, "How much do you suggest we spend?" Then, having committed himself, he's hit with the next question, "What do we get for our money?"

The answers to both questions are 50 percent guesswork and 50 percent education. The marketplace is fluid and constantly changing. Competition is a factor one must (but doesn't always) consider when figuring how to operate in the competitive marketplace. Elements beyond anyone's control also affect public buying patterns. This is all part of the technology that causes product obsolescence even as a product is so carefully being engineered, packaged, and brought to market.

In 1776 the combined advertising budget for every company doing business in what is now called the United States was around $200,000. Practically all of it was spent in newspapers. Since there was no mail service, there was no direct mail budget. There were no trade papers and no electronic media, so no monies were set aside for these.

In 1800 all the companies doing business in this country spent altogether $1 million in advertising, once again almost entirely in newspapers and primarily in announcement-of-product ads. The term "advertising" doesn't really apply to the staid notices of those early days. Announcing dynamically and with a sense of salesmanship what you had for sale was considered undignified.

By 1900, perhaps the turnaround year for advertising, the total amount of money spent was $450 million. The population was about 80 million then; there was substantial industry and public transportation—and a dollar bought far more then than it does now. Annual increases became pronounced, starting with that year. For example, $750 million was spent on advertising by 1904.

With the exception of the years between 1929 and 1936, Americans began an inflationary spiral. Today inflation is a major budgeting factor. An advertiser may announce with great pride that he has increased his advertising budget by 20 percent only to realize that he has barely kept pace with inflation; his $1.2 million projected budget may not even buy him the same exposure next year that his $1 million did this year. He isn't becoming more dominant in the market unless every competitor is reducing his budget, thereby granting him dominance by default. The whole idea in aggressive mass communications is not to win the race by default, but to cause the competition to fail. That's why comparative advertising, naming and defeating competitors, is so effective.

The first billion dollar year was 1909. In 1909 advertising became big business. By 1950 it was over a $5.75 billion business; by 1960, $11.9 billion. By 1976, total U.S. advertising hit $32.4 billion. By 1980, $45 billion. By 1985, $96 billion. The forecast for 1990: $150 billion.

Who the competition is and how competitors advertise are key factors in the advertising budget decision-making process. In many cases, when a company is determining what to spend for advertising, that determination is based solely on what the competition is doing. This policy isn't altogether bad, but it's hardly an aggressive marketing philosophy. It amounts to a chess game in which you checkmate your opponent one move after he checkmates you, because you're making the same moves he makes. Sooner or later, you'll almost win that game, but you'll be one move shy because he'll checkmate you, and you won't be able to make that last move. Hardly a business exists in which an advertiser doesn't say of a competitor, "Hey, look at their ad and look at ours. Look how much better theirs is than ours."

Some advertisers have embraced each other's advertising approach, switching within the same week and forgetting a tenet of advertising codified way back in 1963 by the sagacious advertising guru David Ogilvy:

What you say is more important than how you say it.°

Changing distribution techniques, on the other hand, can give dominance in a different ball game. You might say: "My competition distributes by conventional retail outlets. So I'll distribute by direct selling, or by mail order, because there's no competition in that area." The change in distribution technique dictates a change in advertising.

This move is a conscious and aggressive marketing decision. Some companies, especially in fashion, shoes, cosmetics, and kitchenware, have built huge empires and have even become dominant in their fields by varying the means of distribution. Avon, for example, has proved that a direct seller can market its wares with strength against a conventional retail market. In an extraordinarily competitive field—beauty aids—Avon positions itself by using one of the oldest forms of marketing, direct selling, door-to-door.

This is what direct selling is: I sell to you—one man to one man, or one woman to one woman. Avon, along with Tupperware, has imposed legitimacy on the lagging arena of direct selling, which was pushed out as a means of major distribution by many companies when shopping centers became prominent in the late 1940s.

°Ogilvy, *Confessions of an Advertising Man,* Atheneum, 1963.

Competition can also unwittingly dictate approach. Witness the continuing battle between Tylenol and Datril or between these and conventional aspirin compounds. One makes a move, and the competition—the other one—makes a countermove. Whether the move has to do with price, content, what ailments are relieved, or the speed with which it churns up your stomach, moves are dictated largely by competition. Some companies pay bonuses to employees of competing companies who disclose forthcoming advertising plans. Why? Because they can plan for the onslaught and prepare their own campaign to neutralize it. Ads become a war game.

And in a war, whether you march boldly and openly into the field, as General Braddock did in the Revolutionary War, getting wiped out because that wasn't the way the competition was fighting—or you set off an atom bomb, infiltrate the enemy lines using guerrilla tactics, or employ a fifth column, advertisers justify their unscrupulous and vicious competition with the battle cry, "All's fair in love and war."

Does it work? In a competitive marketplace, you may have to follow the venerable philosophy of Vince Lombardi: "Winning isn't the most important thing; it's the only thing." You forget that you have any friends. You go out into the competitive arena and scratch and claw for your share of business. That could well be the road to success in the 1980s. Some say such actions are not gentlemanly. I submit that writing an ad or campaign that doesn't work is ungentlemanly.

At some point the gloves have to come off, and you become a practicing marketing expert rather than a theoretician. Anyone who reverts back to a limbo that doesn't exist is not going to sell merchandise competitively.

Is there a valid controverting philosophy? Bayer Aspirin traditionally gets top dollar for its product, which differs not at all from St. Joseph's at half the price, or Walgreen's bottle of 100 aspirin, which is perhaps $\frac{1}{8}$ to $\frac{1}{10}$ the price. This suggests a sometime rule of marketing imagery: A product is what it is, plus what the buyer thinks it is.

That rule is both a truism and a complicated facet of marketing. That a doctor in whom a patient has faith can give that person a sugar pill and cure a headache is not mere folklore; it really is so. We live in a psychosomatic age: You put on a dress with a Givenchy label in it, and you walk proudly. You put on a dress with a Three Sisters label in it, and you don't feel well dressed; you hope nobody asks to look at your label. "I hope I don't have an accident today. If they take me to the hospital they might take off my dress and see that label." A product is what it is, plus what the buyer thinks it is.

Just to complicate the marketing milieu a little more, you must also be conscious of shifts in public demand. Most of the current best-selling products in the supermarket weren't there five years ago. Coca-Cola, even with its olympian position in the marketplace, is now heavily into sugar-free beverages. In mid-1985, the company changed its venerable formulation. The "new" Coke was sweeter, more "Pepsi-like." Within months, Coca-Cola restored its original formulation as "Classic Coke." Currently, Americans are a thin-oriented society, so each year sugar-free drinks increase their share of the market-place, and brand loyalty is an erratic way to project next year's sales during the Age of Skepticism.

For years sugar-free beverages all used saccharine as a sweetener. One switched to aspartame (NutraSweet) and advertised it; quickly, all the rest made the same switch.

In almost any field, as technology and public tastes change, products that refuse to change are left behind. How many people have bought a box of Rinso in the last five years? None, because it's not on the market anymore; you can't buy it. Yet only a few years ago, the main Rinso plant was going day and night, turning out soap powder. But soap powder isn't as effective as detergent, and the buyers have learned this. If the producers of Rinso fight public demand, they deserve their lot. This is why top companies more and more frequently underwrite research and development programs to keep them a step ahead of the competition.

A product is what it is plus what the buyer/user thinks it is. That's why Prestone Antifreeze far outsells an almost iden-tical product priced lower and referred to in Prestone's own advertising as "Brand X." Both products are basically ethylene glycol. But Prestone says, "You can trust us." Implication: You cannot trust the unknown brand. And many a buyer, unaware that he parrots the party line—and perhaps quick to say that he doesn't respond to advertising pitches—says, "The reason I use Prestone is I trust them."

With Prestone in his car, he doesn't have to stop every Monday at the gas station and say "Hey check my antifreeze." Prestone has managed to imply that with Brand X, he might.

The very words "IBM-compatible" suggest that a computer takes a secondary position to IBM. In second position, the only advantage one can offer is a lower price.

The Power of Guilt

In this country whenever people don't buy something advertisers think they should, guilt feelings are bought to the fore. Guilt is the major weapon some marketers have against the Age of Skepticism. We have only four great motivators today: Guilt and greed are the most logical for most marketers. Fear also sometimes works, but it can turn on an advertiser like a tiger, and a real marketing pro is needed to use fear successfully as a motivator. (The fourth motivator: exclusivity.)

Sometimes one buys a label. A man's suit with a Bill Blass label in it or a woman's scarf with the name Hermès written on it, for example, costs more because a buyer pays for the use of that name. There may be no difference between that scarf and another at Montgomery Ward, for half the price, but the element of status causes the product to become what it is, plus what the buyer thinks it is.

How To Be Your Own Competitor

In thinking competitively, consider the premise of self-competition: If competition doesn't exist, you can create competition internally and artificially, a discount sale is one such means of self-competition. You say, "Here's what this regularly costs, and this is what we're selling it for now." You've gone into competition with yourself.

What you cannot claim, if untrue, is superiority over

external competition. "Others are selling this for x dollars." Untrue? Then you may not say it. But you still can succeed in the competitive marketplace by saying: "This is what X is supposed to sell for—what it normally sells for" or, "As of October 1, prices revert back to . . . " This is saying I am in competition with the normal course of my own business.

Closeouts, the usual rationale behind buyers' sales, managers' sales, Christmas sales, or end-of-the-season sales, are consistent with the theory of self-competition. The suggestion of scarcity—"This is the last group we have left"—gives the buyer a feeling of urgency.

Choosing an Ad Agency and a Theme

Choosing an agency is often a difficult task. Unlike medicine, in which even the worst practitioner has survived some years of tough schooling, or aviation, in which one cannot get a commercial license without substantial experience and proof of competency, there's no standard by which advertising consultants or agencies become qualified. Anybody who wants to can call himself an advertising expert, but when that expert is proved wrong, it's usually accompanied by the waste of someone else's money.

I'm not suggesting that every advertising person is a phony, but the unwary should be warned that there are yardsticks by which you can measure the worth of an outside consultant or agency, should you reach the logical conclusion that you're best off as a supervisor rather than as your own shirtsleeve practitioner.

First, you should realize that any advertisement can be dissected into four component parts:

1. Theme
2. Copy (or "continuity")
3. Production
4. Media placement

Which is most important? Assuming that the perfect ad totals 100, they can probably be weighted as follows:

1. theme—30
2. copy—25
3. production—20
4. media placement—25

Hey, wait a minute: Media is as important as copy?

You bet it is. Right now, before you forget, reread the Premise, which precedes this chapter. *Where* an ad runs determines whether you've reached the right group—that important First Law of Mass Communications. The most perfectly written ad, aimed at the wrong group, will produce no sales. You might as well recite Shakespeare to cavemen, or submit a report written in French to people who read only Swedish if you're selling something to a group who aren't your primary target: the most people who can and will buy what you have to sell.

Let's start with "theme," which has the heaviest weight. The theme of the ad is its pitch, its appeal, its rationale. Theme doesn't have to mean "We have to sell a hundred cars this week!" That's no theme; that's a goal or a hope. An ad has to realize that goal, but to do it, a theme must motivate the consumer. "We Have to Sell 100 Cars This Week" is a "so-what" ad to consumers, who have their own problems and don't care about yours.

So you reach into the consumer's problems for a theme and try to target the ad to specific potential buyers: "This 1986 Buick: Your 1984 Pontiac and $3000"; "We'll Give You a *Free Calculator* To Figure How Your New Ford Is $500 Less Than Any Other Dealer's Price"; "This Week Only: Buy This Chevette for $500 Below Sticker Price and Get This Pile of Accessories at No Charge!" or "The Bank Says We Have to Sell 100 Cars This Week. Knock $1,000 Off Any Sticker Price."

Determining a theme might be nothing other than saying, "Let's give 'em $25 off on suits under $100 and $50 off on suits over $100." A theme is the offer that generates the possibility of response.

Once a theme is established, the copywriter takes over. He adds credibility and verisimilitude—that is, he makes the offer believable. The reader doesn't care why you're giving him a bargain; he just wants to be sure that it *is* a bargain. Give him the right ammunition and he will not only convince himself, but he'll defend his decision.

The "Campaign" Concept

Not only beginners think in terms of one ad instead of a campaign; some professionals are just as guilty of this type of partial-think, which is sometimes flashy but seldom accomplishes any marketing goal.

The effect is that of planning one play in a football game instead of analyzing field position, opposition, and strength with the intention of scoring a touchdown. One might score a touchdown with one desperate long pass, but the odds aren't favorable, and such planning isn't smart, organized thinking.

Much of campaign thinking is setting up a series of "matches"; an offer is matched to a specific group of potential buyers; an appeal is matched to their known buying habits. This matching is nothing more than an interpretation of Lewis's First Law of Mass Communications.

So the first question the marketer askes himself or herself is: Who's my public? What group might buy this? The marketer then goes with the largest group of potential buyers. Appealing to them seems to mean not advertising automobiles to children or Tinkertoys to senior citizens, but it isn't that simple. You may not know exactly who your public is. Children don't buy bread, but they're the strongest family-member influence on what kind of bread the family buys. Women may not drink as much beer as men, but they buy more, since they're the ones most often in the supermarket.

Isolating a specific public is one key reason local community newspapers can coexist with giant metropolitan newspapers inside the same market; local papers reach a separate market, a separate public, a more selective target group.

In any market situation, you have three possible publics to which you can sell:

1. The mass market is the market consisting of everybody. Daily metropolitan newspapers are the most mass-oriented of

all media, because they cross all barriers of geography in one market area, as well as crossing ethnic origin, income, and age. (Within a newspaper, one has selective areas. Chapter 8 contains a fuller discussion of this.) Prime-time television is also considered "mass," aimed as it is at the entire family. You might advertise ice cream, soap, bicycles, automobile insurance, and sporting goods in mass media without worrying about too much wastage.

2. The selective market is the market consisting of more prospective buyers than nonbuyers. Magazines in general are more selective than newspapers; men's, women's, and sports magazines are more selective than general magazines, and trade magazines are far more selective than consumer magazines. Direct mail (direct response) advertising is the most selective of all mass media, since you can pinpoint exactly the group you want to reach without touching any others.

3. The speculative market is a market that may or may not pay off, because no one really knows how many buyers are there. Advertising sophisticated Christmas gift items in *Popular Mechanics* instead of *The New Yorker* or advertising picture frames in *Time* instead of *Art News* is a speculation that these ads will reach people who otherwise wouldn't think of the product, but the danger of heavy waste lurks close enough to cause constant worry.

Most advertisers who heed Lewis's First Law of Advertising—exhorting them to reach the most people who can and will buy what they have to sell—constantly try to improve their reach within a narrowing selective market as they learn more and more about who buys. But you should take one more step: Since, if they have any brains, the competition advertises in the same marketplace, you have to reach out into the mass group to pull some more buyers who don't see or notice you in the selective advertising marketplace, or who aren't current users of anyone's product or service in your group. This means that when you advertise to your selective group, the ones who most logically can and will buy what you have to sell, you reach them on a level more competitive than the level you'd try for nonusers. To the user, your advertising might say, "Here's why we're better than anyone else in our field"; to the nonuser, it might say, "Here's why you should use this type of product or service."

Any target customer must be reached on his own terms. What does he want? How does he use what you sell? What does he regard as superiority? What gives him status? How can you prove to him you're upgrading his position by causing him to buy your product instead of a competitor's?

If you agree an effective advertisement in today's marketplace has to convince the buyer and not just make wild claims of being "the best" or "the greatest" or "the finest," then you implicitly agree with the Second Law:

> In this Age of Skepticism, cleverness for the sake of cleverness may well be a liability rather than an asset.

Why does this belief imply agreement? Because you have already accepted the *fact* of skepticism and the need to combat it; the method lies in the Second Law, and this is why *comparative advertising* has made such headway in the 1980s. (See Chapters 3 and 12.)

Before reading Chapter 3, the core of this book, do both of us a favor: Reread the three laws of advertising in The Premise one more time.

3

Credibility:
The Key to Persuasion

Some academicians who teach courses in mass communications still work from lecture notes they themselves took in classes in the 1950s, 1960s and 1970s.

With those notes they might as well be teaching a geography class that the earth is flat, an astronomy class that the sun travels around the earth, and an automotive repair class that you can fix almost any problem in your car's engine with a screwdriver.

What has caused the revolution of the 1980s? Most commentators who recognize that the Age of Skepticism has dawned (and not all do) blame television. Television is undoubtedly the largest component of the mix, because it brought into focus the obvious untruth of multiple conflicting claims by multiple conflicting politicians as well as advertisers. But a more comprehensive explanation might be that television has been one contributor to an educational process that has also been fed by newspapers, books, and the youth revolution of the 1960s that led people to feel they're second class citizens unless they've (1) been everywhere and (2) done everything.

Nobody believes anybody in the Age of Skepticism. Does that make the advertiser's job impossible? To the contrary: If advertising is adapted to a new set of rules, a new group of motivators, advertisers can feed on skepticism and make it their weapon.

Look back to 1975 when comparative ads were a novelty. They were cause for sneers. Advertisers said, "Is that the best we can do, attack someone else?" They don't sneer anymore. The comparative ad is a completely valid way to prove superiority in the Age of Skepticism. Names are named, and exhaustive, extensive competitive tests are made with the full intent of proving superiority.

The key to mass communications in the Age of Skepticism, a point I wish you'd write on your mirror, is that noncommunicative advertising dissipates impact. Many people writing ads don't think as communicators but as word-users.

Choosing the Right Word

In the business section of a large metropolitan paper I saw an ad headed, "Buying Short and Selling Short Can Be Very Simple and Very Complicated." If ever there were a meaningless nonspecific, that's it. No matter what you want to sell, it can fit into that framework: Writing ads can be very simple or very complicated, driving one block in an automobile can be very simple or very complicated; trying to analyze a nonsense sentence like this can be very simple or very complicated.

When someone who gets paid for writing ads excretes something like "very simple and very complicated," that writer should be strung up from a post, because the ad is the output of a pro—someone who actually gets paid for this. Some people get enormous salaries for not communicating. That's the cream of the jest in today's communications marketplace. "Boy, that was a great ad I wrote today. It was something I didn't know very much about, but listen to this tremendous phrase I came up with: Buying Short and Selling Short. . . . !"

This kind of nonsense writing reminds me of a speech I once heard: "The past is gone. The present is here. The future is yet to come." And some of the robots in the audience applauded. They noted . . . but weren't motivated, except to mechanical applause.

When you explain a phrase with its own words, all you've done is create gobbledygook. That others do it, that it appears in print, that you hear it on the radio, that you see it on television, that it's in a four-color magazine ad with a 200-line screen, doesn't mean it's good advertising. It just means others are doing what you shouldn't do.

A headline on an ad: "Sometimes you want something badly, and sometimes you don't."

What if this ad had said, "Sometimes you want a cheap suit"? That's a better ad. It's specific. Or, "Sometimes you want a good, cheap suit." Even better. Even more specific. Thomas Riley Marshall was Woodrow Wilson's vice-president, but today he is remembered only for one quotation: "What this country needs is a good five-cent cigar." That was a potent, whole message—concise, well stated.

Consider this ad: "Are you hiding your child's musical talent?" Here again are words; what do they mean? "Are you hiding your child's musical talent?" "Yes," you say, "I stuck it in the closet." Is that what this means? Surely they aren't saying, "Are you *stifling* your child's musical talent?" What a wonderful difference between the two words. When you *hide* something, your action may not necessarily be bad. In fact, it's an obscure kind of action. But when you *stifle*, you damage your child. And if the great motivators today are guilt and greed, this advertising idea is a good guilt pitch, emasculated because of one badly used word.

Positive action words are better than negative, passive words. "We did it" says more and communicates better than "It was done." (It was done by whom?) "It was arranged" sounds like something out of a George Orwell novel, whereas "We set it up for you" is direct and action oriented.

Generalizations also cloud the communications process. Look for the most specific word. *Produced* is better than *made*, and *manufactured* is better than produced.

Innovated? Gave birth to? Created? The word *created* is like the word *quality.* In certain usages it has lost all meaning. Consider the word *quality.* "We carry fine quality furniture." What does this mean? Nothing to anyone, because the word has lost its impact and no longer draws any specific word picture.

Never assume you can convince someone without doing some homework. Think of yourself as a vacuum cleaner salesperson, demonstrating in someone's home. If the sales pitch is based on know-nothing phrases such as, "This is a fine quality machine," or, "She's a beauty, isn't she?" how can you expect someone to buy? Would you?

No responsible vacuum cleaner company would let you loose without filling you full of facts about that machine. You'd quickly know it's made of titanium, and you'd know why titanium is better than steel or aluminum; you'd know how much more suction it has than a Eureka or a Hoover; you'd know what each attachment is for, what innovations and improvements are built into the machine, the length and limitations of the guarantee, and how to demonstrate each feature.

Are vacuum cleaner salespeople that much better at their craft than advertisers? They are when copywriters fail to make use of these same facts when writing ads.

Finding a Good Slogan

Occasionally, a vague slogan does make its point. But such slogans are best used as part of a massive campaign that involves repeated exposure. (This is where a medium like radio can become most effective.) Acceptance comes slowly and occurs only when the slogan becomes automatic through repetition. For example: "Delta is ready when you are." Think back to when you first heard that phrase. You may have thought: "I don't get it"; "I'm not ready"; "Nonsense"; or "Expletive deleted." But we've heard it enough times, for enough years, so that the phrase has become part of our own consciousness. This message now brings immediate identification. The consumer doesn't respond by *doing* something; she responds by forming an image of Delta Airlines. In 1985, Delta decided to replace its 16-year-old jingle: "Delta gets you there." How long does it take, in the communications clutter of the late 1980s, to make a comparable impression on public consciousness?

A jingle is basically a mnemonic device (a mnemonic device helps you to remember), and jingles that tend to be mnemonic have less factual material than do nonjingles. This hasn't always been true. The first memorable jingle was both mnemonic *and* specific:

Pepsi-Cola hits the spot.
Twelve full ounces, that's a lot.
Twice as much for a nickel, too.
Pepsi-Cola is the drink for you.

Look at the specifics! And mnemonic? People still remember the jingle fifty years later.

Today, jingles tend to have tight orchestrations and a lack of specificity, although the best of both possible worlds is to combine the mnemonic value of a jingle with some factual content (see Chapter 7 for a fuller discussion).

How to Use Humor

Humor that calls attention to itself rather than to the product can damage the product. Some of the people who make a specialty of producing humorous commercials lapse into self-glorification instead of product glorification. They want you to say, "Oh, what a clever person that writer is," rather than, "Hey, I want to buy that."

Safety lies in the decision against being a comedian on any level. Call attention to what you sell, not to yourself. On the radio, on television, and in print, you can't put your foot in a wastebasket and tilt a lampshade on your head and sell merchandise. The reason harks back to Lewis's Second Law of Mass Communications, which says that cleverness for the sake of cleverness may be more of a liability than an asset.

What a difficult lesson that is for the ego-driven writer. Do you know how to learn it forever? By writing a noncommunicative "clever" ad that fails to pull. Then out of desperation and frustration, you write a straightforward message that tells the story, presents positive facts, has no puffery—and pulls.

Getting Rid of Add-Nothing Claims

The rule of grammar is simple: An adjective ending in "er" is a comparative. The word suggests a greater degree of

Dare to Compare. Come in. Sit down. Run both PCs. IBM vs. TI. Side by side. Compare how they run powerful software. Like 1-2-3™ from Lotus. Or BPS Business Graphics.™ Or MultiMate.™

Compare speed. Keyboards. Graphics. Service and support. Compare everything a PC can do for you.

And one simple fact will emerge:

"TI is better."

IBM Personal Computer
(1-2-3 from Lotus)

Texas Instruments Professional Computer
(1-2-3 from Lotus)

Take TI's "Dare to Compare" challenge today. Selected dealers want you to see for yourself how the TI Professional makes the best software perform even better. You'll also learn how TI backs you with outstanding service and support, including an optional 24-hour customer support line and extended 1- or 5-year warranties. Call us toll-free at 1-800-527-3500 for your nearest TI dealers.

IBM is a trademark of International Business Machines, Inc. Lotus and 1-2-3 are trademarks of Lotus Development Corporation. BPS Business Graphics is a trademark of Business & Professional Software, Incorporated. MultiMate is a trademark of SoftWord Systems. Copyright © 1984. Texas Instruments Incorporated.

TEXAS INSTRUMENTS
Creating useful products and services for you.

Figure 3-1 If you have product benefits a better-known competitor doesn't have, say so. This ad makes a flat comparative statement of superiority, and the message is straightforward and clear—infinitely better than the weak and nonspecific "Ours is better" claims we see so often, in which the advertiser is afraid or unable to tell us, "better than what?"

something than something else. The suffix "est" is a superlative; it suggests a greater degree of something *than anything else.*

Throughout this book comparative advertising will be endorsed; in fact, it will be embraced as the salvation of advertising credibility. But comparative advertising must make a comparison.

The unexplained comparative is one of the worst atrocities inflicted on the unwitting victims of modern communications. Something is "whiter," but what is it whiter than? A garment that has been soaked in mud? Complete the comparative. Superman isn't faster; he is faster than a speeding bullet. The completed comparison gives the recipient of the message a handle for absolute evaluation. Superman doesn't just leap higher. He leaps higher than tall buildings. The specific completes the "word-image," and the recipient of the message has that basis for judgment.

Muhammad Ali could claim, "I am the greatest," but he had the recognition factor to make others assume automatic completion of the phrase, "I am the greatest prize-fighter in the world." When an advertiser says, "We are the greatest," the reader or viewer not only asks, "The greatest *what?*" but is annoyed by the obvious puffery.

Words such as *best, number one, finest,* and *top quality* have no significance in the Age of Skepticism. They describe nothing, they prove nothing, and they're anachronisms; they're software in an age of hardware.

A word such as *most* means nothing unless it's explained. The most *what?* A face cream doesn't have "the most vitamin E." It has "the most vitamin E per gram of any cleansing cream"—and the advertiser had better be ready to prove it.

"Awareness": The False Prophet

More and more advertising by some of the most sophisticated and supposedly most knowledgeable advertisers seems to be *non*communicative.

Is this an unholy trend, does it reflect the invasion into the ranks of communicators by improperly educated recruits, or does it indicate an even more serious malady—being more interested in people "noticing" the advertising *as advertising* instead of wanting to buy whatever is being sold?

We have too much evidence that this last trend is our problem, which means millions of dollars are being wasted. Some of the giants are making their advertising *half* as effective at *twice* the cost—the reverse of our own intention.

An example is a study of a study prepared for *Adweek* by Video Storyboard Tests/Campaign Monitor, during the 1984 election campaign. After seeing television commercials— expensive ones—prepared by each party, only 43 percent of registered voters said the commercials gave them a better understanding of the Republican platform, and only 31 percent said they had a better understanding of the Democratic platform.

Worse: Of those who saw Walter Mondale's television spots, 19 percent said those spots had increased their interest in voting for the Democratic candidate, but 24 percent said the spots actually decreased their interest in voting for him.

Politics and cynicism go together like ham and eggs, so this field may not be the best example. The classic television way of keeping score, those magic words "noted" and "recall," showed that during a one-month period (July/August 1984) McDonald's advertising had a big 10.8 percent increase in awareness; competitor Burger King had an 8.1 percent drop.

But Restaurant Trends issued survey results showing that during this same period Burger King's sales—*a far more logical way to keep score*—were up 15 percent, while McDonald's were up 9 percent.

One last comment on the silliness of "awareness" as the be-all and end-all of advertising-effectiveness measurement:

Oxtoby-Smith is a research company. It conducted brand awareness surveys for Mrs. Smith's Cake Mix, Dentu-Tight, and Four O'Clock Tea. Scores ranged from 8 percent to 31 percent.

None of these brands exists.

Heroes and Bums

Slavish worshipping of "awareness" leads computer advertisers to use Martina Navratilova and Dom DeLuise as "spokespeople"; are they credible? Who cares? We're aware of them.

Do celebrity endorsements add anything to a selling argument, other than cost? The jury is still out. For the typical small advertiser, my advice can be condensed into three little words:

Save Your Money

The 1984 Olympic games threw the entire concept of celebrity endorsements into cynically sharp focus. When Mary Decker, a runner, fell during her race, one frequent comment was, "There goes a million dollars in product endorsements."

Does the ability to run make an individual an authority on coffee or computers or credit cards? Let's not oversimplify, especially when we realize that when rock singer Michael Jackson was reported to eat bean curds, the sale of bean curds went through the ceiling.

But how many Michael Jacksons are there. We see far more Dom DeLuises and Ivan Lendls.

(Lendl typifies the near-ridiculous commercialism that has hit the tennis world. Wimbledon had a tie-in promotion with Weight Watchers, the "Wimbledon/Weight Watchers Sweepstakes"; Lendl agreed to wear a clothing patch promoting Porsche-Audi during his Wimbledon matches, while Jimmy Connors, already a walking billboard, had a more prosaic extra patch to wear: McDonalds. Martina Navratilova agreed to wear a ComputerLand patch, specified for the left sleeve.)

The new group of celebrities: *business leaders.* Lee Iacocca signed to smoke Don Diego cigars for newspaper ads. Ted Turner, owner of "superstation" WTBS, was a featured television spokesman for an air courier service (DHL) and a

© 1983 Atari, Inc. All rights reserved. W A Warner Communications Company

Figure 3-2 Atari was so proud of having actor Alan Alda as its spokesman that the company ran a color page in many trade magazines, glorifying the spokesman rather than the product. Is this a sign of product weakness, or shrewd maneuvering to induce retailers to push the brand of computer whose spokesman inspires trust?

Figure 3-3 NCR Corp. introduced an IBM-compatible computer with an advertising campaign budgeted between $10 million and $15 million. The spokesman: comedian Dom DeLuise. Might a professional announcer, not known as a buffoon, have been better as a confidence-inspirer, especially for a business product? Or is the recognizability-factor enough to overcome that image? Only NCR knows for sure.

men's shirt manufacturer (Hathaway). Henry Block, founder of H&R Block, explained why he preferred United Airlines. A failed airline founder, Freddie Laker, videotaped commercials for American Telephone & Telegraph.

Even without celebrities, giant companies pay for tie-ins whose commercial worth is pure exposure, not sell—a procedure which can benefit the titans only. Coca-Cola paid $14 million to become "the official soft drink of the 1984 Olympics"; Budweiser was the "official beer"; Fuji was the "official film," but Eastman Kodak, through a judicious deal with ABC, also was the official film owning the bulk of television exposure. One vitamin was the "official vitamin" and another was the "official stress vitamin."

Practice really does make perfect.

Without doubt, Chris Evert-Lloyd is one of the all-time great women tennis players.

Three Wimbledon, six U.S. and five French championships, as well as the Australian Open and five Italian titles, are evidence of Chris's unmatched will to win.

She has always played with metronomic precision. She drives the ball hard and deep with a consistency and accuracy that bear testament to years of practice. An increasing willingness to come to the net and volley with the same ruthless efficiency has raised her game to near perfection.

Chris Evert-Lloyd is a very strong competitor indeed. Those who know how tough the game can be have learned to appreciate her for it.

"For the first few years, I think the crowds were just waiting to see the Ice Queen melt," she says. "And, of course, eventually I lost some matches ... but when they saw I could take it ... that I was human ... then they liked me for it. Now crowds are usually on my side ... and that's nice!"

To Chris Evert-Lloyd, stamina and style count. In her game. In the watch she wears. A Rolex Lady-Datejust. "It's a strong watch," she says. "It's always surprising to me how tough it really is.

"Still, I know Rolex has been making watches for a very long time, and 'practice makes perfect' is something I've always agreed with."

Chris Evert-Lloyd and her Rolex Lady-Datejust. Both made perfect by practice.

ROLEX

The Rolex Lady-Datejust Chronometer. Available in 18kt. gold, with matching bracelet.

Write for brochure. Rolex Watch, U.S.A., Inc., Dept.585, Rolex Building, 665 Fifth Avenue, New York, N.Y. 10022
World headquarters in Geneva. Other offices in Canada and major countries around the world.

SEE READER SERVICE PAGE FOR MORE INFORMATION

Figure 3-4 Advertisers sometimes have to stretch their imaginations to bring the sales message into congruence with the image of the celebrity-endorser. One minor problem here: Chris Evert-Lloyd isn't wearing a Rolex watch in the photograph, even though the copy quotes her as being surprised at "how tough it really is."

Can Celebrities Match Product Benefit?

Procter & Gamble, in dropping celebrity Lauren Bacall as spokesperson for High Point decaffeinated coffee in favor of a straight product presentation, may have signaled the switch that inevitably will result from "celebrity-clutter": "We believe the new ads better convey the benefits of this product than a single spokesperson can."

If you consider using celebrities, whose loyalty to brand or sponsor doesn't extend beyond the arm-patch and who may be seen in a single day promoting computers and Jello (Bill Cosby); swimming pool accessories, oil, and dictating equipment (Arnold Palmer); a stock-brokerage and a fast-food restaurant (John Houseman); or automated teller machines and wristwatches (Chris Evert-Lloyd), I suggest you lay in a supply of those stress vitamins.

4

How to Deal with Suppliers

"I hate farming this out! If only I had a staff writer. . . . "

The businessman who complains that farming out his advertising to freelance sources is costly and uncertain has a point. But he is also enjoying a hidden benefit. Along with the disadvantage of having the writing done by someone who simply can't know as much about his business as a staff writer would, this advertiser has the advantage of having the writing done by someone who simply cannot know as much about his business as a staff writer would.

If this sounds like doubletalk, consider this: The inbreeding of corporate philosophy has undone many an ad campaign, and staff writers often slip into the indolent position of writing the same tired clichés only because competitive instincts are dulled. They don't have to live by their wits. The result can be either constant regurgitation of the same message the writer knows pleases the boss or the assumption that every potential customer knows as much about a product as the company does.

Not that free-lancers are immune to writing to please the guy who hired them, but there's a built-in safeguard: Free-lancers are more likely to be blamed if an ad flops, and they know it. Since they're very much in the cliché marketplace, they usually have a closer touch with trends, changes, and what currently works.

Furthermore, an advertiser is not married to a free-lancer. Along comes Ms. B., who says, "I've seen your ads and I can do better." Mr. A., who has been writing the ads, might well be out if Ms. B's ads pull better and if the businessman has the guts to throw out a loser.

Competition is valuable in choosing writers, and is probably even more so when dealing with artists and printers. I've seen hundreds of circumstances in which production bills creep up and up until a would-be supplier suddenly draws forcible attention to the gouging; then that new source is established as a supplier until bills again creep up. (The most common areas of "packing" a charge are typesetting and photostats.)

One warning: The cheapest isn't always the best. A truism, I know, but it certainly doesn't mean that the most expensive is the best. I hate to report it, but the cheapest is best more often than the most expensive, and that's because the difference in output isn't in ratio to the difference in cost.

Suppose you want to put together an ad about a storewide sale of furniture. A free-lance copywriter writes the ad, and for $20 more, he gives you a copywriter's rough layout, showing the general position of the elements. Now the artist takes over. If there is no illustration to do, the job is largely one of assembly and type specification. From your clipping file, you may have a sample of the style you want or even a similar ad perhaps from another business in a distant city. It would be nonsense to let an artist make a big deal of this project.

And you should remember that if you live on your wits, depending on the type of business you're in, you can get a lot of creative work done free.

How to Get Professional Work Done Cheaply—or Free

These are the components you deal with in creative work:

1. Copywriting
2. Layout
3. Illustration, either art or photography
4. Typesetting
5. Printing
6. Other production—broadcast, for example

In all these areas, the shortest road to getting the work done free is to do it yourself. "Ah," you say, "I'm not a writer

and I'm not an artist and I don't know a thing about typesetting." So what? You read the papers, don't you?

If you take a month's subscription to any newspaper from
a city over 500,000 in population, and at least 500 miles from
you, you'll have a five-year supply of good, usable advertising
ideas for a retail business, including easily adaptable copy and
traceable layouts.

If you're not in a retail business, get copies of publications
in fields unlike your own but with similar marketing problems.
For example, if you sell industrial machinery, there's little
point in copying ads from your own trade publications;
instead, look for approaches used by obliquely related businesses, such as earthmoving equipment, automotive repair
journals that show equipment, and publications that carry ads
for specialized equipment used for bakeries, trucking, or construction. The items and descriptions obviously will be different, but what you're after is the approach.

Let's examine the list, item by item, to see how you can
handle each facet.

1. *Copywriting.* If you're a wholesaler or a retailer, the
job is done. Ask the manufacturer for appropriate copy.
Chances are the company has some on file or has an advertising department that can grind this out for you. You needn't
accept it exactly as written, but you don't have to pay for it.
You can also find a piece of copy you like about anything and
use the same approach for your product or service. Finally, if
advertising courses are taught in a local college, ask the
instructor if he or she wants to moonlight, or, even less expensive, to use your product or service as an assignment in an
advanced class. If a submission is usable, pay a nominal fee to
the winner. (Warning: Don't settle for sophomoric copy.)

2. *Layout.* Layout shows the position of the elements in
an ad. If you have the confidence to recognize that you don't
have to be a polished artist to do layouts, you're halfway there.
Obviously, one way of getting a layout free is to do it yourself,
using as a model an ad of the same size as yours that you find
visually pleasing. Sometimes a newspaper in which you advertise will have a staff artist prepare a semicomprehensive layout

for an ad; this layout is yours, and you should photocopy and file it for possible future use.

3. *Illustration.* This is where the greatest challenge to ingenuity presents itself. Start with the product: If you're a car dealer, you already know that you never need ask a shutter to click or a brush to hit paper; the manufacturer of every car has hundreds of pictures of the product, and they're yours free. If you sell toys or furniture or clothing or many of the products that appear in supermarkets or drugstores, the supplier will give you photographs or line art on request.

If you sell insurance or another intangible, or if you're the manufacturer, you may have another problem. In that case, you can look for free photos—from airlines, from foreign countries, from state and city chambers of commerce—or you can buy stock photographs for a fraction of what your own production cost would be (the Yellow Pages lists stock photo sources), remembering that you may trade away the specificity of subject matter you'd like in exchange for saving money.

There are lots of sources of stock art: professional-quality line drawings of just about everything, done straight or humorous. A whole book of stock art will cost less than $50, and for many advertisers this is a lifetime supply. Almost every issue of Advertising Age carries several ads for stock art sources.

(*Warning:* Don't lift a piece of art from another ad without asking and receiving permission, in writing. You can be sued from here to Canarsie.)

4. *Typesetting.* Getting type set free is a delicate matter. There are only two ways of doing it: (1) Ask a supplier for a finished ad into which you can drop your name, or (2) have a newspaper set the type for you (they'll usually do it at no charge if you're a local advertiser). If the paper sets the type, ask for an extra set of final proofs—smudge-free, proofed samples of the typeset. You then have the type, already set, if you want to use the same copy in a direct mail piece, a magazine ad, or a handout sheet.

Typesetting has the widest range of prices of all aspects of production, varying from a few dollars for type set on a computerized typesetting machine or an IBM composer to many dollars for type set by the old-fashioned hot-type method. You may be in love with an exotic typeface only a very expensive typographer has on hand; the look isn't that different, and unless you're after a Cadillac image, you're better off putting your money into ads or postage than into typesetting.

Resist the urge to use a typewriter as a typesetter. The result invariably is amateurish and cheap.

5. *Printing.* There's no way to get printing done free, unless you can prevail on a primary supplier to print something as part of his cost of doing business with you. Some manufacturers will arrange co-op advertising.

Printing prices vary widely. The advertiser who pays top dollar is the one who either insists on a particular brand and weight of paper, who designs a piece with a lot of paper waste (a tip: work in sizes that can be divided equally into a sheet of paper 17-by-22 inches and you won't have this problem), who has lots of intricate color work, or who prints so few pieces it hardly pays the printer to start the press.

Try to "gang-run" the work, perhaps by printing several months' supply of bulletins together, or if you have a standing headline of a second color, print several issues in that color, which then means you need print only black in the smaller single-issue quantity.

6. *Other production.* If you're planning a broadcast campaign, let the time-salesman sell you. Most radio stations will agree to produce a commercial to give you a feeling for the sound. And most television stations will make a deal on production of videotaped commercials if the spots are run on those stations.

A lot of advertisers include an extra station on a broadcast schedule because that station produced the spot, and even though it's a station they wouldn't normally use, they find that they more than come out ahead since they save so much on the cost of production.

If you accept the spot, you might have to pay a nominal fee to the "talent" whose voice or face is used. But unless you're a big advertiser in a big consumer market, stay away from A.F.T.R.A. (the American Federation of Television and Radio Artists) and S.A.G. (Screen Actors Guild), because your talent cost can eat you alive and because you have to make "use" payments to the talent every 13 weeks.

Barter

There's one additional way to save money and that's to trade. You can trade your product or service for any of the six facets of production just described, for print media space, or for broadcast advertising.

Several companies handle nothing but barter on a percentage basis, or you can deal direct. While the success of barter depends on the value and acceptance of what you have to sell (luggage and automobiles being easier barter material than truck mudguards), some of the barter companies carry "banks" of barter goods and services, so that if the person with whom you are doing business doesn't want the mudguards, he can have tableware from the bank and someone else somewhere else will ultimately want the mudguards.

From 1972 to 1976 radio and television rate cards disintegrated. To the sophisticated buyer, they became a joke. Only yokels paid card rates for broadcast time, and advertising agencies and the news media services began to compete bitterly for accounts based not on creative services but on who could buy at the greatest discount (see the section in this chapter on advertising agencies).

Then in 1976 the squeeze began in television. Suddenly time was tight, rates shot up, and by 1978 advertisers of consumer products were looking to magazines as an alternative for rocketing television rates.

From 1980 to 1985, more and more television buying became concentrated in the hands of media-buying services, who offer instant computer printouts of availabilities and, even better for the advertiser, a rebate of two thirds of the 15 percent agency commissions (see pages 40-41).

In today's marketplace, one-day television-time availabilities are plentiful and the next day availabilities have dried up. For the smaller advertiser looking for discount time, plan changes are as instantaneous as a video arcade game.

As of this writing, discount time during much of the year is often hard to get and television is a more expensive crap game than ever before. But radio remains a great swap shop. Rate cards are still in fragments and may stay that way.

What You Should Pay and When You Should Pay It

The standard party line in advertising agencies is this: "When the client pays us, we'll pay you."

On behalf of the coolies in today's work force, I object to this philosophy. It demands a chain reaction that is neither logical nor healthy. Here's a better plan:

First, what should you, the advertiser, pay for creative help? With the obvious disclaimer that rates depend on geography and market, here are some yardsticks:

Layout for a 7″-by-10″ magazine ad: $50
Layout for a newspaper ad, full page: $60–$100
Layout for a small ad (200 to 1000 lines): $35–$50
Copy for average magazine-page ad: $100–$200
Copy for brochure, average complexity: $400–$600
Copy for business letter up to two full pages: $125–$200
Illustration, black-and-white, nonproduct: $100–$150
Product illustration: $200
Product photograph, black-and-white: $75–$150
Product photograph, color: $100–$200
Written rationale suggesting advertising methodology, 10–20 pages: $250
News release: $100
News-type photograph, not a polaroid: $50 plus travel and laboratory expenses
News-type photograph, polaroid: Nothing

These are average prices based on 1985 costs. Actual costs vary depending on whether you hire a beginner or an old pro, and they also vary depending on how big a spender the creative source thinks you are. These people have great flexibility. If a writer demands $500, and you offer $100, chances are he'll take it.

(A disclaimer is in order here:

These are local prices, for local advertisers. A heavy-weight professional charges $1,000 for a two-page letter, $3,000 to $5,000 for copy and layout of a brochure. Obviously, if you're in that ball game, you aren't concerned about saving money. You're on a different, more elegant plateau, and I salute your dedication to high professionalism instead of economy—while gently suggesting that this book isn't really for you.)

It's just as unfair to refuse to pay until you're satisfied as it is for a source to demand full payment in advance. You'll find logic in both corners. The creative person fears, with ample justification because it has happened before, that he's at your mercy. You can change your mind and reject the work on phony grounds of imperfection, or you can change your mind in the middle of the job and require a whole new approach without paying for it. On your behalf there's absolutely no sense paying in front without seeing some results. The whole relationship becomes cockeyed.

The normal pattern is to pay a creative person with whom you haven't worked before one third in advance, one third on delivery, and one third within 30 days. This system guarantees a flat price and prevents arguments. After you have established a relationship, payment may gradually become more casual.

Never let work on a job start without having an estimate. If the writer says, "Gee, I don't know how long this will take me," reply, "Give me a 'between' figure." And don't be afraid to argue. The comfort you'll have from knowing in advance what a job will cost is part of professionalism on your part. You wouldn't order a piece of machinery or an insurance policy without knowing how much it would cost.

Try to stay away from writers and artists who charge by the hour. Inevitably you wind up paying more, and you may hate yourself because you can't audit the time. If someone brings in a four-line classified ad and says, "I took three hours to write this," how can you argue? Maybe she did. If that writer gets $30 an hour, you might take the vow never to deal with her again, but meanwhile, you're out of the money. Anyone who ever has dealt with building tradespeople such as plumbers, carpenters, and plasterers knows what can happen when they bill by the hour. Pay a flat rate and avoid a flat pocketbook.

Milk the Advertising Agency or They'll Milk You

Does everybody know how advertising agencies work and how they bill? Just in case, here's a quick refresher course: The usual method of agency compensation is 15 percent of the gross. If a magazine charges $100 for an ad, the agency bills the client $100 and pays the magazine $85.

But 15 percent of the gross is 17.65 percent of the net. For example, a printer bills the agency $100 for a job done for you, the agency's client. The agency pays the printer $100 and bills you $117.65. Deduct 15 percent from $117.65; the result is an even $100. This is simple mathematics: 15 percent of the gross equals 17.65 percent of the net.

Why is this important? Because there are alternatives. The ancient edifices of advertising are cracking and crumbling. Even as agencies scream they can't make a profit on 15 percent, they're being undercut by media services who won't have anything to do with the printer—that's not their bag— but who will gladly take that $100 advertising charge from a magazine, pay the magazine $85, and bill the client $90 instead of $100.

These media services are like modern service stations that pump gas and that's all. They don't mess with repairs. They handle volume, which means they develop high efficiency in a specialty that enables them to make a profit and still charge less than the corner garage that isn't yet automated.

The greatest strength of media services is among advertisers of consumer goods and services who use broadcast heavily, but they also have grown strong in magazines and national newspaper campaigns. Full-service agencies battle valiantly on the ground that they provide service and creativity, but they fight for a losing cause when the advertiser has the capability of handling his own creative work.

Usually in this type of battle the media service must win. Since media services make no pretense at being a fully staffed advertising agency with creative and production specialists, they never require the traditional 15 percent commission; the going rate for a media service is four to six percent, which means the advertiser will save 9 to 11 of each hundred dollars he spends on broadcast advertising, provided he handles all his own creative work. Being specialists, media services can track rapidly changing rates and space and broadcast time availabilities on computers and can make instant nationwide buys with great efficiency.

Many major advertisers have switched their media buying to the media services, leaving the creative work in the hands of their advertising agencies. In such cases the advertiser often pays the agency a flat fee, and the buying service gets a nominal percentage.

Smaller advertisers have the problem of settling for freelance or semiprofessional creative work if they suddenly switch from full-service agencies to buying services. But advertisers able to handle their own creative work can realize a substantial savings by seeking competitive prices on media buying, if that's the only outside service needed. And they'd be foolish to pay more than six percent.

Finally, the media, especially magazines, often allow a two percent additional discount for payment within ten days of invoicing, and for some reason (obviously, the possibility of pocketing that discount) a lot of advertising agencies fail to pass along that extra discount.

A suggestion: Pay agency bills promptly and deduct two percent. The agency may argue, but you'll be right in taking the deduction in most cases. Let Standard Rate & Data Service act as mediator. SRDS ratebooks, available at the library if nowhere else, usually indicate whether a medium allows this extra discount. Sometimes the original media bills from the newspaper, magazine, or broadcast station indicate that the discount has been given. (If the agency isn't including the original media bills and you're paying anyway, shame on you.)

The flat fee, the negotiated fee, and the graduated fee are all alternate, contemporary means of compensating advertising agencies. It's as simple as this: The advertiser/client says, "I'll pay you X dollars for writing my ads and doing the art and production work. At the end of ninety days, if one of us is getting hurt, we'll renegotiate or part company."

Some agencies charge the full 15 percent fee but throw in free creative work. This includes copy and layout but not finished art, typography, broadcast production, or outside services that must be bought; they're marked up the usual 17.65 percent. Others charge the 15 percent and creative fees. God bless them if they can get this kind of fee, but after reading this book, you need not ever pay that kind of money again.

Remember, too, that if you're a local advertiser using newspapers, the paper probably has two rate cards and you're spending more just to have an agency place the ads. This condition usually doesn't apply to automobile dealers, employment agencies, and in some cases, amusements, which, for some strange reason no one ever has been able to explain satisfactorily, are billed at the national rate by most metropolitan papers (see Chapter 8 for discussion of "local" or "retail" rates versus "national" or "general" rates).

Usually, all broadcast and magazine advertising is commissionable to recognized advertising agencies.

Hardly an advertiser of any consequence exists who isn't courted continuously by advertising agencies. Since the average length of time an agency holds an account is less than five years, turnovers occur frequently enough to encourage agencies to perform their strange courting ritual.

Suppose you don't have an agency but are considering using one. Phone three or four and ask them to drop in to see you. Chances are a team of two or four people will show up. Their approach may be bold or subtle, but their bottom-line question is, "What's your budget?" If the budget is less than $25,000 a year, including production, an agency probably can't make any money from you. After all, the gross potential for them is 15 percent, $3,750, and if $500 of that sticks as pure profit, it's a well-run agency.

Still, the lemmings must rush to the sea, and agencies must make presentations.

Sometimes an agency will prepare the initial advertising program free, on speculation. On the other hand, many will tell you, "We don't make speculative presentations," and their ethics should be applauded. While you're applauding, find an agency with less ethics and more hunger, because you want to have some indication of what they can do before making a decision.

Warning: Don't go to a relative. Severing the relationship later can be difficult.

Before appointing an agency, ask what their fees are for writing, art, and other services you may need. Don't let the forcefulness of their presentation awe you into postponing that question. The earlier you ask, the lower the fee will be, because agencies love "capitalized fees"*—they look good in industry reports.

Don't sign a contract unless you feel it's to your benefit. If you do, insist on a clause that permits mutual cancellation on 90 days' notice. The worst wastes of advertising dollars come from agency complacency, stemming from either a feeling that you're a minor account and don't deserve top-echelon service once you're safely in the bag, or from the general indolence that creeps around an account like fungus, sooner or later. When complacency occurs, you're taken for granted, like an unpleasant-smelling, sick relative who pays his room rent but isn't really nice to have around when the rent isn't due.

How to Be Your Own Advertising Agency and Save 15 Percent

There was a time when being an advertising agency really meant something. Even the smallest newspapers insisted on complete credit information: You had to have $15,000 in the

---

*Capitalized fees (charges for services, rather than for media placement) show up on agency statements as far greater income than normal commissions. If an agency bills a client $100 for copy done inside the shop, the agency is entitled, by industry practice, to multiply that fee by 6.67 when totaling its billings for the year for inclusion in trade magazines. Thus the $100 becomes $667 and the agency can claim greater "billings," leading to greater applause from its peers and greater numbers of raw, untrained beginners hitting them for jobs starting at $35,000 a year.

bank, you had to submit a list of clients, and a Catch-22 provision insisted that in order to get agency recognition you list clients you already had which you couldn't already have if you weren't already a recognized agency.

Today, anyone with a business card can be an advertising agency; companies big and small have established house agencies to save the 15 percent commission.

Sometimes a house agency is a big mistake. Agency commissions are saved, but professionalism in copy, art, production, and media buying may be sacrificed. If you know what you're doing, you're not sacrificing these necessities because you know as much about them, or as much about where to buy them, as your former agency knows.

If you decide to be your own agency, and if, from reading the first part of this chapter, you feel you know how to buy creative services, you can go ahead, provided you can prove to yourself that you will indeed save money. Keep in mind that the simple media-buying function is available to you at well below 15 percent.

Here is what you need: A letterhead, a phone, and an address, which really should not be identical with that of your regular business. If you are the Jones Manufacturing Company located at 1000 Main Street, then Michael Robert Advertising, Inc. (the first names of your two sons) is located at 500 Eighteenth Street—in the same building, but with another address. The phone number is another line, too.

Trade publications will usually grant agency recognition to anyone who asks for it if the ad is accompanied by a check. The publication is prepared to give agency commissions to someone, and in today's wild marketplace, at least a couple dozen new agencies are formed every day, with the same number folding.

That's the key to the new, unknown agency: Send a check with the order. It's not all bad, because your check for that hundred-dollar ad isn't for $100, or even for $85; it's for $83.33 because you've taken the additional two percent discount for cash.

Most broadcast stations will go along with your claim to be an advertising agency. Newspapers are touchier, but once you run some ads in a few trade papers, a broadcast station or two, and the local newspaper, the few holdouts (at this writing The New York Times, The Chicago Tribune, The Wall Street Journal, and four or five others are the last tough-recognition papers) will send a questionnaire you can easily answer since you will have recognition from others.

This is the domino theory: One magazine gives recognition and ten others fall into line; the ten give recognition and the whole media world goes along. Just send a check with the order and you're way ahead of lots of old-line agencies with bad or no credit.

Depending on the type of business, a house agency might well be a consortium of three or four medium-sized, noncompeting advertisers. If that's the case, hire a copywriter or a media buyer or a one-man gang to operate it, and you will probably save a bundle.

You might look at it this way: If your ads run in commissionable media (broadcast stations, consumer and trade magazines, outdoor or newspaper ads that carry the national rate), if you already have an advertising department or someone charged with this function, if your agency commissions don't seem to be worth the service you get because you make most of the creative decisions and select the media yourself, then it may pay to be your own advertising agency. At worst, your agency disbands and you award the account to another agency; at best you may actually pick up some other accounts.

A Final Note

Saving money in advertising is as simple as squeezing out the fat. It helps if you're clairvoyant, but you have this advantage up front: There is probably more wastage in the advertising business than in any other, and a lot of that wastage is due to plain, ordinary stupidity.

Some of the rest is due to greed that leads to overcharges, and the remaining fragment is due to the client's own lethargy: He tells himself he is going to see whether or not he was overcharged . . . and he never does.

5

How to Make Selling by Mail Pay

In the 1950s, selling by mail went into a tailspin. The cost of doing business seemed to be locked in an endless rise, and profit potential seemed to be trapped in an endless decline. Some of the big Sunday newspapers and monthly magazines that had entire sections of ads selling merchandise by mail slowly shrank these sections into fragments of a single page. Big mailers who flooded the mails with offers went out of business or into conventional retailing.

In the mid 1980s, direct marketing—the new words for selling by mail—was the fastest-growing facet of marketing. Giant companies with long traditions of selling through conventional retail outlets were frantically gearing up to compete in the red-hot marketplace.

What resuscitated mail-order selling? Most of the new generation of direct mail giants credit the computer, which has overcome the impossibly rising costs of production, printing, and postage and has made possible the pinpointing of markets, reaching the most people who can and will buy what they have to sell.

Not only are mailing lists segmented with great accuracy, but the user of the mails can pinpoint specific zip codes, demographic and ethnic groups, and buyer preferences. "Merge-purge," discussed later, eliminates duplication of names, so when a mailer says to his prospect, "This is the only notice you will receive," the statement is true no matter how many lists that name may appear on.

Mail order is in a period of expansion far greater than that of any other mass medium, and today's knowledgeable mailers, using computer augmentation for tests and validation of appeals, can predict after only a modest investment whether or not the program will succeed. Much of the danger has been extracted from direct mail advertising.

(Direct response, direct marketing, and direct mail are terms with differences so subtle and so slight that they are used interchangeably in this book.)

Third Class Mail or Else

Postal costs, on the rise for years now, can cut drastically into profits, so an understanding of the mails helps. Here is a quick review:

First class mail: letters and other mail handled on a priority basis and supposedly delivered without delay
Second class mail: publications and periodicals
Third class mail: everything else
Fourth class mail: parcel post

First class mail is rarely suitable for bulk mailings, because in most cases the cost just isn't justified. First class mail is about twice as expensive as third class, which means that for the same budget you either can deliver circulars a few days earlier or you can print and mail many more of them. The only logical answer in most cases is third class mail, which requires advance planning.

Delay is the villain causing mail that might be dropped third class to be mailed first class. You get it ready too late, and you are then afraid an extra couple of weeks in the mails will kill the promotion. In direct mail, as in every other type of advertising, thinking ahead can save you money.

For example, suppose you have a deadline as an incentive. Something like this appears on the order form:

COUPON VALID ONLY UNTIL OCTOBER 1

Obviously, that kind of wording won't work with third class mail; the piece might not be delivered until October 1 or it might be delivered by September 10, which is too early. What to do? Simple:

COUPON VALID ONLY FOR 15 DAYS AFTER RECEIPT

Here's another way to save money by thinking ahead: Suppose you plan a series of three mailers, all with a common theme. Instead of printing each one separately, print all the envelopes in advance. Even if you change the copy on each one, you still have a single press run instead of three.

If you plan to offer items for sale, then come back at the same buyers later on with the same items at a lower price, print both pieces together, then overprint half the copies in red with the close-out prices you'll offer later. Instead of printing the entire piece twice, you print it once.

Gang-running order forms, which are often small and result in paper wastage, will save paper and presstime; you need only cut them apart and store the ones you plan to use later.

Alert printers and production men can be a big help in saving money. Listen to them.

Some Legal Rules

If you've never used third class mail, don't wait until a mailing is ready and then walk into the post office with two armloads of mail and ask where to dump it. Instead, visit the post office in advance to ask for printed information on third class mail, or deal with a letter shop or professional mailing house familiar with the regulations. Otherwise, you might find yourself with mail that has to go first class because it was printed or sorted wrong.

Some mailers think they have to print a permit number on the upper right corner of the envelope, sadly identifying the envelope as third class. This is unnecessary. If you want to have a stamped look, you can affix precancelled stamps, some of which are just as jazzy as first class stamps.

If you want to imprint a permit number, which is easier because it requires no saliva, obviously you need a permit number; it costs about $20. No matter what imprint or metering or stamp is used, third class mail must be sorted by zip codes. Sorting is no problem if you're dealing with a professional mailer, because his lists are presorted; but if you're handling a mailing yourself and have a "scrambled" list, then you might find it more economical to skip the zip and mail first class.*

There are some other guidelines. Did you ever get an envelope with a red sticker on it, labelled "D"? The post office put it there. "D" means yours was the front envelope in a package of ten or more, all in the same zip code. If the letter had an orange sticker "S," yours was the front envelope of a package of ten or more headed for the same state. A "C" on a yellow background goes to the same city, "3" on a green sticker indicates the first three digits of a zip code area, an "F" on blue, the same firm.

Third class mail must weigh less than one pound per piece; every piece must be identical. You must mail at least 250 pieces or 50 pounds. There is no such thing as third class mail to another country.

The rules change constantly and without logic, so it's wise to discuss a mailing with the local postmaster. If he accepts it, out it goes.

Dealing with letter shops and mailing services can be costly, but you might find that these suppliers can do the job cheaper than you or your employees can, and they know the ropes. Rates from the various suppliers of direct mail services differ widely, so you should get at least two estimates.

Merge-Purge

All big mailing houses have their lists of names on computer tape. Suppose you want to send a mailing to customers and to "cold lists," and you don't want any one individual, or

---

*At this writing, presorting first class mail by zip codes entitles a mailer to a slightly lower postal rate, but the special "indicia" on the envelope gives the mailing a third class look, and some mailers have complained that the postal handling isn't always parallel to standard first class mail.

even any one address, to get two pieces of mail. How do you cull them?

When dealing in thousands of names, culling them used to be an impossible job; today it's a simple, uncomplicated, not particularly expensive trick done by computer check of one list against another. Duplications are kicked out, and even if you mail a million pieces, no one will get more than one. Merge-purge has an obvious value if you're claiming that something is exclusive or hard to get. Imagine that claim being made to someone who is on four lists and receives the same "hard-to-get" offer four separate times.

Most mailers agree, too, that they do more business by mailing once to many prospects than by mailing several times to fewer prospects. Usually merge-purge is worthwhile, but it only can work when the lists being purged against each other are on computer tape; it won't work if you have 5,000 customer names on labels and the cold list you try to merge-purge has 10,000 names on tape.

What you can do, if you can't merge-purge, is avoid duplication of zip codes. At worst, you include a note in the mailing saying you're sending this only to people who have shown an interest in what you have to sell, and if some lucky recipient gets two, please turn one of the two over to a friend who also might be interested.

The merge-purge process may cut down the number of pieces you mail. Suppose you buy the American Express list, the VISA list, and the Diners Club list, all from the ten top zip codes (most buying power) of your area. A merge-purge might find a 10 to 25 percent duplication. Find this out before you settle on the final quantity to be printed.

Buying and Using Mailing Lists

There are hundreds of list brokers, each of whom claims superiority for the lists he manages. "This list worked well for the Jones Company," a list broker will tell you; "It has to work for you, too."

Maybe it will. But there are several reasons why it might

not: Maybe Jones and others like Jones have milked that list so thoroughly that no response is left in it. Maybe Jones doesn't sell quite the way you do, or maybe the product isn't parallel. Maybe Jones has a discount image and you have a class image, or vice versa. Maybe the list was valid when Jones used it six months ago but hasn't been worked since and no longer has any life.

Some mail order operators would sell their souls for one mailing to a competitor's list. Suppose you're approached in a dark alley by an unsavory character who says, "You want your competitor's list? I'll get it for you for a thousand bucks." Don't touch it! Any list worth having is "salted" with fake names put into that list only to prevent exactly what this person is trying to do. The buyer doesn't know which are the salted names, and the moment that piece of mail hits the mailbox you have a lawsuit on your hands, or worse—in some cases theft of a mailing list is considered a criminal act.

If you want a competitor's list, chances are the only way you can get it is to swap; you let him mail to 10,000 of your names and he lets you mail to 10,000 of his. If it works for both parties, you can continue with the entire lists. Obviously, no two lists are the same length, and it's senseless, if you have a thousand names, to try to swap for more than a thousand names of a competitor.

One other way to get a competitor (to use his list for you), and it makes sense if you're starting out and have no list to swap, is called a third-party endorsement. With a third-party endorsement, you don't mail your competition's list—they do. You persuade them to put your piece of literature into an envelope (supplied by you) with their company name on it. The letter, from them, might start out, "We've been able to arrange with The Smith Company to let our buyers have the same offer, on the same terms as their own customers enjoy." The mailing either becomes a joint venture or you pay Jones a commission of 10 to 20 percent on sales to his list. If you're lucky, or if Jones is big enough or cocky enough not to care, the names of the buyers will be turned over to you for fulfillment (filling the order), and you can add the names of those buyers to your own list.

Most lists sell for $45 to $100 per thousand names and are guaranteed accurate within 95 percent. That means you should have no more than five pieces of mail coming back undelivered from each one hundred mailed.

Choosing the Best Time and the Best Prospects

Mail order doesn't differ from other businesses in its best selling season: *Christmas.* Next to Christmas, the best time to mail seems to be January. The whole season from January through May is good; September through November is almost as good; and summertime doesn't seem to pull as well, even though there's less competition in the mail.

Some lists are segmented into sublists. If you can get a "hot-line" segment, it should outpull the rest of the list, because a hot-line name is that of a buyer within the past six months.

Multiple buyers are better than one-time buyers; that is, someone who has bought more than once from the owner of the list is better for you than someone who has bought only once: Multiple buyers are serious buyers.

There are demographic differences, too. People over 35 will buy at a higher rate than those under 35; except for sophisticated merchandise, rural and exurban names will buy more than city names will.

Maximizing the Use of Mailing Lists

Because postal slowness suggests you should not put an absolute deadline on an order form, instead say something such as, "Please return this reservation form within 21 days." Responses will peak the second Monday after the first reply is received; after counting that day's mail, you can assume you have 60 percent of the total response.

"Key" mailings so you know what pulled. You can color-key an order form or you can use "Department A," "Department B," and so on. Without keying, you may never know what worked and what failed.

Testing a list is another important tactic. To test a concept, experts say, you need 25,000 to 40,000 names; to test a list, 5,000 names. This means you get a truer test by mailing 5,000 each to the lists you and the list broker agree are the strongest. Then, you hope, with your winnings from that mailing, you can go on to further testing while you "rollout," or mail, to the list or lists that have worked.

Obviously, with a dollar-short situation, testing may not be possible. And if you're testing, the list isn't the only test to make. Also test:

the offer itself
the price
the approach (whether friendly, formal, feminine, masculine, or casual)
the time of year

With all these possible tests, you can understand why a test mailing by a large mail order company, just to see whether the offer is valid or not, can easily exceed 200,000 pieces. The rollout can number in the millions. I know companies that are still testing after two or three million pieces have been mailed, and sometimes I wonder, when they finally have that offer refined for a rollout, who's left to *get* that rollout.

Some companies, especially publications, make more money renting their lists than they do from any other facet of their operation. That's why some publications constantly solicit new subscribers even when the publication is sent free. The name is money in the bank, and a company might rent out a single name 20 to 50 times a year.

It's probably unrealistic to ask a list broker to withhold from a competitor a list you're using so the recipient won't be swamped by similar offers. Still, it never hurts to ask and sometimes, especially if no one is breaking down the door to get at that list, exclusivity in a field for three months may be granted.

How to Test Without Going Bananas

Although mailing list professionals claim they can't get a valid test of a concept with fewer than 25,000 to 40,000 names or a test of a list with fewer than 5,000 names, not everyone can or wants to do this. Some mailings are simply too small.

Some experts suggest testing a consumer mailing of 10,000 pieces by using 5,000 for the test and 5,000 for the rollout. The 5,000 could be broken into three lists of 1,667 each. To each of those lists, mail the same piece of literature (there is no point in printing three brochures in that quantity because the extra cost would wipe out any chance of profit) with differently pitched letters. As an example, here is how the three might start:

> If the stock market isn't a good investment these days, what is? (Greed)
> Chances are 21,900 to one that you won't die tomorrow. (Fear)
> I was talking with Don Shula the other day—about you. (Testimonial)

The lists of 1,667 would be split into three segments of 556, which is small, in fact too tiny a sample to be tabulated by the giants. But since you're not a giant with this size mailing, you're entitled to maximize your chance for success.

Here are some of the specifics you might test if you have the urge, the money, the know-how, and the objectivity to do it:

1. *Color v. black and white.* You'd be surprised how many times color doesn't pay for itself. I know—I went to school just as you did, and we all learned that color outpulls black and white. Except that it doesn't always, and sometimes, when it does, the difference doesn't equal the added production costs.

How do you know which is better? You test.

2. *Motivators.* The great motivators in the Age of Skepticism are *fear, exclusivity, guilt,* and *greed,* and you'd expect these to outpull everything else. But which one will pull best for your offer? Sometimes a testimonial works better than either guilt or greed, because you need that testimonial to overcome the recipient's ignorance of just who you are. Sometimes no approach other than "only you" can reach a status seeker. Sometimes cold product facts outpull everything else. How do you find out? You test.

3. *Price.* Before you test price, you'd better decide why you're doing it. If you want to add a lot of names to your mailing list, a lower price will bring you those names, and even though you may not make a lot of money on this mailing you can anticipate selling something else to those captive names. On the other hand, a higher price means less shipping, less handling, fewer complaints, less computer time to enter the orders, and probably higher profits. You can test an item at $25, $35, and $45, and find a reason to justify rolling out with any of these prices. The goal should be clear beforehand. Then you test. And be sure the literature is identical except for price; otherwise the test is invalid. If you opt for the lower price, be sure to refund the difference to those who bought at the higher price.

4. *Length of letter.* I once had a six-page letter that pulled reasonably well. On a hunch, we de-puffed it, slashing it down to four pages. It pulled better. I've also had a crisp, short letter that followed every rule of advertising writing; it did nothing compared with a longer letter that threw in everything from poetry to a family reminiscence. How do you know which length works best in your particular situation? You test.

5. *First class v. third class mail.* I know what I said. It's still worth a test.

6. *Male v. female approach.* This is a new one, never seen until around 1978 but increasingly common in the mid-1980s. Having a business letter to consumers (not to a business list) written by a woman seems to pull better in some cases than the same type of letter written by a man. Notice that I said, "the same type of letter," not "the same letter." A letter signed by a woman should have a feminine aura to it; if you have a male copywriter, have a woman check it to see whether she would use the same phrases. Ask her to suggest an anecdote or two; they'll be a different type of anecdote from ones a man might use. Does a woman outpull a man? Test and see.

7. *Lists.* In this context consider testing at least one speculative list together with the old standbys. The lists most certain to pull are those rented from publications in the field to which you are mailing. Next are those that have been used by others mailing to similar targets; after those are lists of people

Figure 5-1 This mailing is almost a textbook of direct mail psychology and mechanical techniques. The computer personalization prints the name in many sizes; the mailing offers the possibility of winning one million dollars, or maybe twice that amount; the spokesman is a TV personality. What this mailer is selling—magazine subscriptions—isn't mentioned at all. (Envelope copy has just one purpose: to get the envelope opened.)

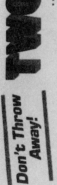

Figure 5-2 Reverse side of the envelope shown in Figure 5-1.

who have bought merchandise similar to the merchandise you're selling. If you're lucky enough to get a list of people who have bought merchandise exactly like yours, move that list to the top of the class.

8. *Envelope color and treatment.* This isn't a rule, but a suggestion: Put a "teaser" message on the envelope. Sample messages might read, "A personal invitation from John Jones," "Open this immediately," "This is the information you asked for," or "Our president wants to discuss something with you." Usually this message is handwritten, but occasionally excellent results come from typing the first two or three sentences from the inside letter on the outside envelope, ending with the words "(continued inside)." If you realize that the purpose of envelope treatment is to get the receiver to open the envelope to see what's inside—a huge percentage of the people who get third class mail never open it at all or open it only to verify that it's an unsolicited mailing and then throw it away—you understand the importance of envelope treatment. Testing colored envelopes against the standard white ones also pays off. Manila envelopes work well, too, because they seem to display less pomposity, or maybe less sophistication, than white ones do.

9. *Means of ordering.* Would response improve if you offered a "send no money now" option? Or if you added VISA or Mastercard as a means of payment? Or if no monies are due for 30 days after the buyer has the product? Test them and see.

10. *Number of enclosures.* During mail order's dark days, a letter, a brochure, an order form, and a business reply envelope (BRE) were all the enclosures anyone used. Today, who knows what kicks that hot button? So test with a question-and-answer sheet, a page of testimonials, a reprint of a magazine article (perhaps planted in that magazine by you), some technical reports of performance, or some trade references. When you have it working, you then test by omitting one enclosure at a time; you'll find out soon enough which one has been pushing the buyers' hot button.

11. *Postage paid v. buyer pays return postage.* The BRE has been standard and probably will continue to be standard because the buyer, acting on impulse (the core of direct

response success), has only to put the order form into the envelope or fold the order form/envelope and seal it. He then doesn't have to fish around for a stamp. If he doesn't have a stamp, that alone could kill the sale. Or could it? If you have lots of guts, test a "place stamp here" on your envelope. You may save a lot of postage, but be warned: It's dangerous.

Incidentally, when unsure how to get the permit number printed on a BRE, just show up at the post office. When you leave five minutes later, you'll have a number. If you get a lot of business reply mail, you may have to deposit some earnest money with the post office to avoid paying a premium, but this is only a deposit, and it's the best way of handling this relationship.

12. *One-step v. two-step conversion.* What's the difference? Sometimes when you go for the jugular on a cold mailing, you turn off the recipient. Subliminally, he forms a "How dare you!" reaction to the frenzy of the pitch. It may be you should play it cool and go for a two-step conversion: The recipient can't order from the materials you send him; all he can do is reply to qualify for materials from which he can order. This is the "Send coupon for full details" approach, which might work because the first mailing, for inquiries only, need not be elaborate; for the same money you can mail many more pieces. If this procedure of one-step v. two-step seems sensible, try it. You should know that usually, in cold list mailings, a one-step is more successful than a two-step conversion, but there are exceptions and maybe you're one of them.

Other areas also could be tested. But should you test even these twelve? If you want to go broke, sure. Otherwise, pick one or two, test those, and let fly. Instincts have to be worth something, or you wouldn't be in business in the first place.

How to Make Sure Your Mailing Piece Stays Out of the Wastebasket

A few years ago, David Ogilvy, surely one of the Grand Old Men of advertising, addressed a direct marketing conference. Two things he said bear repeating: "If an advertising man has served his apprenticeship in direct response, he will be able to keep his feet on the ground for the rest of his life," and "The trouble is that many copywriters, perhaps most of them, do not think in terms of actually selling a product. Until they have written a direct response advertisement, they have not tasted blood."

A practicing direct mailer doesn't need a maestro of advertising to realize that he stands or falls on the success of his package, which is measured not only by the number of people he persuades to order but also by how much was spent against how much was received back—which means the game can't be won by heavy production and gimmicks alone.

Years ago, I published a list of rules for direct response letters. Some of the key rules are more important today than they ever were. If you're a windbag letter writer, this list will be of some help even if it only controls the mad urge to overwrite:

1. *Fire your biggest gun first.* (Sure, there are exceptions, and I can specify two of them: (1) If your letter is designed to educate customers to a state of mind you know they lack without the education of that letter, and (2) if you suspect the recipient is hostile. Otherwise, haul out the cannon and fire.)

Which of these openings would you guess will motivate the most prospects to lift the phone and call?

> Dear Fleet Operator,
>
> We've been serving fleet owners like you for more than a quarter of a century, and in that time we've proved at least one point: You'll get better service from us, and we'll save you as much as 20 percent on every car you buy.

Or this, which names the big specific benefit immediately?

> I'll save you $1,000 on the next car you buy. And the next one. And the next one. And if you buy ten cars, you'll have $10,000 in your pocket that wouldn't be there if you did business with someone else.

Whatever your bomb is, heave it. The chance of having a

recipient read the letter all the way through is slim, so don't decrease the chance further by boring him or sneaking up on a point he's impatient to learn.

2. *Fill the letter with "you,"* not "we," unless the "we" is a reference to what *we* will do to benefit *you.*

3. *Use no paragraphs longer than seven lines.* Does this rule sound difficult? It isn't. It's the easiest rule you'll ever have to follow, because all you have to do is count. If you don't believe this rule, check your own reading habits and fatigue level. It needn't be with a letter; it can be with a book. For example, this paragraph is harder to read than the paragraph just above it, because that paragraph is shorter.

4. *Include some validation of your claim.* If you don't have one, get a testimonial, and that testimonial doesn't have to be from a celebrity. Here's an example:

> I showed this knife to my wife. She's an expert on kitchen knives. Showing it was a mistake, because she kept it and won't give it back. I'm proud, but I'm getting tired of her showing her friends how it slices through bones in the roast as though they were made of cardboard.

Here's another:

> Art consultant Johann Karlsen had this to say about the painting: "A masterpiece. He has Picasso's eye for color and Dali's incredible talent for detail."

Who is "art consultant" Johann Karlsen? Probably the artist who pasted up the brochure.

5. *Don't be afraid to write notes in the margin or to hand-write a p.s.* These should be printed in a second color for emphasis; a good idea is to write the notes and your signature in blue, a common ink color, suggesting that you wrote those notes by hand on each letter and then signed it. What can the notes say? Anything from "Read this!" or "This is my personal invitation to you" to "I must have your answer by December 1."

6. *Be personal, not stiff.* Use contractions. Say, "I don't," not "I do not." Write the way people talk. Don't sign the letter "Yours truly." The single word "Sincerely" is fine.

7. *Don't clown around.* Tell anecdotes but not jokes. Here's the difference between an anecdote and a joke:

> The idea for this project came to me during a trip my wife and I took to the Holy Land this summer . . .

These words begin an anecdote. You're telling a story, telling it personally and treating the recipient like a friend.

> A funny thing happened to me on the way to Jerusalem. I went up to the man renting camel rides, and he asked me, "One hump or two?"

You're a clown. The reader isn't with you; he's above you because you're nothing but a borscht-belt comedian.

8. *Make the letter as long as necessary to tell the story.* It might be one page, two pages, four pages, six pages—whatever it takes. People *will* read long letters if you use the space to explain benefits to them.

9. *Big benefits, such as price breaks or free offers, should be described and repeated at least twice.* Repetition of benefits builds confidence; the reader knows he hasn't misunderstood and is sure you and he agree on what he's getting.

10. *Don't double-space a letter.* Single-space, with two spaces between paragraphs. Indent an occasional paragraph and have one or two only one line long. This spacing breaks up the letter into readable blocks and is a psychological "plus" contributing to readability.

11. *Here's a safe approach to mail order letters.* It works when no other approach will; it's a promise that brings signatures to the order forms:

a. Everybody wants it.
b. Nobody can get it.
c. Except you.

This approach spells out exclusivity and greed, a potent combination. Telling the reader what he'll miss if he doesn't respond can be a heavy thumb on his hot button.

12. *The p.s. on a letter is more important than any part of the letter except the first sentence.* Everyone reads the p.s., even if he doesn't read the letter all the way through. Use the p.s.

for a final killer-argument. If you haven't been appending a p.s. to your letters, start now.

13. *This is the most important rule of all: experiment.* Experiment with handwritten teaser copy at the top of the letter. Experiment with occasional handwritten words and marginal notes. Experiment with indentations. Experiment with "Plain Ol' Country Boy" verbiage. But however you experiment, don't violate Rule 7.

As for the literature itself, picture what you're selling as beautifully and comprehensively as you can. If the product is a coat, show the coat worn by a model; show the lining; show several people wearing them; show a closeup of the weave or surface; include a swatch of material if you can. Show it being worn to a party, to an office, to a football game, getting into a car, to school, at an airport.

But don't misrepresent the product in photographs or artwork. You may fool someone into ordering, but the rate of returns will be so high it will wipe out profits.

Returns aren't the bane of mail order any more than they're the curse of conventional retail selling. Every department store has an adjustment department, and every mail order company takes returns as a matter of course. As long as returns average under five percent, don't complain.

Offer a refund guarantee in the copy. Give the buyer 10 to 20 days to inspect the merchandise during which he can return it "for a full refund." This guarantee (set it in a formal guarantee-type border for emphasis) of refund will improve sales far beyond the amount you ever will refund, and most sellers would give an unhappy buyer his money back on demand even without advertising it. You might as well cash in on the psychological benefit of risk-free inspection.

Sell on the order form. Don't just list the merchandise, although you should cover every option in size, color, fabric, or anything you've mentioned elsewhere. Keep selling.

Offering buyers the option of charging the purchase to a major charge card will increase the sale of high-ticket items 20 to 40 percent.

Direct response marketers went through a computer letter period from 1967, when computerized personalization first was used by *Reader's Digest,* through 1978, when computer personalization became so "in" it was "out." Although big magazine circulation drives still use computer letters, for the smaller mailer today the extra cost of computer personalization may not justify itself.

The BRE can be a help, too. Instead of simply printing "Jones Company" on it, address it to "Mr. John Jones, President, Jones Company." The personalization will improve the response.

One sad note about selling by mail: While it's fine for fund raising, there's one exception. It's brutally hard to raise money for a political candidate by mail. It just doesn't seem to pay for itself, unless the candidate is a political extremist. For example, it worked for Ronald Reagan but not for Jimmy Carter.

As you use the mails, you undoubtedly will eliminate some of these rules and come up with some new ones—provided you watch the response and keep careful score of what works best and then try to improve from there.

Mail Order Advertising in Media

When advertising in newspapers or magazines, test ads with an A/B split, which means that every other copy of a publication has the other ad. Suppose you're considering two headlines for an ad. One says, "First Time Below $25!" and the other says, "You Get All 12 of These for $19.95!" Testing with an A/B split shows which ad pulls better. Note that the A/B split is every other copy; don't buy a split that replates in the middle of the run, so that the first half of the copies get one ad and the second half the other. That's not a true test, because all the copies going to one zip code probably will get the same ad. You want absolutely random testing.

In a few publications, you can A/B-test color against black and white. If you run this type of test, copy should be the same to avoid diluting test results.

Here are a few general rules for print media mail order advertising:

1. *A right-hand page is better than a left-hand page.* Ask for but don't demand this position. If you demand it, the publication will add a position charge.

2. *The front of a magazine is usually better than the back.* Unfortunately for mail order sellers, their ads are usually placed in the back, but researcher Daniel Starch reports that a front position is read by ten percent more people than is the middle or the back. One thought, though, that might temper this consideration: The mail order buyer is used to looking for such ads in the back of the publication.

3. *The outside of a page is better than the inside, especially if you have a coupon in your ad.* That coupon will almost always increase the pull enough to pay for its space and then some. Some advertisers claim a coupon will double or triple the pull.

4. *When trying insert cards, ask for the first one in the issue.* Invariably, each succeeding card in a publication pulls a little worse than the one before it, but most advertisers don't know this and won't ask for the first card.

5. *When advertising on television as a mail order marketer, don't let yourself be sold a lengthy schedule.* Buy it week by week so you can get out when the pull drops below the profit level. The pull will be lower each week; it won't get better, so don't hang around to bury your investment in television.

Most television advertisers want to be in or near high-rated shows, even though time costs far more in those time periods. As a mail order marketer, you don't. People are less likely to respond to you during a program of high Relative Attention Ratio (see Chapter 6) than during a program of low Relative Attention Ratio. They may love what you're selling, but they won't pick up the phone or a pencil for fear of missing the next murder, the next touchdown, or the next joke. A definite benefit pertains to the mail order seller in advertising on lower-rated programs. Not only do they cost far less, which makes the break-even point more realistic, but viewers are more apt to take the time to respond. The later into the evening one goes, the more relaxed the viewers are, which makes fringe time a good possibility for mail order sellers.

Go Where the Money Is

Even before the introduction of the pocket calculator, mail order sellers were costing themselves many thousands of dollars they might have been earning, by misusing statistics. Mail order operators deal in percentages. A product should cost no more than 25 to 33 percent of selling price. Mailings and media advertising should pull double the break-even point.

But he who lives by percentages alone must die by percentages. An advertiser tests publications. In one, he spends $1,000 and nets $1,200; in another he spends $3,000 and nets $3,400. "Aha!" he says. "I made 20 percent on the $1,000 ad, and I only made 13.3 percent on the $3,000 ad. I'll discontinue that $3,000 ad and run the $1,000 ad."

Right?

Wrong.

That's the way an accountant might look at it, and it's why accountants have tunnel vision relative to so many businesses. In both cases the advertiser got his money back. In one case he made $200 and in the other $400. Which would you rather have, $200 or $400? *Raw dollar differential* is what counts, not percentages, and if you understand this one point, you can deduct the cost of this book from the much higher taxes you'll pay on your much higher income.

There's another way, overlooked by many mail order sellers, to make money. The magic word is "bounce-back." A bounce-back is an offer enclosed with the merchandise shipped from the buyer's first order. Has the customer ordered seat covers? Enclose a bounce-back for floor mats that match the seat covers. Has he ordered collector's plates? Enclose a bounce-back for display stands. Has he ordered art prints? Enclose a bounce-back for frames. She's ordered an arthritis remedy? Enclose a bounce-back for a giant-size refill. They've ordered luggage? Enclose a bounce-back for a clothing bag.

The bounce-back doesn't have to be for an allied product, although such an appeal is logical. For example, you needn't give up if you can't bounce-back curtain rods when someone orders curtains. A bounce-back for dishes might do even better. And remember: Bounce-backs don't even cost postage, since they're included with a product. If you haven't been bouncing back, start now: It's found money.

When working on an inquiry rather than on a sale basis—that is, when going for the name rather than the sale—how many times should you mail to a name before giving up? Some tests show that the second through fourth mailings pull as well as the first. I've seldom found this to be true, but enough others have to convince me, and I hope you, to keep mailing. The first offer may have turned off a prospect. If so, send him another one. After the fourth mailing, though, response drops off so fast it's probably more economical to mail a "cold" name than to send a fifth mailing to a nonresponsive inquiry.

You can appreciate the many disciplines forced onto the mail order seller not required of other types of advertising. Ogilvy may have been only partly right when he said, "Until they have written a direct response advertisement, they have not tasted blood." He could have added one word: "Until they have written a *successful* direct response advertisement, they have not tasted blood."

6

Caution: TV Advertising
Can Be Hazardous
to Your Wealth

For the marketer who advertises to show off rather than to sell something, television is the perfect medium. No other mechanical invention in history is so capable of emptying a pocketbook, bringing peculiar results in which competitors are helped as much as you are, or building the advertiser's ego if not his business.

In the early days of television—the golden days from 1948 until about 1955—local advertisers were the mainstays of television stations. Until 1952 there wasn't even a nationwide cable hookup for a network, which meant that stations west of Chicago (or east of Chicago, depending on where the show originated) had to be fed by kinescope (there was no videotape yet, either). There was no color, which meant that low-cost black-and-white commercials were used by the giant advertisers as well as the little guys. And so many commercials were live that the number of goofs in big-budget commercials sometimes gave the little guy even more than equality in image.

No more.

When viewers regularly see spots that cost $500,000 to $1 million to produce, what does a primitive ad on slides look like? And the car dealer who used to sponsor an entire movie from 8 to 10 P.M. now can't even find an opening in the schedule for his spot until 10:30 P.M., when one 30-second spot costs 25 times as much as sponsoring the whole movie did in 1952.

Certainly television has spawned some staggeringly profitable success stories. On a mass consumer-goods level, a product can't achieve high visibility without it. For example, most people can name almost every cigarette that was a major television advertiser until the 1973 ban but can't name ten brands introduced since then.

How to Waste Lots of Money in Commercial Production

To the advertiser with a $10 million budget, spending $100,000 on a commercial represents one percent of the total. If 30 percent waste occurs in that production figure, it amounts to $30,000—a good day's pay—but it's only three tenths of one percent. So what?

So the acceptance of waste by the giant advertisers causes waste by the little guys who emulate them or who inherit their sets of rules.

The little guys can also inherit the big advertisers' compliance with rules by trade and talent unions, and that can be even more damaging since no one can really point a finger at anyone else and say, "Look what you did." The acceptance of skyrocketing wage demands, under the pressure of refusal to perform, buckles the giant advertisers and their agencies somewhat, but the rules aren't adapted at all to the small advertiser who can't survive with these restrictions. The situation is similar to General Motors accepting a pact with the auto workers that includes contributions, retirement, no layoffs, guaranteed hours, a 25-year employment limit, and overtime after 25 hours; G.M. can absorb this and even pass it on to their consumers, but when the union then goes to Glutzz Motor Company, which makes 80 cars a year, and enforces these same demands, Glutzz folds. So think carefully about the following rules for wasting money:

Rule One for wasting money: Follow the union rules of the

biggies. This means shooting commercials in the large studios. These places have lots of people to bring you coffee, pretty receptionists to ogle, and tons of equipment that help build up the overhead. A crew will consist of a director of cinematography, a camera operator, an assistant, a boom man, a recordist, two electricians, a grip (dolly-pusher), and several apprentices (called "gophers" because they "go-fer" things). There will also be a director and an assistant director. None of these people can touch anything operated by another, and all of them get "time-and-a-half" as of 5:31 P.M.

Rule Two for wasting money: Use union talent. Excluded from this rule is "name" or celebrity talent because this type of individual might actually be valuable. The technique for using them is discussed elsewhere. Instead, this rule refers to journeyman members of the Screen Actors Guild or the American Federation of Television and Radio Artists. The typical member works for his talent guild, not for you. For every 13 weeks in which he appears in a commercial (even if it is only used once within that 13-week cycle), a new payment is due.

What can that cost you?

Here are the current rates as of this writing. By the time you read this, they will probably have gone up. You needn't worry about their going down.

Screen Actors Guild, which controls talent for film, calls its people "Players." The American Federation of Television and Radio Artists, which controls talent for videotape, calls them "principals." Just about every actor and announcer belongs to both. On camera the talent gets a basic fee of $333.27, called the session fee. This fee enables the sponsor to use the commercial once on a network; if it's on a spot basis, it can be used up to five times in a small, local market; once in Boston or San Francisco, (which count as five-units), not quite once in Philadelphia (which counts as six units). A separate formula applies in Chicago, New York, and Los Angeles, each of which counts as many cities.

Cable TV has a separate rate. Fifteen-second spots have a separate rate. Pension and welfare payments depend on the length of the spot and where it runs.

An "extra" gets $243.96, which is ridiculous for the small

advertiser. Off-camera announcers get $250.61 against use payments. And after 13 weeks, everything starts over.

As a curiosity, the table of current rates follows. If you find it confusing, you're in good company; some of the large advertising agencies have not only entire departments, but sometimes subsidiary companies, that do nothing but figure out talent payments. From the chart, though, you can see that if a spot runs on a network once a week for 13 weeks, you'll pay $1,526.69 to each person who appears on camera; if you run the spot just once in Detroit (four units) and Philadelphia—a total of ten units—you'll pay $455.57 for that one spot.

CLASS A PROGRAM (On Camera)		
(number of times)		
Use	*Per Use*	*Total*
1	$333.27	$333.27
2	122.68	455.95
3	97.34	553.29
4	97.34	650.63
5	97.34	747.97
6	97.34	845.31
7	97.34	942.65
8	97.34	1039.99
9	97.34	1137.33
10	97.34	1234.67
11	97.34	1332.01
12	97.34	1429.35
13	97.34	1526.69
14–18	91.99 each	

SPOT (On-Camera)	
Units (example)	*Unit Rate*
1	$333.27
25	665.75
100	1043.73
150	1295.72

You can see why the big advertising agencies have entire departments whose only job is trying to keep track of "use payments."

Rule Three for wasting money: Use a big studio. Your commercial might consist of a close-up of a smiling druggist holding a bottle of suntan lotion. You shoot it in a studio 100 × 200 feet; there's a huge crane, which you don't use; a hundred lights, which you don't use; a gigantic cyclorama (limbo background), which you don't use; a sound-mixing facility capable of mixing twelve separate tracks, which you don't use; and a colossal overhead, which you do help pay.

Rule Four for wasting money: Change commercials every two weeks. A man named Rosser Reeves, who used to run Ted Bates & Co., an advertising agency, long ago wrote a book about advertising.[1] In it he makes a cogent point: "If you find something that works, keep it on the air until it doesn't work any more." But once the typical advertiser has screened a commercial for his wife, his office staff, his friends, and himself, he's already sick of it; the novelty has disappeared, and he can't visualize it from the position of a consumer who may have seen it at most once or twice. He spends money on a new spot instead of on television time to get mileage out of the existing one. When you get the urge to change a commercial because you've seen it too often, congratulations! You've found another way to waste money.

And how do you save money in commercial production? In one sentence: Find a production facility that treats its clients fairly, doesn't show off with equipment and people you pay for but don't use, and has a solid base of professionalism.

Where do you find such people? I suggest looking at the film and videotape facilities of smaller television stations. They almost invariably charge less than commercial studios and producers. There are stations in St. Petersburg, Florida; in Rockford, Illinois; in Tucson, Arizona; in Minneapolis, Minnesota— all with sophisticated videotape equipment, with adequate film equipment, and with the desire to produce commercials

---

[1]Reality in Advertising, Alfred A. Knopf, 1961.

that represent a little more than you're paying for. Local cable companies are often a good bet.

Obviously, the advertiser obsessed with production instead of marketing can't survive in these waters; he'll strangle for lack of oxygen. It's difficult to lower production sights to a point of sanity, especially when the advertising publications seem to glorify only those commercials that cost a lot of money, not those that sell a lot of merchandise. Some of the more expensive spots, including the famous six million dollar Pepsi-Cola "Michael Jackson" commercial, are discussed later in this chapter. But this book is about a sensible approach to advertising, not a bigshot approach. If you can spend six million dollars for a commercial and not feel it, you're far beyond needing my advice.

The Short Happy Life of Novelty

Mighty Dog has achieved steady market inroads since the day the first spot was aired, and it hasn't switched from its basic format. Visine overpowered long-time champion Murine with just one commercial that ran for two years. The Anacin spot, with the famous hammer-in-the-skull, has been off the air for a long time but is still remembered; it ran for about nine years.

Having just said that switching away from a commercial that pulls is a bad idea, I have to temper this remark with the comment that not only do commercials wear out like a suit that becomes threadbare, but commercials based on novelty wear out even faster, like a Nehru jacket both threadbare and out of fashion.

A few years ago Stan Freberg spent $165,000 of the H. J. Heinz Company's money to produce a whopper of a commercial. Starring vintage dancer Ann Miller, it was patterned after a Busby Berkeley musical. Not only was its life span short, but most of the admen I know remember it as a Campbell Soup commercial, which doesn't do Heinz a lot of good.

Some of the novelty commercials, especially those with a cartoon format, have tremendous wallop the first time they are viewed. From that point, though, because the medium dominates the message, it's like hearing the same joke twice, three times, a dozen times: Its impact is weaker each time it appears. The best commercial is one that makes a point, makes it again, and hammers it home a third time, without becoming pompous, boring, dull, preachy, or too cute. It's possible to be lively and entertaining and still make a point.

Replacing Spectacle with Sincerity

For every $100 an advertiser spent in 1975, by 1983 he had to spend $276 to reach the same number of people on evening network television. (As a comparison, radio was up to $176, magazines up to $179.)

One way in which the cost of television exposure has outstripped normal inflation and price-rises by thousands of percent has been in the cost of producing commercials. As recently as 1979, the industry was aghast at the $250,000 Levi Strauss spent on a single commercial.

$250,000? Chicken feed.

At this writing, the current cost champion is the commercial produced in 1984 by Pepsi-Cola, starring rock singer Michael Jackson (whose actual appearance on camera is only for a few seconds). Pepsi spent a million dollars on the spot—*not* including the estimated five million dollars paid to Jackson. The incredible numbers dwarfed Apple Computer's estimated $600,000 production cost for the spot introducing the Macintosh Computer, a spot which ran less than half a dozen times.

(Writing in *Adweek*, Mary Alice Kellogg commented, "I forced myself to watch the legendary Michael Jackson Pepsi commercials, masochist that I am. I barely saw three seconds of Jackson. I barely saw three seconds of the product. I did, however, have fun dancing around my living room—but not on my head. I saw lots of footage of kids breakdancing and a tiny shot of Michael doing something that looked like the '80s version of the Funky chicken.")

For Pepsi-Cola, a soft drink company, currently regarded as one of the world's smarter merchandisers through shrewd

Figure 6-1 Key scenes from the controversial commercial introducing the Apple Macintosh computer. Product never appeared in the commercial, which had a cast of 200 people. Cost was estimated at $600,000. Whether because of this introduction or not, Apple's Macintosh had a strong initial reception.

appeals to younger buyers, the commercial may have built the image they were after. But I'd hate to see a lesser advertiser decide to spend that kind of money on the grounds that the more expensive a commercial is, the more effective it is. Arm & Hammer's baking soda-in-the-refrigerator commercial was neither complicated nor expensive, but 30 million households were moved to put a box of baking soda in the refrigerator.

Where a lot of advertisers, even big ones, go awry is in overlooking television's superiority to other media. That superiority doesn't lie in spectacle—a 16-page insert with pop-ups or scents can make the claim of spectacle. Rather, television offers the opportunity to *demonstrate.*

Demonstrations don't require a multiplicity of commercials, and they don't require heavy production for a single commercial; but they do sell. Through demonstration a wild claim becomes truth; through demonstration the complicated becomes easy; through demonstration skepticism can be turned to admiration.

This is especially true if you avoid the urge to make something big out of something little. The smaller advertiser has the edge, because he isn't so impressed with himself he'll think an uncomplicated, straightforward demonstration isn't jazzy enough for him.

The Tools and the Costs

Even making simple commercials requires some technical information:

16mm film. Film is the most flexible production method, because a small 16mm camera can go anywhere. Cameras such as Bolex, Eclair, and Arriflex give perfectly adequate results and aren't expensive, which means a lower overhead. Right now synchronous sound (sound recorded as someone talks instead of a voice-over—see Appendix 2) costs less in a small-station videotape studio, but sometimes there is no small station available. Film runs at 24 frames per second; 16mm film has 40 frames per foot, which means that a 60-second commercial is 36 feet of film, plus leader. The sound is advanced

26 frames ahead of the picture, and for reasons that are logical but not worth your time, television stations don't want the sound to start until $1\frac{1}{2}$ seconds into the commercial; this silent opening is called unmod, for unmodulated sound track.

Every station has 16mm projectors. The film most commonly used is Eastman 7294, a negative color film with reasonable speed and fine grain. If someone asks whether you want optical or magnetic track on the film, give him an "Are you crazy?" look and answer "Optical sound, of course."

All professional color film is balanced for 3,200 degrees Kelvin, the color temperature of quartz lights and other professional film lights. To shoot outdoors, use an 85-B filter, which every camera store sells.

35mm film. If you have a lot of optical effects, you might prefer to shoot 35mm instead of 16mm. That's because you'll be making "dupe negatives" to achieve your effects, and each generation of film picks up grain, giving the final print a coarse, grainy look. Not so when you have a 35mm original and reduce to 16mm, because the 35mm image isn't twice as large as 16mm; it's four times as large.

Only the largest television stations, usually network origination-points, have 35mm projectors. All sound film except super-8 runs at 24 frames per second, but 35mm has only 16 frames to a foot and crashes through the projector at 90 feet a minute. It's substantially more expensive in equipment, film stock, and laboratory, and because most 35mm production houses are unionized, it may be substantially more expensive in labor too.

The current choice of film in 35mm is 5294, identical to the 16mm 7294 except for the size. The 35mm film has four sprocket holes per picture, but it has the advantage of being a size you can look at without squinting.

8mm film. Avoid it. It isn't professional, and most stations can't project it.

Two-inch videotape. Videotape itself isn't that old, but there's already a generation of old-timers who claim that anything smaller than two-inch videotape is unprofessional. All the big console machines by Ampex and RCA were that size, and almost every station has at least one two-inch machine.

The tape rushes through the unit at 15 inches per second, and with a two-inch unit you can count on professional results.

One-inch videotape. Constantly improving, one-inch tape seems to be the size that one day will be the standard of the industry. Obviously, one-inch equipment isn't as expensive as two-inch, and the difference in quality, for the average advertiser, is negligible. You can record a spot in one-inch and transfer it to two-inch, or vice versa, with no noticeable loss of quality. Much of the progress in computerized editing is in the one-inch size, together with cassettes.

$\frac{3}{4}$-*inch videotape cassettes.* The bargain-priced production houses record on $\frac{3}{4}$-inch tapes but the size is standard for projection. A spot is produced on one-inch or two-inch tape and then dubbed onto a cassette, which is $\frac{3}{4}$-inch. Computer editing has hit this size in force. Electronic signals are put onto a tape as it's dubbed from the larger size onto a cassette. An editor cuts the larger size, and a playback unit transmits the signals from the cut version onto the cassette, resulting in a one-piece commercial with the right scenes. The cassette is slapped into a tape cassette player—such as the one in your home, except for size—and it can be televised onto the air without the mess and possibility of mistakes one can encounter with reel-to-reel videotape.

This process sounds like something out of the movie *2010,* but videotape editing onto cassettes is a common occurrence and is improving so fast that the biggest problem is obsolescence.

$\frac{1}{2}$-*inch videotape cassettes.* These are for your home videotape player, and although in a pinch a station might be able to use them, they aren't considered professional.

Slides. There's absolutely nothing wrong with a commercial composed in part or in entirety of slides. They're the cheapest means of presentation.

There is no sound on slides. A separately recorded voice tape is prepared or the local announcer reads the copy that matches the slides.

A slide shouldn't just sit there for more than five seconds unless it's an address slide requiring reading time. As many as 30 words can be put on a slide. Use an easily read typeface that doesn't have hairline serifs and it will be readable even on a small television set. Slides should be 35mm, in two × two-inch mounts, covered by glass. Be sure they're square and mounted evenly.

What Should Production Cost?

Production costs change constantly, seemingly always upward, and anyone who tries to suggest an average cost invites criticism from production houses that think he's quoting too high, or too low, based on their own production costs.

There are three rules to consider in figuring costs:

1. Nobody is a big shot—not the client (that's you); not the advertising agency, if any; not the production house; and not the talent.

2. There will be no attempt to cover imaginative sterility with a host of mechanical or optical tricks that add cost and flash but not salesmanship.

3. There won't be any mind-changing halfway through the shooting.

Here are some estimates of what costs should be for television spots. These figures are based on 1985 prices (costs appear to increase about ten percent a year).

A 60-second commercial, with a 30-second lift, in 16mm color with voiceover sound, no music, normal product photography, a little production—a kitchen set, a living room, some panning around in close-ups—and no optical effects (straight-on card titles are included) should cost $2,000 to $4,000.

A three-hour videotape session, including two cameras, boom man on the microphone, lighting man, grip or electrician, and normal control-room gang, should cost $500 to $1,500. In the three-hour session, you can and should record at least two or three commercials if the talent is properly rehearsed. On average, add $500 for videotape editing.

A commercial using location photographs (an automobile showroom, a street scene, a storefront, factory scenes, office shots) will cost $500 to $700 more depending on how much is shot inside, where portable quartz lights may be necessary.

Slides should cost about $50 to $75 each, including art or photography and reduction to 35mm size. Making slides from art you already have costs only a few dollars.

Are these prices low? You bet they are. The entire low-budget concept goes out the window if you're geared to process photography, chroma-key, wild cutting, location video-tape with Minicams, or multiple-take synchronous sound on film.

If you're considering animation, figure on $175 to $200 per 35mm foot, which means that a 60-second commercial (90 feet) can easily cost $18,000. If you must have animation, please don't consider a full 60 seconds of it anyway. The commercial will be all novelty instead of a sane combination of novelty and sell.

I might as well make another unpopular suggestion: Don't use your family as talent in the commercials, and don't try to shoot the spots yourself unless you really know what you're doing. If you've never lit a glass of beer or a shiny automobile, don't try it.

Incidentally, shoot still photographs of the rehearsal (not the takes—the still camera makes noise). You might be able to use those stills in print ads.

The Right Way to Buy TV Time

A time-buyer looks at the rate for a local television station in the current issue of Television Rates & Data. "Ah," he says. "WXXX charges $100 for a 60-second spot." He calls WXXX. "I want to buy a dozen 60-second spots. I understand they're $100 each." "Yes, sir," says the time-salesman. "I'll put you on the air."

Would you hire this person to buy time for you?

A buyer using this approach wouldn't last a day in a high-powered advertising shop. Station salesmen to the contrary, rate cards today are merely a point of departure. Not only are there lots of ways to use discounts the station offers (so it's possible to buy ten spots and pay less than you would for five), but the availability of discount time has shattered previous notions of what television time costs.

Here is how ten spots can cost less than five: One to six spots are $100 each; six to eleven are $75 each. The five spots, on the *ten*-time rate, go down from $500 to $375. To reach ten spots for the discount, buy five of the cheapest spots the station has: Spots at 2 A.M., which, at the ten-time rate, are $20 each. These rates give you a total of ten spots instead of five at a cost of $475 instead of $500.

Stations will tailor a package for an advertiser. No one pays the one-time rate. And only the beginners try to buy 60-second spots between Seven and Ten in the evening on network-affiliated stations, because there aren't any for any advertiser except for program sponsors. And you don't want to be one of those.

The first thing to do, when considering the purchase of television time, is to look for a discount source. Several big companies deal in discount time. One is CPM, Inc.; another is Media General; a third is Media Associates. These discount time-buyers may not have an office in your town, but they do have them in New York, Chicago, Los Angeles, and maybe other places, and it could be well worth a long distance call to get their ideas. There are others, by the way, besides the ones just named.

Another way to buy discount time is to put an advertising agency to work. Call three agencies. Tell them you're thinking of going on television, and you want to know how much clout they have with the local stations. You might say, "I have $1,000 budgeted each week for a six-week campaign. Give me your media schedule." But don't do this to an agency unless you plan to hire one of them—assuming that one of the three has some notion of how to buy time.

There's one big danger in all this, and that's winding up on the station these guys deal with the most. For example, a media-buying service may have lots of time available to them on station WZZZ, but that's a low-powered UHF station with only religious programming. Another may have a potful of commercial time on an obscure cable channel nobody watches.

So try to get a rounded schedule, not all on one station unless there's only one station in the marketplace. Try to reach the most people who can and will buy what you have to sell. Otherwise, you're in the station's trick bag, buying time you really shouldn't have. Yes, women buy cars; no, you don't want spots in a cooking show. Yes, the whole family buys cereal; no, you don't want to sell cereal through spots on the midnight movie.

The safest time, in general, is the movie that starts at 10:30 or 11:30 P.M. In many cases it's the best mass/class audience available. Husbands and wives both watch. If your schedule calls for a spot a night in that movie, Monday through Friday, be sure the station promises to rotate the spot. That way, you'll have at least one spot in the early part of the movie, which has the most viewers.

What Length Should a Commercial Be?

Almost no commercials were 30 seconds long in 1965; by 1985, 80 percent of all spots were 30 seconds. This change occurred not only because television's impossible rising costs forced 60-second advertisers to go the shorter length but also because the typical 30-second spot costs about five-eighths as much as a 60-second spot but has far more than five-eighths the impact.

If you accept the belief generally held by television experts that an effective spot makes one single point and doesn't attack a multiplicity of themes, it's easier to accept the 30-second spot as an optimum length. Too many first-time television advertisers try to cram their whole corporate story into a single spot. There have been spots for supermarket chains that list about 15 prices. The argument advanced by the advertiser is that a housewife might not be interested in detergent but might be interested in lamb chops, and that by including specials from every department, the advertiser reaches everyone's interest.

Ah, but does he?

$E^2 = 0$. Might it not be better, instead of having one spot advertising a box of detergent for $1.09, lamb chops for $3.98 a pound, bananas for 29 cents a pound, and as many as a dozen other items, all of which sap interest away from one another, to have a schedule of ten-second spots, each of which hammered on one item? Which would have the greatest impact? Which would suggest that when the next spot hits the tube, you'd better watch because here comes a new bargain?

Most veteran advertisers operate in many spot-lengths. An advertiser might kick off a campaign with a schedule of 60-second spots. After the first week or two he switches to 30s, in the completely valid belief that the viewer will associate the shorter message with the longer one—and will, in fact, not realize that a shorter spot has been substituted.

But consider this: The average viewer believes that all spots are 60s. Invariably, when test groups are asked to estimate the number of commercial minutes they've seen in the last hour, they guess too high. If there are 12 commercial minutes, they guess 20; if there are 9, they still guess 20.

In relation to what might be called the Relative Attention Ratio, they're probably right.

The Relative Attention Ratio is the amount of attention focused on the advertising message to which the viewer is being exposed. An R.A.R. of 100 might be achieved under hypnosis but nowhere else, because only under hypnosis can anyone be forced to pay attention to one message (the operator's voice) and nothing else. At the other end is an R.A.R. of five to ten—almost subliminal, because 90 to 95 percent of one's attention is focused on something else; this low R.A.R. applies to a lot of outdoor advertising and to ads that aren't seen because the viewer is reading a publication he doesn't really care to read, i.e., a magazine in a doctor's office. A television viewer's R.A.R. is probably somewhere between 35 and 70, which isn't bad, but when that viewer is hit with a solid stack of commercials, the R.A.R. declines, and it declines fast.

A program ends with two spots; at the station break there are three more; and the next show opens with two. That's seven commercials, practically unseparated, each clamoring for attention. It's like a group of gunshots: If one gun is fired, an R.A.R. is perhaps 90; if a hundred shots are fired in staccato fashion, the R.A.R. would be fractional for each after the first few.

Some of the big advertisers are clamoring for—and getting from the stations—"split 30s." These advertisers give half the commercial to one product they make, the other half to another. Result: one advertiser, but two commercials. The 15-second spot is becoming epidemic.

What does this mean in terms of proper spot length? Since a spot will be buried anyway, and since most viewers will *think* they saw a 60-second one, you might as well go with the shorter length. It costs less, it may well produce an R.A.R. way above five-eighths that of a 60 (which also would be buried among other spots, albeit perhaps fewer in total number), and you have far greater flexibility as to when the spot can run.

Ten-second spots are great, if you can compress your message into one. A ten-second spot in no way lasts ten seconds. The picture length is eight seconds; the sound begins $1\frac{1}{2}$ seconds late and ends $\frac{1}{2}$ second early, so with six seconds of sound, can you deliver the message without sounding stupidly rushed? If so, try tens, because a station can squeeze tens into slots where nothing else will fit.

Until 30s leaped into prominence, the most popular length was the 20-second spot. In the station-break space of about 26 seconds between network shows, a station could cram a 20 (with 18 seconds of sound) and a 10 (with 6 seconds of sound); the 10 was, and still is, designed to correct any error of timing, with a 7-second freeze on the final scene—usually, the product name. Twenty-second spots are making a comeback as stations cram more and more spots into the same time availabilities.

Some shows, such as sports spectaculars and network nighttime talk shows, include commercial breaks for both network and local advertisers. A 60 might get into one of those, but on the other hand, it might not. You might have to stand in line to spend your money, a denigrating position for any advertiser.

When producing commercials, think not only in terms of the schedule you've already bought but also of the schedule you might buy later. This could dictate a quick extra take for a spot of a different length. At the very least, if using film, shoot some extra takes or footage of each scene so you can, when buying some different lengths later, cut together proper spots without having to go to the expense and reduced quality of dupe negatives (literally, a printed duplicate of the film negative that went through the camera) of the existing spot. In fact, if you're going up from 30s to 60s instead of down from 60s to 30s, you just won't have enough footage to do it any other way short of reshooting.

Deciding How to Make and How to Run Spots

Just in case you can't decide what to say in a commercial, what to show, or what length the spots should be, here are a dozen rules. Like most of the rules in this book, they're right down the middle: You won't be a bold pioneer, but you won't get into trouble.

1. No spot should have more than 30 percent entertainment. The rest must be sell.
2. Sincerity always works.
3. A spokesperson should enhance the product, but that person should not be so strong that the product becomes secondary.
4. To make any impact, repetition is necessary. This is absolutely generic to commercials in both television and radio.
5. If Rule 4 makes sense, it's obvious that testing a commercial with just one airing is insufficient grounds for exhilaration or depression regarding its effectiveness.
6. If you air your spot once and it bombs, get ready for radical surgery.
7. Bulk run-of-station spots are better for the small advertiser than one intense prime-time spot. It's better to saturate logical buyers than to reach everyone once or twice (reread Rule 4).
8. Repetition of a novelty is a paradox. Each repetition makes it less novel.
9. A gimmick must relate to the product. Speedy Alka-Seltzer, for example, worked better than ethnic humor would for this product.
10. Making too many points in a television commercial is a perfect violation of Lewis's Third Law.

11. Don't produce or appear in your own commercial, and that goes for your family, too.
12. Never pay retail for television time.

Some of these rules are contrary to what the giant advertising agencies and their clients practice. They test commercials in single screenings to test groups in screening rooms, and by overlooking the build-up potential of frequency, they often err. In an article in *Advertising Age*, Raymond Tortolani, vice-president of marketing of Rumrill-Hoyt, Inc., commented on this fallacy:

> Why is all the major advertising preresearch testing performed on the basis of one-time exposure? Why should we be surprised when we often get enormous inconsistencies between test results and market performance?
>
> . . . We found some commercials which performed very well (using various pre/post scores, attitude measures, recall devices, etc.) on a one-time showing, which deteriorated badly on multiple exposure.
>
> Conversely, there were other commercials which scored low on the basis of the standard one-exposure method, but when tested on a double-exposure method, they did better, on a triple-exposure method, still better, and better still on four exposures . . .
>
> The traditional method of single-exposure testing has serious limitations, which can produce grave errors in commercial pretesting and which can be dangerous to advertisers and to the overall creative process.

Replacing Spectacle with Sincerity

You not only don't need a tap-dancer scurrying across soup cans, you might actually lose your position in the marketplace if you film one.

Giant advertisers of automobiles, beer, and coffeemakers, whose products often lack comparative differences, try to create them with the spokespersons they use: They hope to ride the coattails of the likes of Joe DiMaggio (who could ever dislike Joltin' Joe?) or Danny Thomas. But many who remember the Danny Thomas commercial don't remember what brand of coffee or coffeemaker he was selling. The glorification, then, is of the spokesperson and not of the product.

Who is credible? Opinion intermixed with fact helps to answer that question.

Muhammad Ali is instantly recognizable but not credible. Wayne Gretzky is neither recognizable nor credible. Gene Kelly is completely credible. Arnold Palmer is credible but overused. Candice Bergen is credible and Petula Clark isn't (in fact, all these persons scored this way in a researcher's test). O.J. Simpson is credible. Robert Blake isn't. Catherine Deneuve is credible for perfumes, but not for automobiles.

Children have a different credibility quotient. Ronald McDonald, who strikes adults as foolish, is credible to children because they don't fear him. Ditto Bugs Bunny.

What do you learn from this? That logic does enter into talent decisions. Don't yield to the agent who says, "I can get you Robert Blake." Instead, ask whether the choice of spokesperson matches the target-buyers you hope to nail. If it doesn't, pass, and use the money to buy time to show the product.

A coterie exists for everyone who appears on television, if only because these people are celebrities, but so much money is wasted on celebrities (money that could instead go into time) that the new advertiser, the inexperienced advertiser, and the low-budget advertiser should follow any instinct that tells him, "This person doesn't match my product or my audience." Instead, if you need an on-camera spokesperson, hold auditions (in a non-AFTRA city) and choose one. Choose on the basis of sincerity—that almost palpable immediate emotional link with the viewer—that so few celebrities, who have no emotional tie with what they're selling, can project.

One final rule: Show the product prominently. Then show it again. Then show it a third time. You'd be surprised how many commercials work their way to the very end before they even let the viewer know what the product is.

7

Radio: Sometimes Your Best Buy

Why is it that the first-time users of radio insist on commercials *they* think are funny? Humor, as we've already seen, can be a potent selling aid, although humor alone isn't strong enough to close a sale; it's an attention-getter that needs a big brother to turn interest into desire. At the very least, an announcer should be brought in to give direction to the attention the humor has generated.

When you write a commercial you think is funny, before putting it on the air change the product name and ask someone whose opinion you respect to give you a comment. Unless that person makes a positive comment about image or sell, scrap it.

Also, look out for words that can have two meanings. Words such as "know," "hoarse," and "too" can be pronounced perfectly and mean "no," "horse," and "two" to your audience.

Here is a commercial someone undoubtedly thought was funny. Read it, thinking of how it sounds on the air and the impact it's supposed to achieve (For broadcast commercials, "announcer" is usually entered as "ANNC."):

ANNC.:   Listen, my children, and you shall hear of the midnight ride of Paul Revere.

SOUND: (HORSE GALLOP)

ANNC.:   Of course, there would have been no reason for Paul to wake the whole household at that ridiculous hour—if there had been a Meggett Printing Company in the colonies.

	All he had to do was let Meggett print the message. Then he could have quietly slipped it under the door in every Middlesex village and town. The result—no shouting 'til he was hoarse. And all the facts would be in writing. None of that confusion about how many by land and how many by sea. And even though it would have been a rush order, Paul would have received the same thoughtful attention to details, the same creative ideas, that make Meggett Printing stand apart. Next time you have an important message to announce—use your horse sense.
SOUND:	(HORSE WHINNY)
ANNC.:	Don't shout it, print it. Gallop down to the Meggett Printing Company in Washington Heights, behind the Quinex Motel, where there's plenty of hitching room. Meggett is spelled M-E-double G-E-double T.

What is this supposed to do? What motivation has this advertiser superimposed? And what is the listener's opinion of Meggett? Is it seen as a strong, dignified, capable printing company? As one with favorable prices? As a better source than the listener's present printer? Or none of the above?

Remember The Second Law: In this Age of Skepticism, cleverness for the sake of cleverness may well be a liability rather than an asset, as appears to be the case here.

How to Produce an Effective Radio Commercial

The biggest problem a radio commercial faces is being unheard. Most people like a little noise. They're uncomfortable in dead quiet. They turn on their radios in order to feel more comfortable, then pay no attention to what is on the air.

Proof? How many times have you turned on the radio specifically to hear the time or weather and then come out of a stupor 10 or 15 minutes later realizing that the time or weather has gone right past you without you hearing it?

Consciously or unconsciously, producers of radio spots try to overcome the noise-tolerance problem by adding more noise, so they'll be noticed. Sometimes they only increase the tolerance level, which suggests that producing spots that move in the other direction—away from noise—can be just as effective or more so.

The second biggest problem a radio commercial faces is idiotic humor. The guidelines on the subject in Chapter 6 apply here.

The third biggest problem a radio commercial faces is lack of sincerity. The commercial is so wrapped up in its desire to entertain that it forgets its purpose—to convince you of something.

Overcome these three problems and chances are you'll have an effective commercial.

Since we laid out some rules for television spots, it's only fair to list a dozen rules for radio spots:

1. Don't be funny at the expense of sincerity.
2. If you become your own announcer, talk as though you're explaining something to your mother; pronounce the word "the" as "thuh" before a word starting with a consonant, "thee" before a word starting with a vowel, and pronounce "a" as "uh."
3. Don't produce a drama; just tell the story.
4. Repeat the product or service name constantly.
5. If the spot ends with a phone number, build up to it: "Have a pencil? Write down this number so you won't forget it: 555-6000. Did you get that? Just in case, here it is again: 555-6000." Then remind the listener that the phone number is in the Yellow (or White) Pages.
6. Use a jingle as a memory jogger, but never use a jingle as the entire spot unless the commercial is ten seconds long.
7. If your commercial emphasizes prices, try to mention only one price.
8. Use simple, straightforward sentences. On radio, for example, you would rephrase this poem for clarity: "The village smithy stands under the spreading chestnut tree."
9. When giving an address, help with a mnemonic device: "Three-oh-three Main Street—across from the Blevins Hotel."

10. In the script write out numbers so the announcer can't stumble. For example, don't write "1,001 reasons," but rather, "a thousand and one reasons"; don't write "9400 E. State St.," but "ninety-four-hundred East State Street."

11. Read the commercial aloud several times to get rid of words that don't "sound": words with "s" and "l" often sound slurpy and slippery; "Louisiana Legislature" is hard to pronounce (lots of l's plus a five-syllable word followed by a four-syllable word); words such as "fastest" and "comfortable" are hard to pronounce, and words like "banal" and "elongated" are often mispronounced.

12. Before producing a commercial, try it out on a child and ask the child to synopsize it for you. If the child can't do it, reexamine the commercial for clarity.

How to Write for Radio

I suppose another list could be started with another dozen rules that might overlap the ones you're still puzzling over. Instead of a list, think of a single rule: Be logical. That's really all there is to effective radio writing.

It's logical, for example, to use short, direct sentences when trying to communicate with someone who isn't really listening and whose Relative Attention Ratio is well below 50.

It's logical to have one theme, to give the listener one point to remember or to buy, to offer one big benefit.

It's logical to have no more than two clauses per sentence.

It's logical to eliminate nonsense sentences ("Look into a new gas oven!"); the word "we" when an announcer is reading the spot (is "we" the announcer or the advertiser?); and mixed-up syntax (this spot for a restaurant actually ran on the air: "You'll find every dish was more delicious than the next").

It's also logical to eliminate the overused words and phrases on this list:

Remember	You'll also like . . .
Quality	Friendly service
Interesting	Convenience
Great	You know
Wonderful	I mean
One of the best things about . . .	Well

Adding Interest and Attention

A second voice is sometimes a good idea, because the second voice might be a testimonial, always potent in broadcast (unless it's a semiliterate sports hero who pronounces "a" as "ay"). A second voice also works to recover audience-drift, which causes the listener to unconsciously lower his Relative Attention Ratio and start to daydream just as the single-voice announcement comes to its most important component. A dialogue between two voices, crisply done and without the confusion that is the curse of overproduced spots, can increase the Relative Attention Ratio, especially during longer commercials.

One easy way to add interest and attention to a commercial is to open it with a question. Usually, the question should not be one to which the listener will answer "No!" but that rule isn't universal.

Jingles are usually more effective at the end of a commercial than they are at the beginning, because they put a button on the product name and help tie the message together for possible recall later.

Many heavily produced commercials have a neatness complex: They open with a jingle, hold the background music under the announcer's pitch and then close with the jingle. They are tied together, but the symmetry draws attention to itself as a commercial and not to the commercial message, which weakens the impact.

Multiple voices on a jingle can become incomprehensible unless one voice is featured, another reason to overlay a jingle with an announcer delivering a clear "sell" message.

When running a comparative ad as a radio spot, the message must be extraordinarily clear. Toyota is being compared with Volkswagen, or Schick with Norelco, or your hamburgers with McDonald's. There's no picture, just the words that can't be recalled for checking. Unless superiority is spelled out, repeated, and then repeated a second time, the listener may not remember which product was the positive name.

When giving a time limit, repeat it:

"Today, and today only!"

"This week, and only this week!"
"Call now. Tomorrow you won't qualify."

Convincing the Listener

The most important communications rule that relates to radio is to tell the listeners why you're on the air. What's the purpose of running a spot in the first place? Wasting dollars for radio time used for pure image is nonsense. When on the air, sell something.

Naiveté never dies. I'm always surprised to hear a commercial come and go without ever telling me what this guy is selling. Oh, sure, there's some value in repetition of the name. Someone may say, "I've heard of you." But how can that compete with having someone say, "I want to buy that"? Why are you in business? To sell something. Radio costs less per thousand people reached than any other mass medium except outdoor. You've chosen the right vehicle; now sell something.

Don't be scared out of doing your own spots. Radio, after all, isn't parallel to television, because you're only heard, not seen. Giving a polished performance is far easier when only your voice represents you. No one will notice your dangling hands and nervous fingers, your awkward stride, your overfocused attention on the cue card slightly off-camera. Just be yourself—a businessperson who wants to do business, who sounds sincere, and who will bring in buyers. If you do go on the air yourself, don't pretend to be a polished announcer. Sincerity pays, so be yourself. You're the entrepreneur, and your greatest communicative power lies in commercials that convey this sort of message: "Come in and talk to me. I'm not a salesman, I'm the owner, and I want to see you and do business with you." This certainly is preferable to some of the pomposity— or worse, elephantine humor—that seems to represent most of the self-aggrandizing commercials in which people in business give their own pitches.

When talking to the buyers, give them a reason to believe you. "We're short of cash," makes more sense than the old cliche, "We're crammed wall-to-wall with merchandise we have to unload." "We have about 200 suits we'll take a loss to unload. Maybe you'll get lucky and one will fit you," is better than, "We're overstocked." The difference in both cases is empathy: You've admitted to an Achilles' heel; you've come down to earth; you've become credible. This is merely a primitive application of some of the rules of communication specified in Chapter 3.

The most common mistake has been saved for last: *overwriting.*

Classes in mass communications have taught for years that a 60-second radio spot can have 150 words. While that may be true, it excludes some effects, music, and pace. Two and one-half words per second should be the maximum, and any number beyond that will lead to confusion.

But don't think that by cutting a 60-second commercial to 75 words the impact is improved. This only leads to "dead air," which makes the listener uncomfortable. The listener is noise oriented, which is probably why he turned on the radio in the first place.

Help the pace of a commercial by giving cues to the announcer, just in case the spot is read live rather than being recorded. Generally, words written entirely in capital letters are not to be read; those written in upper and lower case are to be read. Sometimes failing to make this distinction can result in spots that are hilarious to hear, disastrous to the advertiser. In the middle of a spot, I once heard an announcer say, "Chuckle," which was supposed to be his cue, not his word.

How to Buy Radio Time

Even more than in television, radio rate cards are in fragments. This is an era of wheels and deals, and except for the most popular shows (usually, one program in town, from 6 to 9 A.M., dominates the ratings) you can put together a package at a discount price that makes radio the lowest mass medium in cost-per-thousand.

With one exception, all rate cards are at their highest between 6 and 9 A.M.—morning drive-time. The next highest rate is 4 to 7 P.M.—evening drive-time. Between 7 and 10 P.M., stations are swimming in unsold time, because that is television prime time and that is where the people are. Many stations have more listeners between midnight and 2 A.M. than they do from 7 to 10 P.M.

The exception is the teen-oriented station, the one featuring rock music. This station has its highest audience from 8 to 10 P.M., because the high school and junior high school student, who gets home at about 4 P.M., is stuck with evening drive-time and family listening until after dinner. Upstairs, doing homework, the young people turn on their radios and an enormous marketplace mushrooms for a couple of hours.

During morning drive-time the audience is not only at its largest because everyone wants to know the weather and local news, but it also is the most polyglot, because breakfast and dinner are often the only times a family is together.

When audiences are biggest, rate cards are highest. This may be logical, but some of the commercials one hears aren't. A spot during morning drive-time should recognize that the business day is ahead, that the grocery-buying day is ahead, that the school day is ahead, and perhaps, that plans for the evening are being made. The wording of this spot is important to its success. "How did you sleep last night?" is better than "How will you sleep tonight?" because last night is still closer than tonight. "On your way home tonight," may or may not work because the memory will not go that far; such a message is better during evening drive-time.

In dealing with station time-salesmen or with a discount source, don't fly blind. Know what the rate card says. That rate card is absolutely the most you can pay; you work downward from there. If you don't know what the printed rate is, you have no negotiating position.

You can't say to a station salesman, "I'll tell you what I'll do: I won't pay ten dollars for those spots; I'll give you six dollars each." What you can say is that you have had spot-packages submitted by several stations, and while you personally favor this station, you need to see a favorable package that will enable you to "come out o.k. on this."

There's an ethical and professional rule to buying discount time from a source other than the station itself; most stations won't deal with a barter or discount seller representing any advertiser who has bought time directly from the station within the past year.

That means not only that you should not (and often cannot) switch in the middle of a spot schedule from spots bought directly to spots bought outside the station's own orbit; it also means you shouldn't ask the station's own salesmen and a discount source to compete with each other. What you can do is tell one you're thinking of dealing with the other, and ask whether the one to whom you're talking can sell spots at a price competitive with the other. At the very least you'll be labeled a sophisticated buyer; at the very best you can buy spots for less than you would otherwise.

Don't assume the barterer or discounter offers the advantage of a multiplicity of stations. The edge is thin, because the discounter may well push the station that gives him the best deal. The discounter may also have no availabilities on the station you want.

And which station do you want? Except for direct mail, radio is the most easily tailored of all consumer media. You can aim rifle bullets instead of buckshot and hit sports buffs, children, housewives, intellectuals, retirees, ethnic groups, people who don't speak English, teen-agers, insomniacs and people who work nights, those interested in the stock market—almost every vertical group has its own programming. But, except for drive-time, never make the mistake of thinking you can reach them all on the same station.

This implies that buying spots during morning drive-time on the highest-rated station, even at card rate, may be the wisest move to make. While it's true that this represents the biggest single audience in town, don't buy this way if you violate the First Law: Effective advertising is that which reaches, at the lowest possible cost, the most people who can and will buy what you have to sell.

When selling a stock-market ticker that plugs into the wall at home, a retirement village in Florida, or a rock record album, buying the biggest mass audience probably won't result in the proper targets at the lowest possible cost. You're paying for too much wastage.

Per-Inquiry Advertising

Right after World War II, when radio was moribund because of the sudden splurt of television stations and because of the overnight sprouting of new radio stations that helped drain the cream off the marketplace, per-inquiry advertising was a big factor in the incomes of many stations.

Per-inquiry advertising is self-explanatory. Instead of paying by the spot, one pays by the inquiry. Michigan Bulb Company, a major per-inquiry advertiser in those days, paid the stations $2 per inquiry. The company neither knew nor cared when its spots ran. If a station forwarded one inquiry, it was paid $2; if it forwarded a thousand, it was paid $2,000.

There isn't a lot of per-inquiry advertising any more, except for some vendors of Bibles and arthritis remedies who have survived the slow death of "P.I. Deals," as the trade calls them. Even if a station accepts a P.I. deal, that station probably will schedule the spot in fringe time where it just can't pull enough inquiries to be worth anything to the station or to you. The spot runs two or three times and is then pulled.

(Some cable TV stations accept P.I. deals, but usually on a "Catch-22" basis: They'll only make the deal for something for which the advertiser has already bought straight time successfully.)

Don't give up because a station refuses to run a P.I. deal. If you can't get in the front door, go around to the back. Tell the station: "I don't want morning drive-time because that's not my best shot, since people have to write in and they won't take the time to do it in the morning. (Translation: "I'm not going to try for time you can sell at straight card-rate.") But I notice your spots from 10:30 P.M. to midnight cost $10 each. I'll pay that. And I know from previous advertising that a $10 spot should bring five sales at $8.95 each. The only thing I ask is that if your spot doesn't pull five sales you give me courtesy spots to bring me to that number. If you'll guarantee the pulling power of your station, I'll guarantee to buy five spots a night, five nights a week."

What have you done here? You've set up a P.I. deal, but you've done it on terms the station can accept. You're paying straight card rate—$10 a spot, $50 a night, $250 a week—

but in exchange the station has to deliver 125 leads. You have a P.I. deal, paying $2 per lead or per sale, depending on what you have.

How does the station know whether the number of leads or sales is what it's supposed to be? Simple: Mail and phone calls go to the station ("Send a card to "Bible—that's B-I-B-L-E—care of this station").

Just two warnings here: (1) Make it possible for the station to make money (in some cases, a strong station will run one spot and be able to bill for five), and (2) pay the station the same day you get leads or sales, so you don't ruin the marketplace for those who follow you.

Getting the Best Mileage out of Radio

A dozen radio spots can be run in most markets for the same cost as a single television spot. Since all broadcast effectiveness is built on repetition, the cumulative impact and gross rating points might well be far higher. But just as you shouldn't abandon a broadcast campaign too soon, neither should you ride a dead horse. One advertiser, buying saturation spots on a local FM station and seeing no results after 13 weeks, decided to renew. When asked why, he said, "What the heck. The spots are only $3 each."

Almost all broadcast advertising is commissionable to advertising agencies. A few more dollars might be saved by establishing a house agency, but finding an advertising agency you trust and letting their people ride shotgun for you is better. Let them be the ones to make the rate-breaking propositions, and have them present several spot-packages to you. Not only does this take you off the firing line, but it gives you the benefit of professionalism at no real cost.

Radio is underrated and often underpriced. Make the most of it.

8

Newspaper Advertising

Newspapers were the first form of mass communication, with the possible exceptions of the town crier and smoke signals. While newspapers usually are considered a local medium because they circulate within a specific geographic area, this isn't always true. Some newspapers, such as the *Christian Science Monitor* and *Grit*, are national; some, such as the *Wall Street Journal* and *U.S.A. Today*, are national but printed in several parts of the country to make local and regional advertising possible.

Standard Rate & Data Service says that to be considered a daily newspaper, a publication must be issued at least four times a week. Most dailies are published at least six times a week, with Sunday being the exception for some smaller dailies whose readership would abandon a Sunday issue in favor of a major metropolitan newspaper covering the same area.

Community newspapers are either weekly or semi-weekly, although a smattering of local daily newspapers serve the suburbs of some of the larger cities. There are also "shopper" papers, which may be almost 100 percent advertising.

McGraw-Hill conducts a "Laboratory of Advertising Performance," which a few years ago conducted a study that concluded that the average full-page newspaper ad will be read by 16 percent of the readers of that issue; the average two-page spread, by 22 percent of readers. The conclusion projected was that by running larger ads, you reach more people.

Yet, that very statistic, when examined, proves specious. An ad costing twice as much pulls only $37\frac{1}{2}$ percent more readers, suggesting that the larger ad was a substantially poorer investment, unless an advertiser was in mail order and had nowhere else to spend his money. A caution: Measure ads by response, not readership. The only real way to keep score: x dollars spent, y dollars coming in.

The prospective newspaper advertiser must determine the optimum size and frequency of ads. Instead of running one page on Sunday, is it better to run half a page Sunday and three columns Monday? Might this not pull a greater number of responses? Usually, frequency is better than a single blast, but there are plenty of exceptions.

Only experimentation can supply the proper mix. One rule that does seem to pertain is that each time an ad is repeated within a one-month period, response goes down. This dictates a policy of changing the offer, the product, or the benefit in each ad in order to pull the most response.

What statistics such as McGraw-Hill's laboratory conclusions do teach is that it's arrogant to assume that because you run a great big full-page ad, everyone in town knows about your offer, or even that everyone who has the newspaper knows it. The *best-read* ad in one of America's most respected newspapers, checked in a recent issue, was read by only 36 percent of the people who bought that paper.

So when newspaper promotion departments cry, "Look at the lack of recall (their way of keeping score) of broadcast commercials aired less than an hour ago," in turn the broadcaster can say, "Yeah, but look at the low readership of a full-page newspaper ad—16 or 17 percent is average, and that's for a page. What about the poor fish who can't afford a whole page?"

The giant retailer on a discounted big-volume contract can afford an eight-page insert, but the typical advertiser who bases his fortunes on a five-inch ad had better have lots of communication skills. Here are eight pages for the mattress department of a retail chain; you sell mattresses, too, but you have one five-inch ad. What chance do you have? You have a darn good chance, because every advertiser lives by his wits. Size alone is no assurance of readership, and some one-inch ads grab the eye with greater strength than ads 20 times their size.

Sometimes advertisers despair: "There must be a filter over the page with my ad on it!" If less than one person in four reads (literally, "sees") a two-page spread, it means the other three are blinded to it. This is called "selective reading."

A bigger problem for the newspaper advertiser is that the amount of reading time remains relatively constant regardless of the number of pages in the paper. If you don't believe this, analyze your own readership patterns. Chances are you read the morning paper in a set pattern five days a week; the sixth day you might not read it at all, or you may give it more time. The seventh day you allow substantially more time in a different atmosphere—possibly more relaxed, perhaps in concert with someone else. Rarely does a reader break the pattern.

If you read the morning paper between 7:00 and 7:23 A.M. (and it sometimes is that close) you'll read the paper for that length of time no matter how many pages are in it. And as readers move toward the time of year when elections and Christmas occur, and the paper automatically gets fatter, any specific page gets less attention.

This might lead you to think that newspapers with fewer pages are better read than fat papers, but that isn't the case, because people read a newspaper (or a magazine or a book, for that matter) selectively; they pick their spots. They linger over one section and reread one story and never glance at the section or story next to it, depending on their interests (which, in turn, depend on their experiential backgrounds).

Why the Retailer Is Safe in the Newspaper

Retailers, who wax and wane on radio and dabble with television sporadically, are both safe and at home in the newspaper. The retailer has four logical reasons to hawk his wares in his local newspaper:

1. The circulation matches his marketing area closer than that of any other medium.
2. Newspapers encourage retail advertising by offering retailers lower rates than national advertisers pay.
3. Production costs are low or nonexistent, since most papers will set type and even prepare basic artwork free for local advertisers.
4. An advertiser can choose a position within the paper, so his ad can reach the reader most likely to buy—through loca-

tion in the main news section, the women's section, the sports section, the feature section, the business section, and in many cases, the new young adult section. (Newspapers also have classified sections, which are perhaps the best consistent match of buyer and seller; the Yellow Pages may have greater absolute specificity, but there's no immediacy to any offer made in those pages.)

Two terms apply to the advertiser's fiduciary relationship with the newspaper: *rebate*, or money refunded because you exceeded the minimum number of inches of advertising to qualify for the next lowest rate, and *short rate*, or additional charges brought to bear because you didn't run enough inches of advertising during the contract period to qualify for the rate for which you contracted. I'll say more about these two terms a little later, but basically you're better off being short-rated than being rebated.

An advantage to the retailer is implicit in the availability of rebate and short rate: the more ads he runs, the lower the rate. This is also true of national advertisers, but they're paying a far higher rate to start with.

Advertisers are usually billed by column inches (if your paper still bills by "lines," there are 14 lines per column inch), and the local rate is usually dramatically lower than the national rate. This means that the same size ad might be billed at $140 for a national ad, or $80 for a local ad.

Most of the daily newspapers in the top 40 market areas have "neighborhood" sections. The most common days for neighborhood sections are Thursday and Sunday (Thursday to take advantage of weekend shopping plans as well as to compete with weekly community newspapers. and Sunday because of the intensity of readership and the start-of-the-week syndrome). If they publish neighborhood sections three days a week, the third day is usually Tuesday.

Suppose you're a retailer in Long Island City. The chances of your getting business from the Bronx are so slim that every Bronx reader you pay for is probably wasted circulation. But if there's a Queens insert, you pay only for the readers who are geographically desirable, and since those inserts are inserted only into copies circulating in a specific geographic area, you aren't paying the metropolitan rate.

The same is true in Chicago, where both papers have a South, Southwest, West, and North edition. Each edition stretches far into the suburbs in that general direction and is especially valuable to a restaurant, service business, neighborhood clothing store, or specialty shop that never could draw from the entire metropolitan area the way a downtown store or a chain with stores in shopping centers all over the metropolitan area would draw.

How to Get the Most Attention in the Smallest Possible Space

Ever look at a newspaper page and see a small ad that grabbed your eye far more intensely than a big ad next to it?

You sure have, and so has everyone else. Size isn't the only key to attention. There are three ways a small-space ad can reach out with brawny fingers to grab the reader's eye:

1. Border treatment
2. Typography
3. Reverses

You can't make a big mistake if you take an iron vow to put a border around every ad smaller than a page. And don't let the typesetter or the newspaper talk you into a one-point rule around the ad. At the very least, ask for a six-point border; at most, ask for a three-point border inside a 12-point border.

If an ad is only one inch high, slap a 12-point border around it and watch the readers' eyes go straight to it despite its position far to the left and below a half-page ad with no border. The space-salesman will tell you it's inartistic, funereal, ugly, or impossible. Stand your ground, and while you may not win an art director's award, you will create an ad that stands a chance of being noticed despite its diminutive size.

Don't assume that because an ad is small, it needs 6-point type. Putting tiny type in a tiny ad only has a negative synergistic effect: The ad appears even smaller than it is. If you must, cut the number of words and use larger type. If you're one of those advertisers who writes an ad first and then arbitrarily says, "Let's cut it down from four columns by ten inches to three columns by six inches," and refuses to cut copy, something has to give. Don't think you can put the same length message into smaller space; at some point the ad becomes altogether unreadable. Think the other way: Cut the explanation and leave the meat of the argument. You may find you can use larger type in smaller space.

Reversing is the third suggestion for drawing attention to a small space. Reversing means using a black background with white type. But if you're going into reverses, avoid reversing any type smaller than 10-point. Reverses are harder to read than black type, and they also have the mechanical curse of ink bleeding into the white area after the newspaper has run about a hundred thousand copies on that soft newsprint. If body type is smaller than 10-point, reverse the headline and let the rest run in black.

Some advertisers think they can beat the system by reversing the entire ad. They'll put together half-page ads consisting entirely of type in one big reverse block. In a lot of those ads, the advertiser has outbluffed himself by making it impossible for the reader to know what he, the advertiser, thinks is important. The reader's eye may go to that ad, but as soon as the reader's mind registers the ghastly fact that the whole ad is a reverse, the chance of intensive readership goes down. This invariably happens when an advertiser values form instead of substance, design instead of communication.

How to Get Far More Ads for Far Less Money

A three-word sentence tells an advertiser how to get far more ads for far less money: Get a contract.

All rate cards suggest contract rates, but too often a space salesman is either untrained (since local advertising is a training ground, itself a paradox because local advertisers need far more creative and technical help than do national advertisers), greedy (which would cause him to suggest a one-time rate because this shortsighted suggestion will bring him higher immediate commissions from the higher per-inch rate), or ignorant (it's astonishing how many space salesmen don't know the intricacies of their own rate cards, which might give lower contract rates to book dealers, entertainment, travel, restaurants, mail-order advertisers, or garden ads).

Back to rebates and short rates: You're rebated if you've overpaid for advertising, and you're short rated if you've underpaid. If you've underpaid, you've had the use of the newspaper's money, some of it for most of the year if you're working on an annual contract.

Some papers won't want the arm's-length transaction and not only won't short-rate you, but, in fear of losing your good-will, will write it off and ask you to sign an identical contract for the next year, when you very well might pull the same stunt again.

Contracts guarantee rates too, and increases come to you last if you have a contract. Before the runaway rate increases of the 1970s, newspapers gave ample advance notice—usually three months or more—of rate changes. Some papers now have two or three rate increases a year, and the unlucky advertiser with a fixed budget can find himself 10 to 20 percent short if he doesn't have rate protection.

A contract tends to guarantee the rate specified in that contract; I say "tends to" because protection of contract advertisers is less and less sure as publications themselves are hit with sudden increases in the cost of newsprint or strange union demands that can prod their operating costs upward sharply and quickly. Still, almost every paper will grant protection to contract advertisers for three months or so, which is more security than no protection at all.

Another rule—a harsh one—for getting far more ads for less money is to not let the sellers get away with anything. If an ad runs wrong, if there are typographic errors in type set by the paper, if the ad isn't in the section you asked for (always put this in writing), demand a rerun.

Newspapers prefer to give a partial credit for their mistakes. "Yeah, one word was misspelled in the headline. We'll give you a credit for three inches of space."

Not good enough.

(Truthfully, a misspelled word can destroy your image

with key prospective buyers. That's why copy going to the typesetter has to be absolutely perfect in both grammar and spelling. If a submission is sloppy, how can you blame the paper? A reputation for consistent accuracy in the original copy makes it easier to press a claim.)

Don't settle for a partial credit. Ask to discuss the problem with someone higher up, and hold out for a full credit. If you delivered damaged merchandise to a buyer, you couldn't say, "I'll give you five dollars credit. After all, only one thread was pulled."

Sometimes a paper will offer a free rerun of an improperly produced or placed ad. That's up to you. Days will have gone by. If the ad needed particular timing it might be that running it again a week later won't help.

A reciprocal point: If you don't pay your advertising bill, no matter how good a person you might be the paper will cut off your ads. So when you've been wronged by the paper, reverse the procedure and refuse to pay them. Never do this arbitrarily and always state the exact reason.

Obviously, it doesn't pay to get a reputation for being an impossible fusspot who looks for trouble. Sooner or later, a paper will say "We don't want your ads," although legally they can be in trouble for such a remark. In demanding what is rightfully yours, though, Leo Durocher's maxim makes sense: "Nice guys finish last."

A third rule: Get the lowest possible rate.

The smaller the paper, the more flexible its rates. Negotiating for the end rate (the lowest possible rate with all possible discounts figured in) may not be practical with *The New York Times*, but it might be a fruitful negotiation with the *East Podunk Courier*. In between all types of deals are there to be made.

Read the rate card carefully. You may find discounts you (and the space representative) didn't know existed. You might qualify not only for a volume discount but also for a different category that might cost less.

It is also possible, strangely, to actually pay less for running *more* ads than you now run, because most newspapers not only have a volume discount but a frequency discount. A 20-

inch ad runs Monday, Wednesday, and Friday at a rate of five dollars an inch. By running a one-inch or two-inch rate-holder ad the other days, which would apparently increase the cost by $15 to $20 a week, you might qualify for a frequency discount that drives down the cost per inch by 50 cents, meaning that the 20-inch ads each cost $10 less—$30 a week saved. Against that you pay an extra $4.50 for each one-inch ad, since all ads, regardless of size, qualify for the frequency discount. That comes to $18.

You're saving $30 on regular ads and paying $18 for the rate-holder ads, which means a net saving of $12 each week for being in the paper every day.

In the case of weeklies, the frequency discount invariably applies to 13-, 26-, and 52-week advertisers. The key is that the discount applies regardless of the size of the ad, and one-inch rate-holders can save plenty.

Sometimes even classified ads, offering an extra shot at the buyer in a different marketplace, are permitted as rate-holders.

If you're not sure what discounts might benefit you, make a lunch date with the advertising manager of the paper. He is not only in a position to approve or override deals made by his salespeople, but he can make new deals, and at the very least he's the contact you should have when the inevitable argument with the paper reaches the point at which you need a friend.

Types of Space-Buys

One type of space-buy that can drive the rate way down is the "band-together" buy. This buy makes sense for a group of merchants in a specific area such as a shopping center, or a group of similar businesses that aren't directly competitive because they serve different geographic areas.

Suppose you're an exterminator. You serve the north suburbs, and you've been advertising in the north-suburban section, which costs about 40 percent as much as an ad run in the main news section citywide. A competitor who serves the south suburbs runs in the south-suburban section; another exterminator in the western part of the metropolitan area runs in that neighborhood section, and a fourth, east, uses radio and the Yellow Pages only.

If all four formed the Metropolitan Pest Control Association and ran ads in the main news section, listing all four addresses and phones, the cost would be 25 percent for each participant. Your savings would be $\frac{15}{40}$ ($\frac{3}{8}$), or $37\frac{1}{2}$ percent. If only the three now in the newspaper participated, your savings would be $17\frac{1}{2}$ percent. You would also be in the main news section, with the benefit of better position and a larger ad.

Depending on what you sell and how successful the paper is, there's a bare possibility that you can persuade the paper to run your ad on a P.I. basis. This is a bare possibility because P.I. deals are far less common in print media than in electronic media. Newspapers are a local medium, and word that a paper accepts P.I. deals could be disastrous to conventional space sales; also, a radio station will be on the air whether its time is sold or not, and a P.I. deal is better than nothing, but a newspaper can tailor the number of pages to the amount of advertising it has.

Gearing payment to the number of units sold is effective primarily for mail order, anyway, but you can still try to strike a bargain.

Remnants, mostly associated with magazines and discussed at length in Chapter 9, are unsold space left at presstime and are harder to come by in newspapers than in magazines, because the concept of unsold space at presstime isn't really a factor with a daily or even a weekly newspaper. The fact that publications such as *Parade* sell remnants and are components of newspapers isn't parallel, since *Parade,* like *TV Guide,* has many local editions, closes earlier than a Sunday paper, and has almost a computerlike control over the amount of empty space at presstime.

Some of the larger metropolitan dailies offer remnants—which they call "standbys"—to a handful of advertisers and agencies who agree in advance to use the space that becomes available. The advertiser tells the newspaper the size of his ad and then "stands by"; he can ask for, but not demand, a specific day of the week. The discount can be as much as 40 to 60 percent below rate card.

If you can convince a paper to sell you whatever space exists at presstime, be sure you get a whopping discount. In turn have an ad ready and standing; in fact, to be safe, have your ad ready in several sizes. Also, make no demands for position. This type of ad runs where it runs, at the paper's option.

How to Lay Out an Ad When You Can't Draw

Thinking in terms of layout instead of communication when planning a newspaper ad is a total mistake; it is like paying attention to background music but not the message in a radio spot. Still, if you can create a visually pleasing ad, why not do it?

Sometimes, seeking visual strength, even a professional layout artist will emphasize too many elements. To avoid this and other common errors, here are a few rules of layout:

1. Don't split an ad into equal vertical halves. It lessens the visual impact. If an ad has a big photograph and not much copy, use two thirds of the space for the photo and one third for the copy. This construction builds an ad people will stop to see.
2. Unless you want a "schlock" effect, don't have more than one reverse in the ad.
3. Use one typeface, in various sizes and weights, to avoid a clash of faces that don't look good together.
4. Don't try to draw the ad in detail. Just roughly block out where elements go, thereby saving time and reputation. Showing a newspaper artist or typographer where you want elements and letting him do the work gets a better ad, anyway.
5. The same principle as rule 4 applies to type. Write or letter in the display words only. Don't write in the words for the copy block: It not only marks you as an amateur; it's messy, time consuming, and of no value to whoever will set the type. Simply draw horizontal lines to show where the body copy goes.

6. Square shapes are weak; round shapes stop the eye; vertical shapes are more pleasing visually than horizontal shapes.

Start to clip out ads you think look good. Forget what they're selling, forget what the illustration shows, forget where the ad ran. You're interested only in the position of elements in the ad—that's what a layout is. When formulating your next ad, take another look at the ones you admire. If the headline is set with caps and lower case letters, that's what you do. If an illustration runs all the way down the right side of the ad, then copy it. Is the name of the company set in an oval reverse block?

When your ad is set and finished, it should look pretty much like the ad you adapted the idea from, although obviously the product and sell will differ. You're at the mercy of that ad's length of copy, though, and if you're selling short, squat prefabricated buildings, you may suffer from having to run a tall, thin illustration, so think flexibly in adapting an ad layout to your products.

One overriding rule of layout should prevail: Write the copy first. If you find yourself tailoring the number of words in a headline, the length of copy, and the size and shape of an illustration because of what someone else did to sell something else, the medium has become more important than the message, always a mistake.

Remember David Ogilvy's edict: What you say is more important than how you say it. If an ad makes sense, it's a good layout.

9

How to Make
the Yellow Pages Pay Off

Neither the climate nor the readership of the Yellow Pages parallels that of a newspaper, a magazine, or broadcast advertising. In those media the target-reader or target-listener is attacked suddenly, without his prior consent. He isn't expecting to see or hear the message.

The one parallel to the Yellow Pages is the classified-advertising section. Both are marketplaces in which the buyer aggressively seeks the seller. Within each section, all ads are competitive with each other.

Don't waste time selling a prospective customer on the concept of what you offer; instead, use every heavy gun selling that prospect on doing business with you instead of with a competitor.

The Yellow Pages are the only media advertising for many businessmen; yet some steadfastly refuse to understand this marketplace, do no research or investigation into its effectiveness for them, automatically renew when their salesman demands it, and have no idea whether they are under- or overadvertising.

In most business areas 100 percent of the merchants in the geographic area served by a Yellow Pages section advertise in that section. Perhaps one third of them may use direct mail, 10 percent use the newspapers, and one or two individual companies might use broadcast. But everyone is in the Yellow Pages, and this is true of just about every field, especially since in most directories every company gets a free lightface listing.

The Yellow Pages as a Marketplace

A survey of the pest-control industry revealed that 36 cents of every dollar spent by businessmen in this field went to Yellow Pages advertising, a ratio high in the business community as a whole but not out of line for a local service business in which there are no name brands and in which a potential buyer starts to look for a source of help when there's trouble. Television repair, plumbers, and automobile towing are typical of businesses who assume that most of their new business comes from exposure in the Yellow Pages.

The key to Yellow Pages advertising philosophy, and to a successful determination to beat a system that militates toward flat, nonselling, punchless advertising, is to compete head-on with every competitor you've ever heard of, plus some you haven't. There is no such thing as a noncompetitive Yellow Pages ad, so your battle cry must be, "Outsell 'em!"

Yellow Pages salesmen are highly paid and well trained in two directions. The first area of training, which involves how to oversell space to you, is one you must resist; the second, which is free advice on copy and layout, should win your conditional acceptance as long as you aren't swayed by such nonsense as, "You don't want to say that; it isn't dignified" or "Our advertisers have had better luck with less copy. People look for the first name that pops out."

It's true that people—some people—just take names in rotation, calling them to get a price or a time or information, and, if unsatisfied, will go on to the next name. That is bad for you if they start with AAAA and your name happens to be ZZZZ, but if you analyze the Yellow Pages you'll quickly realize that some of the very smallest one-man companies are those whose names consist of a string of A's. There are lots of categories in which someone calls himself AAAA-Aaron Typewriter Repair or AAAA-Able Television Service, because this might give him the first listing. In major cities, though, this is self-defeating, because there will be a dozen or so names in one category, each of which looks about the same. No buyer loyalty can be built up when the buyer doesn't remember whether he called AAAA-Aaron or AAAA-Absalom the last time.

Free assistance from the Yellow Pages salesman is best used in the form of a production man who will translate your original ideas into print. He will come back—at no charge—with a layout once you've given him the copy. His layout will be on a large sheet of paper with lovely empty space all around it. Make a photocopy, put it in position on a typical page, and then photocopy the whole page again to give you an idea of how your ad really will look.

Don't be afraid to turn down an idea or a layout you think doesn't sell, but do allow yourself this luxury by planning far enough ahead to avoid the typical problem of losing out to a deadline. "The section closes in three days, and if your ad isn't ready, maybe you had better just repeat what you—."

Incidentally, if you're just going into business, the telephone number itself can be important. Some numbers, such as direct sequences (1-2-3-4, 6-7-8-9), are easier to remember than scrambled numbers. Two numbers repeated are also easy to remember (2-2-4-4, 5-5-9-9). Numbers ending in double zeroes are the easiest to remember, and they suggest a big company, but chances are these will be spoken for long before you hit the scene. Still, it never hurts to ask.

Four kinds of ad can be bought in most Yellow Pages sections:

1. The basic ad is a listing. Normally, you get one listing, in regular type, free. If you want a boldface listing, it costs, and if you want to be listed in more than one category (such as in advertising and in public relations), you pay more. For additional payment you can also include a no-answer number ("If no answer call . . . ") or extra-line information, up to 25 words of description that appears directly under your listing.

2. Space ads are available, usually from ½-inch to two inches high and one column wide. These ads have a hairline border and usually allow up to 18-point type.

The phone number in space ads is set in boldface, which helps a little, and the company name is set in capital letters, boldface, which also helps. Usually, in a half-inch ad, you have room for your name across the top, about three lines of description, and a line for your address and phone number.

3. Display ads are available in sizes from one quarter of a column to one quarter of a page. Usually, a quarter page is the

largest ad allowed in the Yellow Pages, whose publishers wisely recognize that otherwise the giant advertisers would swamp the smaller ones, to the ultimate detriment of the Yellow Pages.

Depending on the size of a display ad, type up to 48 points can be used; artwork and Ben Day screens are also available. A bold border is acceptable. But seldom are you permitted to use a reverse or some major eye-catching device. Together with a display ad you'll often get a free bonus: An anchor listing which appears in the alphabetical listings in the section together with the booster, "See Advertisement This Classification."

Many directories now offer a second ink color—red—as an extra-cost option. Although the red-on-yellow effect is neither artistic nor emphatic, many users report greatly enhanced response.

4. Trademark listings group together dealers of a brand name. For example, the Ford or Amana or RCA logo will be shown together with all participating dealers in the area. Usually, the parent company pays for the master "Where To Buy It" listing, which includes a regional office phone number. Each dealer decides whether or not he wants to add a listing for himself. (Undecided? This is one place you should be.)

Living with Arbitrary Rules

If you're a prime candidate for the Yellow Pages, be sure you understand the principles of comparative advertising outlined in Chapters 3 and 12. On the other hand, if you try to run the kind of comparative ad deemed perfectly okay by the Federal Trade Commission and by local newspapers and broadcast stations, you may get stomped on by Yellow Pages advertising regulations designed to protect the purity of their marketplace.

Sometimes I think the publishers of the Yellow Pages would be in heaven if every advertiser took a quarter-page ad and used it only to print his name and phone number (no address, please: We want people to lift the phone, not to write or come in).

Small Yellow Pages ads pose few problems in decision making. Type sizes are specified, and there's little space to do much except follow the standard pattern. Where the maverick advertiser often runs into an argument is in larger ads.

For example, a Yellow Pages book of specifications lays out these rules for a two-inch space listing:

1. Text must be placed in a box $3\frac{1}{2}$ picas square, bordered by a one-point rule. Only one such box may appear in the ad, and it must be only in the upper center or upper-left quarter. Copy in the box must be typeset, and may not run at an angle.
2. Maximum typesize is 24 point, and this size can be used only if just one line of copy is used; if you use two lines, 14-point type is the maximum, and so on.
3. Multiple use of punctuation symbols is forbidden (I agree with this one!!!).
4. No reverses or artwork; these are allowed in larger ads, but a reverse can be used for a logo only.

All these rules are mechanical. What about copy restrictions? There are many.

Most important, the comparative ad is absolutely verboten. You may not discredit a competitor, no matter how true the claim of superiority may be. This is an odd and paradoxical regulation. While there may be a need for dignity in an exhibit hall that crowds competitors together, this particular marketplace might not suffer if it had a more liberal set of rules or a more free-wheeling atmosphere.

Logically, unexplained superlatives are usually disallowed. Policing within the Yellow Pages is not universal, however, and one section may be crawling with ads saying "Fastest service in town" or "Best by far," while the supervisor of another section bans all such references.

If you're a service company that offers a guarantee, you may or may not be able to specify that guarantee in the Yellow Pages. Most sections permit the mention of a guarantee only if every nuance and condition of it is spelled out; in fact, some advertisers have been forced to say, "Ask about our conditional guarantee." Huh? Conditional instead of unconditional? Since you know the public rejects any but the most powerful

and specific claims, you're better off saying nothing about a
guarantee than inserting a promotionally valueless statement
such as that.

   If you're prepared to kill a lot of space explaining a guarantee, go ahead, but don't let restrictions cow you. Within
their limitations say all you possibly can. Censorship and editing are individual matters, administered by Yellow Pages
bureaucrats, and you just might happen across one who
doesn't endorse a rigid interpretation of the rules.

How to Make Your Ad Pay Off

   Here are some headings on Yellow Pages quarter-page
display ads. Check the ones you think are good:

   Friendly Efficient Service
   One-Stop Shopping
   We Aim to Please
   Your Happiness Is Our Success
   Call the Professionals
   Where the Values Are
   New Kid in Town?
   The Team that Tries Harder to Please You
   We Service What We Sell
   Home of "No Unhappy Owners"
   We're Going to Be Number 1
   A Neighborhood Dealer with a National Reputation for
      Excellence
   Where More than the Price is Right
   Where Your Savings Add Up Faster
   Our Customers Today Get Us Our Customers Tomorrow
   Your Best Buy
   The Blue Ribbon People
   Come & Visit a Public-Minded Business On the Move
   Compare Our Quality and Prices Before You Buy
   No Job Too Big, No Customer Too Small
   Quick and Quality
   Place Your Confidence in An Alert, Progressive Firm
   For All Your Needs
   Staffed by Experts

> For the Finest in Service
> Serving the Metropolitan Area
> Famous for Reliability and Service
> A Tradition of Quality
> For Fast Service See Pat
> Olde World Craftsmanship
> We Invite Comparison
> Quality Material and Workmanship at a Fair Price
> Quality Has No Substitute

Okay, how many did you check? Ten? Five? Two? If you checked any, go back and read chapter 3 again. None of these has any competitive value, and the Yellow Pages are a purely competitive marketplace.

Complicating the problem is the attitude of Yellow Pages salesmen, who surely endorse (or perhaps wrote) many of these nonsense phrases. What's the common denominator of all of them? They all lack sell. They all avoid offering a specific reason to lift that phone and make that call.

Can you imagine someone leafing through the Yellow Pages reacting to copy such as

WE DO IT RIGHT!

or

EXPERT INSTALLATION AND SERVICE

except with a yawn?

How can you make an ad in the Yellow Pages pay off? Part of the answer lies in the use of specifics, covered in the next-to-the-last section of this chapter. The rest lies in adherence to at least some of these guidelines:

1. Always ask yourself, "What's my unique selling proposition? How can I outsell the competition, knowing that the Yellow Pages reader who sees my ad sees everyone's ad?"
2. Don't use fine-line artwork that won't reproduce well in the soft yellow newsprint.
3. If you're afraid to ask questions of the Yellow Pages salesman because you think it's an admission of ignorance, you're costing yourself the immeasurable ammunition this information represents.

Figures 9-1 and 9-2 These two ads appeared on the same page of a classified directory. Professional Vision Associates lists its doctors, mentions insurance participation, shows the credit cards it honors, and specifies the types of lenses available.

Dr. Sam Katz has a specific—"While-U-Wait Service"—but this is subordinated to the meaningless headline: "Our specialty—serving you, and your optical needs. Complete quality service and personalized professional care in a friendly atmosphere." Nothing to chew on here.

**Waterfield Insurance
Agency Inc.**

Complete Insurance Service

**AUTO, HOMEOWNERS, MARINE, HEALTH, LIFE, BUSINESS
ALL INSURANCE NEEDS ARE NOT THE SAME
WE TAILOR PROGRAMS TO FIT YOUR INSURANCE NEEDS**

232-6931

1001 E. JEFF BLVD
SOUTH BEND

674-9957

1106 LWW
OSCEOLA

Figure 9-3 Except for the listing of types of insurance—and none is unique—this Yellow Pages advertiser has wasted his money. The word *needs* appears twice, and in both cases it has neither significance nor impact. In a competitive atmosphere such as the Yellow Pages, thoughtless advertising is more than a waste; it drives business to competitors.

4. Do what you can to have a memorable phone number.

5. If you have two strong selling points (e.g., "Open 24 Hours" and "Delivery Within One Hour"), consider two separate ads instead of one.

6. Fight for your rights. Don't abandon a good piece of selling copy because the salesman says, "I don't think they'll accept that."

7. Unless you're in a city that has separate directories for consumer and commercial use, aim your copy at consumers if you service both types of buyers. In such circumstances business clients are probably better recruited through direct mail or personal solicitation.

8. If Yellow Pages regulations force dilution of your sales pitch or a complex explanation of a claim, you may be better off dropping it. This kind of copy, watered down by a lot of explanation, lacks punch and may kill off calls.

9. If you're in a zoned area or one with tolls, either establish a local phone number that eliminates the toll or invite collect calls. Local suppliers are always favored.

10. Don't use dumb cartoons, puns, unclever slogans, or your children's pictures. People looking in the Yellow Pages are hot buyers looking for a professional source.

11. Use strong borders—the blackest allowed. Lump type into smaller areas to give emphasis to those areas, and try to keep type away from the border. The reader's eye will go to your ad.
12. Line illustrations usually reproduce better than photographs, but don't clown. Cartoons are for the comic strips, not the Yellow Pages.
13. Don't be too sharp. The serious buyer resents smug cleverness. Copy should be warm but businesslike.
14. Don't rerun last year's ad because you're at deadline and last year's ad is available.
15. Don't be afraid of long copy. Research shows that long copy outpulls short copy in the Yellow Pages.
16. Plan ahead. Analyze what works and what doesn't. Ask every new customer: "How did you hear about us?" Learn what the customer wants, and gradually bend your copy approach to give a positive answer to those wants.

How to Go Broke by Advertising in the Yellow Pages

The new Yellow Pages directory was just issued. There's your ad, just as the salesman said it would be. It's expensive, but . . .

Who is that man in the outer office? The representative from the Yellow Pages? But it just came out. Oh, not those Yellow Pages, the north suburban Yellow Pages.

Some businesses, such as restaurants, business services, contractors, foreign (and even domestic) car dealers, movers, hotels, and schools have a peculiar advertising problem. They have one location, and their clientele may be not only citywide but areawide. Their problem is where to advertise. In almost every market there is not only the major metropolitan directory but also a host of Yellow Pages sections covering the suburbs. Each section is assembled separately; closings aren't uniform (probably by design), and you're never sure, in a lumped telephone bill, just how much you're spending for what. There are some guidelines to help, if you use multiple insertions.

Never, never use as an excuse for overadvertising your inability to decipher the charges. You're the buyer. If this were a shipment of merchandise, you'd know to the penny what it cost and how much you're making on it. Pretend the truth: This is an advertising expense, and it's your money.

Determine as quickly as you can, certainly within the first six months (which still gives you plenty of time before the next closing), whether each separate insertion is paying off or not. Adjust up or down accordingly. You may want to increase rather than decrease, but you must have a base of information. Try to have a local phone number in each area in which you advertise, but if that isn't possible, be sure to mention the name of the community prominently in your ad. One good argument for the local phone number is that you can tell quickly whether that community is sending you any business.

The breakup of AT&T accelerated the growth of the national Yellow Pages directories. If you do business nationally, consider these ("Business" or "Consumer"), but because they're so expensive, track their effectiveness supercautiously.

If your business is drawn from one entire metropolitan area, the big metropolitan Yellow Pages are the best marketplace; be sure you're in them before experimenting with peripheral surburban phone books and independent directories. If your business is drawn primarily from a specific suburb or group of suburbs, load up on your primary area before considering expansion into the city directory. Be sure your biggest blast is where you want to do the most business. That way, you still will be in business when the next directory is issued.

You also may have to decide about advertising within several categories of a single directory. You might be listed under "Automobile Dealers—New Cars"; "Automobile Dealers—Used Cars"; "Automobile Repairing & Service"; and another batch of categories under "Trucks." You should have at least a lightface listing under every category within which you do business, but one of those ads should have some flair and size, if possible.

Some advertisers hang on to ads that have ceased to do them any good because of the "seniority rule": the advertiser with the greatest longevity gets the best position. Consider the Yellow Pages advertiser who has been in the directory for 20 years and is on the second or third page of his section because so many other advertisers have been in there for 30 years. It's a fair system, I suppose, but a lottery for space would be a lot more exciting. Meanwhile, advertisers buy these ads hoping to move up in position.

Don't forgo advertising in a prime Yellow Pages section for a speculative ad or a single listing in the main directory. You can be seduced by a salesperson for independent directories, other communities, or boldface listings in the White Pages. These are all speculative: In fact, the boldface listing in the White Pages, on analysis, only makes your name and number easier to find for the person who is looking only for you and who will surely find you anyway.

One argument in favor of the large-space ad in the Yellow Pages is that the buyer isn't coming to see you; he's going to phone you.

This suggests two important considerations for the advertiser:

First, in the Yellow Pages, you're as big, as well established, and as dominant as your ad. A smaller company with a big ad can appear to be bigger than a far larger company with a smaller ad. Second, since your Yellow Pages ad is intended to bring business inquiries from people who have never called before, take your best shot and train whoever answers your phone to be as warm, but businesslike, as the image you hope your ad projects. Never let a person who answers your phone sound tired, surly, bored, smug, or annoyed. Put a big sign in front of her or him: "Smile as you answer, and remember: "We're all professionals here, including you."

Using Specifics When You Really Have None

Between the restrictions on selling copy and the problem you may have with every competitor being able to make the same claims, establishing a position in the Yellow Pages isn't easy. What can you use as a selling argument? Here are a few Yellow Pages hot buttons that motivate the users of this medium.

1. *Fast service.* Of all the motivators, this is the strongest. Think about it for a moment: Why are people looking in the Yellow Pages? Chances are better than even that they need

something fast. As obvious as this point may be if you're a plumber, an automobile-towing company, or a television-repair shop, it's not that different if you're a tax consultant, a printer, a car dealer, or a folding-box distributor. People want action, and you should advertise your capability of giving it.

Tell exactly how fast the service is. "One-hour service" is far superior to "Fast Service" as a call-grabber. "In and out in one day" is better than "Fast service"; "Immediate radio-dispatched couriers" is better than "Fast service"; "Fast service" is better than "Dependable service" or "Known for service" or no reference at all.

2. *Availability.* If you have 24-hour service, say so; if you take calls on weekends, say so, especially if you can make a big point of no extra charge for weekend service. You may think this isn't a big deal, but think as a Yellow Pages user thinks (for example, as you thought the last time you used the Yellow Pages) and you'll understand the huggy-blanket aspect of availability to someone hunting for help.

3. *Professionalism.* This isn't easy to prove. Sure, you can claim it, especially if yours is the type of business in which licenses or memberships can be claimed. If you don't have that kind of business, or if you're not a member of some official association, claim longevity. The company doesn't have to be in business for 25 years for you to claim "A quarter-century of experience" if you yourself have been in the profession that long.

4. *Guarantee/warranty.* This point is a weak fourth. It isn't all that important in the Yellow Pages, and a good thing, too, since, as was noted earlier in this chapter, you can wind up with such nonsense claims as, "Ask about our conditional guarantee."

Whether your guarantee or warranty is a potent selling weapon depends on how you put it. What you say depends on the amount of policing by the local Yellow Pages honcho, and if you have to spell out your guarantee in 50 or 60 words, you're better off saying nothing, since saying nothing is stronger than an overexplained guarantee. The strong guarantee is the short, absolute guarantee, such as "No charge until work is finished to your complete satisfaction," or "If we can't make it run in one day, there's no charge." You can go broke with these claims if you can't operate profitably inside them, so don't use these lines of copy unless they make sense for you.

5. *Free.* Everyone offers free estimates, but if you have a free water-hardness testing kit, a free mileage chart for every call, free wheel balancing with every tire, or a free atlas with every fill-up or policy, you're now talking in tangible terms. You do have to live with such an offer for a whole year, until the next directory is issued—or even longer than that, since it takes three months for a new directory to filter into full use.

6. *Specialization.* Instead of a quarter-page ad headed, "Foreign Car Specialists," try a whole bunch of smaller ads for every brand of foreign car: "Jensen Specialists," "Mercedes-Benz Specialists," "Subaru Specialists," "Toyota Specialists," and "Volvo Specialists." These are all for the same repair company, but mentioning the specific make of car is more powerful than a larger ad listing every make in one hunk. How can the same ad make the claim that you're a Citroen specialist and a Fiat specialist? The individual listings build buyer confidence.

7. *Absolute specificity.* Even if you can get away with copy such as, "Number One in the City," what good has it done you? In what way are you number one? Are you the biggest? The oldest? The fastest? Say so, and be prepared to prove it.

8. *Big Daddy.* Tell buyers what they want to hear. This is as simple as asking yourself, "What can I say to a buyer that will convince him I'm the right company with which to do business? Then tell him that. You usually can't quote prices in Yellow Pages ads, which is probably a good thing, since you would be stuck with those prices for a whole year. You can suggest ease of payment, remembering that you don't want to rub a customer's nose in costs before he decides to call you. "Your budget is our budget," while horribly weak, is still better than, "Low monthly terms," which suggests you're so expensive that he'll be paying forever.

9. *Hours.* State when you're open. It may salvage a customer who, otherwise, getting no answer, will call someone else. For example, if you're a restaurant and your ad reads,

"Open from 11 a.m. to 11 p.m.,"you may get the business of a party of 12 whose spokesperson looks in those pages at 10 A.M., whereas, if you have no reference to hours, he may phone, get no answer, and then call someone else.

10. *Superiority.* If your ad for a real estate company says, "We're the publishers of the Tri-Cities Commercial-Industrial Real Estate Guide," you've given yourself automatic dominance. Obviously, you'd better have such a guide, but it may not be that much more work than a helpful guide you already use as an automatic, unpromoted handout. Superiority is hard to claim directly in the Yellow Pages, not only because you can't run a comparative ad but also because you can't make the direct claim. Think of the whiskies that claim superiority with statements such as, "By appointment to her majesty, Queen Elizabeth II," or even with references to some long-dead ruler. This is good Yellow Pages copy.

Conclusion

All these comments about Yellow Pages advertising can be condensed into a single sentence:

Think like a buyer when you design and place your ad.

10

Using Magazines

A few years ago many advertising-agency media departments regarded magazines as obsolete. This was because some of the giants of the first half of the twentieth century—*Life, Look, Liberty, Collier's,* and *The Saturday Evening Post*—gradually lost circulation during the 1950s and 1960s, then vanished.

What the demise of these once-great publications indicated, a trend that if anything has intensified as we move toward 1990, isn't that magazines are obsolete; rather, *general interest* magazines are obsolete.

So in today's marketplace, magazines such as *PC World,* catering to a vertical-interest group, can have 600 to 700 pages each issue, while magazines without a specialty to support a hard-core readership scrabble around for discount subscribers and for the thin end of advertising budgets.

Magazines have a unique position in the advertising mix, based on a combination of force-communication factors no other medium can offer in a single package. Like television, they can show a product, in color, looking just as it looks in life. Unlike television, they can't show that product in motion, but along with this implicit disadvantage is an explicit advantage: The picture can be enhanced, retouched, and made more glamorous. Also, the recipient of the advertising message can return at will to study the advertising message.

Magazines don't have the timeliness of newspapers, but that isn't the marketplace they should invade. Even weekly magazines can't begin to compete with newspapers for short deadlines, and the advertiser who regards a newspaper's 72-hour deadline as unreasonable would go mad with the 17-day deadline of *The New Yorker*, short though that deadline is. If because of the nature of your business you can't decide what to advertise at least several weeks in advance, you can't use magazines. They close too far ahead.

How Magazines Differ from Other Media

What magazines have that neither newspapers nor television have is class. They reach a more selective marketplace, and invariably that marketplace has more dollars to spend than does the more generalized market of television and newspapers.

The advantage of magazines, then, is that they tend to reach more people who can and will buy what you have to sell. To reach those people at the lowest possible cost, you have to know how to buy magazine space, which is no marketplace for beginners.

Whereas newspapers circulate to almost everyone within a given geographic area regardless of social, economic, ethnic, or professional background, consumer magazines tend to choose specific individuals as readers regardless of geographic area. Thus, magazines in general deliver a more selective readership and can command a higher cost-per-reader.

This trans-area reach isn't universally true. Some magazines cover as limited a geographic area as do newspapers. Every major city has a magazine, and some, such as *Chicago* or *Los Angeles*, are highly successful despite their obvious local circulation. Why? For the same reason that so many consumer magazines now offer local or regional editions. Since magazines invariably offer higher-income readership than newspapers do, especially for higher-ticket items, they reach a greater percentage of readers who can and will buy what their advertisers have to sell. If an advertiser whose product sells best to high-income groups spends four dollars per thousand in a newspaper, 30 percent of whose readership can even afford to buy what he has to sell, he would make a better buy in a local magazine at eight dollars per thousand if that magazine could deliver 61 percent or better in qualified readership; and the reproduction and longevity of the magazine are superior to that of a newspaper.

Some magazines, ostensibly local, achieve a national circulation. *The New Yorker* and *New York* sell many copies outside the New York metropolitan area; *Sunset*, published for the Southwest, is distributed widely across the country. Yet, this "outside" circulation isn't always sought because distant readers aren't necessarily buyers, particularly if the product advertised is local or if the advertiser is a retailer.

Dollar for dollar, an advertiser not dependent on buyer-reaction within a single day probably would prefer magazine advertising to newspaper advertising. The quality of printing is better; most magazines will take halftones from 100 to 150 lines per inch, compared to the coarse 65-line screens newspapers accept. From a marketing point of view, there's a more profound advantage: A magazine is alive for a week to a month, or even longer, while a newspaper dies the next day.

Sometimes the dividing line between newspapers and magazines isn't easy to establish. For example, some weekly tabloid or smaller-than-tabloid publications qualify as both, although the technique of distribution would identify them as newspapers. *The New York Times Magazine*, distributed each Sunday as part of that newspaper, calls itself a magazine both in name and in its trade advertising. It claims to carry more lines of advertising than any other magazine—even though its readers, however loyal, pay nothing for the magazine, nor can they buy it without getting the rest of the Sunday *New York Times* thrown in. Is it a magazine?

Parade, distributed free with many Sunday newspapers, is also a magazine, although no one "buys" it; it's free with the newspaper that contracts to distribute it. Because it's more mass than class it can't command the cost-per-thousand-readers a paid-for magazine can.

Inches of advertising carried is one way to gauge the success of a magazine, but it isn't always a valid way, since weekly magazines, with 52 issues a year, have a powerful edge over monthlies that publish only 12 issues.

Another factor is intensity of readership, the result of

reader loyalty that bleeds over from the editorial content into the advertising. How much time is spent reading the publication each week or each month? And of that, how much readership do the ads enjoy?

Since magazine ads usually are more professionally produced than newspaper ads, it's a more competitive marketplace for an advertiser trying to get attention. This greater emphasis on production isn't only the result of a higher cost-per-thousand, it also is the result of the policy among magazines to grant a 15 percent advertising-agency commission to all ads, which means the advertiser can employ an advertising agency without spending any more for the space. That same retailer who commands the considerably lower local rate in *The New York Post* pays the same rate as national advertisers in *New York Magazine;* he might as well place the ad through an agency, which tends to bring about a slicker job of production.

The Decline of General Magazines

For the first half of the twentieth century, the general magazines were the kings. They sold the most copies; they paid their writers the most; they carried the most color; and they were the most thoroughly read. That these giants—*The Saturday Evening Post, Collier's, Life, Look, Liberty*—have expired (although the *Post* continues as a thin, low-circulation monthly and *Life* has been revived, also as a monthly) is due not only to their inability to adapt to a changing society but also to the obsolescence of the general magazine as a genre. Those stories that were so avidly read in the *Post* or *Collier's* are grist for television series today. Those startling photographs in *Life* are old hat when satellites can pick up instant news film from around the world and every fumble on a Saturday afternoon is dissected, replayed, and shown from a different angle in slow motion by 17 color-television cameras located all over the football stadium.

Even the weekly news magazines, *Time, Newsweek,* and *U.S. News and World Report,* have adapted their coverage to become feature- rather than news-oriented, in order to hold onto circulation. In magazine publishing, being a giant is no grounds for security in an age of future shock, when the very reason for your existence can vanish under the onslaught of the next round of technology.

How to Buy Magazine Space for Half the Rate Card Prices

There's a magic word that can save you half the cost of an ad, giving you twice as much advertising for the same amount of money. The word is *remnant.*

Not every magazine offers them, however, and some would rather go to press with Smoky the Bear fillers than sell space at a discount. To the shrewd buyer, though, remnants make the difference between a profitable ad or a losing one, since many advertisers, especially in mail order, use cost-per-lead as the only criterion of success.

A remnant is space left unsold, and apparently doomed to remain unsold, as an issue approaches presstime. The advertising manager offers this space at a discount—first-come, first-served. For weekly magazines, between one and two weeks of lead time is allowed to prepare the ad, once you agree to take the space. Here are the rules for buying remnants:

1. You must take the space offered. If a publication has a half page available, and all you have ready to go is a full-page ad, you either revise that ad or take a pass.
2. Your commitment means the ad will be there on time. You don't have the post-deadline excuses regular contract advertisers use.
3. If the magazine publishes regional editions, you may have the option to take all or some of the markets. For example, you may be told: "I have Philadelphia, Pittsburgh, the Great Lakes, all the Southeast and Southwest, and Seattle open." You might answer, "I'll buy everything except the Southwest." The number of dollars is based entirely on the number of circulated copies that carry your ad. The advertising department then goes off to find someone to pick up the Southwest region of that issue; if they can't find someone, in goes Smoky the Bear.

4. Because you're a discount buyer, you have no say as to which page the ad is on, nor can you expect to see proofs before publication. Safety lies in one direction only: Sending the publication a completely pasted-up, ready-to-go ad, which they can throw into the open slot without production problems.
5. If you want to get on a list of remnant buyers, deal through an advertising agency knowledgeable in this type of buying. On your own, you'd get last choice, which means you might wait for months before something opens up. Most of the remnant-buying agencies are in New York or Chicago, and their value is that they're the ones the publications call first when space becomes available.

The big weeklies with multiple editions most often have remnants available. For examples, *Plane & Pilot*, has one national edition, and all ads appear in every copy printed. The magazine closes months before publication. The panic and rush are over well in advance, and the publication would seldom offer a discount because chances are that discount would be to a regular advertiser who, were there no discount, would pay card rate for the space. But *TV Guide* is a different ball game. This mammoth (in circulation; its size is tiny) weekly has so many local editions and combinations of advertiser options the salesmen themselves have trouble remembering them all. It swarms with national and regional advertisers, and the computer that determines what pages go where has to be working nights. In comes an advertiser who locks up the Northeast. Once the pages are committed to him, it's possible—especially since this is a weekly—to be almost at deadline with openings in some of the other editions. This is what you want.

Within the magazine there are no physical differences whatever between space bought for the full rate and space bought at half price. What you must remember, if you're in this sophisticated avenue of marketing, is to have an ad ready to go. What size? Best is to have ads in six sizes:

Half page, digest (*TV Guide* size)
Full page, digest
Half page, standard (seven by ten inches)
Full page, standard
Half page, vertical tabloid (Sunday Supplement)
Full page, tabloid

Prepare remnant ads in black and white. Even though about half the remnant availabilities are in color, you can buy these in black and white. But if you have a four-color ad and the availability is for a black-and-white page, you have production problems and costs.

Here is how easy it is to figure the value of remnants: You sell beer coolers by mail. You can afford to spend $100 per sale. You bought a page for $10,000 and you sold only 80 coolers. You needed to sell 100, so you lost money. The sales cost you $125 each. Ah, but now consider that same page at remant price. Your ad still exists. The page costs you $5,000, and you sell 80 coolers. The sales cost you $62.50 each, and you've made a better-than-average profit on the same ad, in the same publication.

There are also two other ways to buy magazine space at a discount. First is per-inquiry advertising, discussed in the chapter on radio advertising. Few magazines offer such deals, but you can always ask. Second is the request for end rate— the lowest contract rate—even though you're buying an ad only once, "as a test." Some magazines will say yes and some no, but it never hurts to ask.

Producing a Magazine Ad

Magazines rarely give the production help newspapers do. Magazines won't set type, won't make negatives or plates, won't provide art or paste-up services, and scream in fury and outrage if an ad doesn't match their production guidelines exactly. The smaller the publication, the more willing it probably is to be helpful. A small magazine may set some type or do some paste-up for you and charge you very little.

When dealing directly with a publication, ask the production department to send the exact specifications of the ad, or look for the specifications on the rate card.

Also, never produce an ad for a magazine without first inspecting an issue. There's nothing wrong if your ad doesn't match the others, but something is surely wrong if your ad is the wrong size or will look ridiculous in that publication.

Almost all magazines are printed offset, and if you don't

have any ready source of offset negatives, send the magazine the original pasted-up ad. Yes, this is dangerous, not only because the paste-ups can be bent or cracked in the mails, but also because they can be lost. It's probably the cheapest way, since invariably the publication can make its printing materials cheaper than you can—and, having made them, can't blame you for a poor reproduction. A "velox" reproduction of the ad will usually suffice; that way, you can keep the original past-up safe.

If you know absolutely nothing about production, you'd better deal with an advertising agency or an art studio. That way, you have someone else to nail for unwitting mistakes or lost materials.

If an ad is running in several publications with similar production techniques and identical sizes—such as *Time* and *Newsweek*—if possible have one publication service the other. Send the materials to one with instructions for them to send it on to the other before a specified date, at least two weeks before deadline. They may not like it, but they'll do it.

In producing an ad, be sure the halftones are the right fineness of screen. While most magazine printing on machine-finish paper can accept any degree of screening from 110 to 133, some can take a much finer screen—sometimes up to 200—and you might as well get the benefit of better production.

There's less reason to put a heavy border around a magazine ad than a newspaper ad, since there's less chance of being buried on the page—but the chance does exist, especially for advertisers using less than a page. As a general rule: The smaller the ad, the greater the need for a border. Full-page ads might use the white paper itself as part of a "bleed" effect, making the ad look larger.

Magazine space is usually sold by the inch or in multiples of $\frac{1}{12}$ page. A standard 7-by-10 inch magazine has three columns, each $2\frac{1}{3}$ inches wide. Thus, a $\frac{1}{6}$-page ad would be 5 inches high and $2\frac{1}{3}$ inches wide. Usually, you can't buy an ad wider than it is high, but this isn't a universal rule.

All the large-format magazines—those of jumbo size— offer what is called a "junior page." This page is the same size as a standard seven-by-ten-inch page. Offering the junior page enables these magazines to accept ads prepared for standard-size publications without expensive plate changes; if they didn't offer this option, undoubtedly many advertisers would regard the additional production cost of ads to fit their formats as a questionable expenditure of money. As it is, the number of magazines with a larger than 7-by-10-inch page shrinks every year.

If you buy a junior page in an oversize or tabloid publication, demand firmly on the insertion order that no other ads will appear on that page. This demand can be the best of all possible magazine-advertising ploys. Usually the publication will honor your request. It isn't easy to position other ads on a page carrying a 7-by-10 inch ad anyway.

Magazines as a Source of Market Research

Should your ad run in *House Beautiful* or *Better Homes?* *Woman's Day* or *Family Circle?* *Playboy* or *Penthouse?* *Cosmopolitan* or *Glamour?* *Ladies' Home Journal* or *Good Housekeeping?*

The demographics of each publication differ enough from even its closest competitor to justify selectivity for the space-buyer. One publication within a field, and only one, can claim lowest overall cost-per-thousand. Yet, since the rule is not just to reach the most people, but the most people who can and will buy what you have to sell, bulk circulation is only one yardstick by which to gauge potential advertising success.

Almost every consumer magazine has statistical support for its use by advertisers. One will furnish research proving its readers will buy more automobiles during the coming year than will the readers of any of its competitors; another will make the same claim about refrigerators; a third will show serious evidence that the gross income of its readership is the highest within its field.°

°An old rule of circulation-recruitment is still valid: When a publication offers inducements and discounts, or engages in a widespread campaign to recruit subscribers, the buying power of the average subscriber goes down.

But suppose you, the advertiser, aren't selling cars or refrigerators, and you really don't know what levels of income are the best prospects. In that case call the magazine or its local representative (major magazines list their representatives in SRDS; most have offices in New York, Chicago, San Francisco, Los Angeles, Dallas, and Atlanta). "I'm putting together a schedule for our line of expensive men's wear," you tell him, "and I'd like some demographic information showing me where your publication fits in."

The space-salesman may do nothing other than check his file for other men's-wear manufacturers who have used those pages and send you photocopies of their ads as proof the publication works for advertisers in your field. If some of the more respected companies in the field have used the publication consistently, you must assume they've checked its pulling power. If they once ran ads but no longer do, that's a danger signal.

An alert publication will ask who your target-buyers are. If you're able to answer the question—and you should be, since you're the entrepreneur—the publication will dig for statistics that match its readership with your buyer. Or the publication may show you other avenues of advertising or point out other buyers you haven't considered, which makes that magazine a speculative rather than selective buy.

When making speculative buys, never tie yourself to a long-term contract. The very nature of speculation suggests a situation in which month after month you're desperately adapting your ad to find buyers whose tastes you hope will match your line of merchandise. And since you and the publication agree this is a speculative buy, perhaps the magazine can be convinced to give you the end rate as an inducement to try its pages.

No reputable magazine will invent demographic statistics. This is less a matter of ethics than protection against having every claim it ever makes suspect. You can rely on the statistical base or the background information you get from magazines, provided the reliance is coupled with an understanding of how to interpret statistics that glorify the positives and eliminate the negatives.

Choosing the Right Buyer Group

Don't just run an ad on the assumption that consumer magazines are consumer magazines and you'll hit the group you're after. If that supposition were true, *Liberty* and *Collier's* would still be titans of publishing. From the moment a person is born *(Parents)*, as he reaches the preschool age *(Cricket)*, enters school *(Scholastic)*, enters puberty *(Teen* and then *Seventeen)*, goes to college *(Penthouse, Rolling Stone)*, becomes an adult *(Cosmopolitan)*, marries *(Modern Bride)*, perhaps works on the farm° *(Farm Journal)* or in an office *(Business Week)*, starts rearing his own children *(Good Housekeeping)*, becomes a middle-class suburbanite *(Better Homes & Gardens)*, and reaches the golden years *(Modern Maturity)*, there are magazines aiming themselves at various cycles of one's life. Nor is this by any means the end of it. There are even more vertical publications for special interests. *Sports Illustrated* is edited for the would-be macho; *Art News* is aimed at those whose interest lies in fine art; *Ebony* reaches affluent blacks; *Marvel Comics* hits millions of comic-book readers with enough buying power to order by mail the toys, games, knives, and magical tricks advertised in its pages; *People* appeals to the voyeur in each of us; *Motor Trend* reaches young tinkerers and automobile buffs—and this is only a sampler.

Within a chosen group of publications, the safest place to advertise is usually the highest-circulation magazine in that group, but because some publications knock their brains out recruiting readers regardless of the utility of those readers as buyers, this isn't always true.

Reader's Digest, which sells more copies per issue than any other magazine, alone seems to know how to recruit subscribers without damaging its image. Once a year, a mammoth promotional campaign directs mail to almost every home in this country; invariably included is an incentive to subscribe, and usually other media, especially television, are used to

---

°Standard Rate & Data combines consumer and farm publications within a single volume, but in different sections. Farm magazines are consumer-oriented, since farmers are consumers, but these consumers are to be reached within their own professional atmosphere in farm publications.

underscore the importance of the offer. This annual promotion is an event that even mail order professionals look forward to.

Even though it circulates about as many copies per issue as *TV Guide, Reader's Digest* lags far behind *TV Guide* in total annual circulation largely because, as a weekly, *TV Guide* is issued 4.3 times as often as the monthly *Reader's Digest*. Greater total annual circulation or ad linage doesn't mean greater, per-ad impact.

An equivalent argument for dealing with one of the lesser publications within a field is that not only are rates lower, which means a test can be mounted at less cost, but these are also the magazines most likely to be cooperative with requests for good position, end rates, and production help.

The obvious suggestion for the first-time advertiser in consumer magazines is to obtain a second-hand copy of the Standard Rate & Data volume listing both consumer and farm magazines. Leafing through this book invariably gives even hardened admen new promotional ideas, because previously unconsidered reader-targets present themselves.

11

Trade Publications

Two changes in the world of professional, industrial, commercial, and technical publications began in the 1950s and now have become almost uniform. First, trade publications, in editorial format and the appearance and wording of their advertising, lost their formality and adopted the look of consumer publications. Second, most trade publications are now free.

The first change was usually generated by one leading publication in each group. That leader modernized its format, achieved dominance by so doing, and forced competitors to pay similar attention to layout and typography. Recognition that the same individual who reads *Time* and *Better Homes & Gardens* in the evening reads *Iron Age, Journal of the American Medical Association,* and *Purchasing Magazine* during the day (and perhaps also at night) has brought some trade publications to a level of typographic excellence that many consumer magazines envy.

This upgrading not only spills over to advertising, but it often results from it. There is no longer a heavy dividing line between industrial and consumer advertising agencies, because there is no longer a difference in appearance or even in approach between trade and consumer advertising.

How to Use Standard Rate & Data Service

Except for Direct Mail Lists, perhaps the thickest monthly volume issued from the Wilmette, Illinois, headquarters of Standard Rate & Data Service is the one titled "Business Publications." Here, each group of publications is classified according to the marketplace that group reaches. Within a group, publications are listed as audited, which means the circulation is verified by the Audit Bureau of Circulation if subscribers pay to receive the publication or by the Business Press Audit if copies are "controlled," or circulated free; or unaudited, which means the publication's publisher offers an unverified report of the circulation.

Categories are listed alphabetically, from No. 1 (Advertising & Marketing) to No. 159 (Woodworking). Not all numbers are covered; there's no No. 8, for example, but there are lots of subnumbers to keep the alphabetical listing proper. No. 5, for example, is Arts, and No. 6 is Automotive. Between them is 5a, Automatic Data Systems. Between 15, Books & Book Trade, and 16, Brewing, is 15a, Bottling.

Even those inside a business or industry rarely know all the publications in the field. In category No. 6, Automotive, for example, there are at this writing 35 audited publications and 39 unaudited publications, 74 possible publications to carry your message to the automotive trade. There are 51 banking publications, many of them limited to a single state *(Tennessee Banker)* or region *(Mountain States Banker)*. Category 35b, Discount Marketing, lists only four publications; 35c, Display, has but one.

In which publication should you advertise? You're running your first ad to a professional bakers' group, and you don't know whether to use *Baker's Digest, Bakery Production and Marketing,* or *Baking Industry*—three of the nine publications listed under category 9, Baking.

Under each magazine's individual listing are up to 19 numbered sections.° These numbers are always the same. No. 11 is always classified ads, for example, and if there is no classified section, No. 11 won't appear in that listing. (If No. 11 does appear, the rates are in a small separate Standard Rate & Data book.)

Any decision should be based on how closely that publication's demographics conform to the First Law of Advertis-

---

°Numbers run from 1 to 18; if applicable, there is a 5a for combination rates.

ing—can you, through its pages, and at the lowest possible cost, reach the most people who can and will buy what you have to sell?

First, note that the publications aren't parallel. *Bakers Digest* charges $1,465 (section 5) for a 7-by-10-inch page (section 15), to reach 6,100 subscribers. The listing gives no breakdown as to how many are bakery owners and executives; how many are production superintendents, plant managers, and production departments; and how many are allied trades (section 18).

Bakery Production and Marketing is obviously the giant in the field. Its 7-by-10-inch page costs $2,960 to reach more than 30,000 controlled-circulation, nonpaid subscribers, of whom some 16,000 are with manufacturing bakeries, 11,000 with wholesale or retail bakeries, 1,800 with distributors of ingredients and equipment, and 1,000 with manufacturers of ingredients and equipment.

Baking Industry charges $1,635 for the same size page and has about 20,000 subscribers, of whom 10,000 are manufacturing bakeries, 4,200 retail bakeries, and the rest scattered.

On a bulk basis, *Bakery Production and Marketing* seems to be the best bet. Spending $2,960 to reach 30,000, one pays $98 per thousand; *Bakers Digest*, at $1,465 to reach 6,100 subscribers, costs $240 per thousand; *Baking Industry*, charging $1,635 to reach 20,000 subscribers, costs $82 per thousand—a slightly lower per-thousand rate than *Bakery Production and Marketing*, but with only about half the circulation. And Baking Industry is a tabloid, which means your "standard" page isn't a full page.

So, to reach the most people, *Bakery Production and Marketing* is the best buy. But suppose your strongest target is the retail baker? Less than a third of the circulation of *Bakery Production and Marketing* goes to retail bakers. You need another choice. Suppose you want to reach the production supervisors at bakeries? Industry sources say *Bakers Digest* sends almost 60 percent of its copies to these readers, who aren't even listed as a subcategory but are lumped into "manufacturing bakeries" by *Bakery Production and Marketing*. Too, you might not want to jump in with an expensive ad. Then consider that

Bakers Digest is a bimonthly that closes on the 15th of the month preceding each issue (section 16 of the SRDS listing); *Bakery Production and Marketing* is a monthly that closes 30 days ahead; *Baking Industry* is also a monthly that closes on the 15th of the preceding month.

Which one will run your news releases? Which might give you the 6- or 12-time rate for a single test insertion? Which might give you a cover at regular page rate? Most important, which penetrates the target-groups you're trying to sell with the least possible waste?

And these are only three of the nine listed publications. You can see the need for the information carried in the Standard Rate & Data and the confusion that would result from a marketplace lacking such single-volume information.

How to Reach the Right Buyers

The rules for trade advertising parallel those of consumer advertising, and adherence to the three laws of mass communications don't vary at all. While some trade advertising is inferior in its insistence on nonspecificity and name/image repetition, on the stuffiest and most pompous level reached by any advertising anywhere, the giants don't do this. With the exception of goodwill advertising, which is often a public-relations function rather than an advertising function, their print promotion to their customers is direct, specific, dynamic, and colorful.

Remove an ad from a trade publication these days, and often you can't tell easily whether the ad ran in a trade or a consumer magazine. The dividing lines no longer exist; what should also exist is the same recognition as in consumer media that an ad in a trade publication should reach the most people who can and will buy what the advertising has to sell.

Why are so many trade publications distributed free? If someone is advertising in a trade publication directed to computer and data processing equipment buyers, he wants to have a chance to reach all those buyers. The publications are sent to the title, not to the individual; so if John Jones, director of purchasing, leaves, John Smith will take his place—and still receive the publication in which the ad appears. If Jones has paid for that subscription, two problems arise: (1) The subscription goes with him, and (2) there is no way to penetrate 100 percent of the potential buyership, since a far smaller percentage will pay to receive a trade publication.

The corollary of the rule of free distribution is control. In fact, within the trade, publications distributed free are called controlled-circulation publications.

Control is exercised not only by sending copies regardless of payment, but also by refusing copies to those who don't qualify. You can't get a subscription to *Meetings & Conventions* unless you plan meetings and conventions. A request for copies of *General Aviation News* will be ignored unless you can prove you're in aviation manufacturing, services, or maintenance.

Some powerful publications that still demand and get subscription money—such as *Advertising Age*—have the best of all possible worlds. They are the spokesmen for their industries, and yet they are able to command subscription dollars. This situation invariably exists only where one publication dominates a particular field with little or no competition.

Paid-circulation trade publications sometimes take the position that controlled-circulation publications are inferior, maintaining that when an individual has paid for some reading matter he is more likely to read it. Yet most readership studies disprove this; readership isn't based on whether the recipient has paid for the publication but on how much he values the information in that publication. Once the subscription check has been sent, the reader forgets about any difference between paid and controlled; the publication either has information helpful to him or it doesn't; the ads are for products and services he wants to know about or they aren't. Meanwhile, the advertiser rests secure in his knowledge that since the publication's circulation depends on that publication's own decision that the recipient is a valid target, there won't be any sudden drop in circulation or "holes" in the distribution.

Some big corporations, normally business-publication advertisers, have diverted advertising dollars to consumer media. A study showed that if consumers have great familiarity with a company and positive attitudes toward its products, they not only are three times as likely to buy its products but they also are far more willing to take management's word in labor disputes, pay a higher price to get products with that company's components, and buy the company's stock.

The Danger of Unprofessional Trade Advertising

The incidence of unprofessional advertising is far lower in consumer magazines than in trade publications. Part of this unquestionably is due to the high incidence of agency-produced ads, which may not improve content but usually assures visual slickness. Trade advertising has a high incidence of unprofessionalism, not only because these same advertising agencies are ill at ease in a vertical-interest marketplace peopled by readers with a technical background the agency writer doesn't possess, but also because so many trade ads spring from ego instead of the recognition that the ad is supposed to transmit information. Possibly the biggest single cause of trade advertising failure is the "everyone-knows-who-we-are" attitude that causes an ad to structure its message around the dead core of company ego instead of comparative fact.

Years ago, teachers of advertising courses talked about a three-stage maturation process for advertising. The first was the pioneer stage, in which a company tried to educate message-recipients about the company and its product, building familiarity and confidence. The second was the competitive stage, in which the company slugged for business against others in its field. The third was the retentive stage, in which the company protected its dominance by a more statesmanlike type of advertising message that sailed above the grubby competitive world.

Anyone still teaching these ideas is more than out-of-date; he is setting up those who listen to waste a lot of advertising dollars. Today's marketplace allows no time for pioneering and no dollars for retention. An advertiser lives on his wits, and safety lies in one direction only: *competitive advertising*, in which advantages are stated, restated, and proved with solid fact.

The same reader who doesn't really mind such nonsensical ads as a television station's "The Best Movies in Pittsburgh," which he reads in the morning newspaper before going off to work, is annoyed to find a similar message in *Broadcasting* Magazine. He reads that magazine not as a torpid consumer but as a businessman in a position to decide where his advertising dollar will go.

It's true that the dividing line between consumer and trade advertising has shrunk to a hairline thinness during the past ten years. It's untrue that unprofessional, fuzzy advertising messages are of any value in trade-publication advertising.

Adherence to three rules should eliminate the danger of lapsing into unprofessionalism in trade advertising:

1. Never run an ad that doesn't give the reader a reason to do business with you.
2. Never run an ad that looks typographically unattractive (the simplest way to avoid this: Set the whole ad in variations of one Roman face).
3. Don't change ads every issue unless you're running a coherent series with a similar format. Such changes only obscure and confuse the selling job the ads are supposed to do.

How to Have Trade Publications Do Your Research for You

A trade publication feels an obligation to be the spokesman for its trade or industry. The whole *raison d'etre* for an editorial staff—many of whom are contributing editors from the outside—is to provide information even those earning their livings in the field don't have. (In fact, if you've amassed some useful information, you can positively count on one of the publications in the field printing that information with full credit to you, provided the information is beneficial to the whole industry and not just to you. This is discussed in detail in the next section.)

As an advertiser, you can ask the publication for information. You'll invariably be surprised at the depth of information already on hand. Most publications know the size of their field, the number of practitioners, the total annual volume, the strong and weak areas, and even who is buying what. If they don't, they'll listen carefully when you suggest that the publication mount a research project to determine just who is buying vinyl, industrial cleaning compounds, or tennis racquet-restringing equipment.

If the information they might obtain would be unusually beneficial to you, you might offer to help pay for the project, perhaps covering the cost of business reply cards bound into an issue to bring in the survey results. But this is a dangerous offer to make, because betraying your interest to that extent can damage your bargaining power. It isn't a weapon you should unsheath too early.

Many publications have a formal research department. It may be one person, or part of one person, but the very title suggests information is on hand—information you can use in marketing. Many researchers love what they do, although this can be a pain in the neck for a marketer who isn't interested in research unadulterated by commercial pollutants. You aren't a theoretician, as are many of the researchers; you're someone trying to sell something and there are three areas of primary interest:

1. Who is buying what?
2. What is your present and anticipated market position?
3. What are the foreseeable market trends?

As a first move, ask the publication for any information it may have already. Most of it may have appeared in print over the last two years, but if you missed it, misfiled it, or didn't care about it at the time, you'll find a coherent background in the package the publication may send you.

A logical and often beneficial aid to your relationship with the publication is to suggest areas of research. The publication may have lost touch with the type of information its advertisers want, while overattending the type of information it thinks its readers want. Before spending your dollars on research, discuss the benefit with the publication. No harm comes from asking. Just remember the one disadvantage: The information won't be yours exclusively; others will also be exposed to it. The counterargument is that since it was your idea, by the time they understand the information you'll have used it and gone on to something else.

How to Use the Weapon of Advertising to Get Editorial Coverage

All magazines, consumer or trade, have only two types of content: (1) editorial matter aimed at a specific type of readership and (2) advertising aimed at a specific type of readership.

These two components are parallel in that they both, properly prepared, will appeal to the same reader. The text of a publication is supposed to reach the same demographic group the advertising reaches.

Implicit in this truism is a potential benefit to the advertiser, one even sophisticated advertisers often overlook. This benefit is the ability to reach the publication's readers not only through advertising but also through editorial coverage. (The word "editorial" is used to mean all textual matter, not necessarily a group of opinions by the executives of the publication.)

In this area, advertising and public relations functions overlap. You, the advertiser, can and should demand and get editorial coverage.°

You should know the method, the logic, and the benefits. The benefits are obvious: First, editorial coverage is free. You pay nothing for the space it occupies, and this is the best of all possible worlds because of the second benefit: Readers believe the articles and news matter more than they believe the ads. What you say in an ad is your opinion. You represent a commercial entity trying to sell a reader something, and you and he both know it. Distrust is implicit, and the Herculean job of building rapport and selling something in a single ad or series of ads is usually only partially successful; it remains for personal contact to complete that rapport.

°The subject is treated with greater depth in a previous book (*How to Handle Your Own Public Relations,* Nelson-Hall, 1976).

The logic, then, is that you need editorial coverage to complete the psychological arsenal you're turning loose on the buyer. For the publication to give you press coverage is equally logical, with one huge exception we'll come to in a moment.

The logic, from the publication's point of view, is that the field it serves is comprised of people who want to know about the very item you advertise. If the magazine is *Office Equipment News,* and you've developed and are advertising a new high-speed word processor, that's news. If you're an advertiser in *Insurance Sentinel,* and you have a new approach to retirement policies, this is grist not just for your ad but is also worthy of editorial coverage.

Now for that exception: Don't ever demand editorial coverage for a story you would regard as trivial, unworthy, or an ad thinly covered by the varnish of the editorial columns, were that story about a competitor. Whether you submit a completed article, with photographs and proper format, or send facts for a staff writer to digest and regurgitate in print, be sure your story is more than a lightweight piece of puffery. If you're a major advertiser the publication may use it anyway, but they'll hate you. Worse, every story of this type weakens the editorial hold a publication has on its readers, making the marketplace less effective for all advertisers in those pages.

To submit an article or article idea, call the editor or the publisher. Don't worry, he or she will take your call. When you identify yourself, even to a secretary, the company name will carry weight if you've advertised before. All you say is, "Mr. Brown (or "Harry," if he calls you by your first name; if he doesn't, invite him to), you probably know we're advertisers in your magazine. We have a new piece of machinery I think is worthy of a story. Do you mind if I send the material on to you? I'd appreciate it if you could squeeze something into an early issue, since we plan to promote this heavily."

What are the rules? That piece of machinery had better be new, and it must represent some sort of improvement or progress to the readers. If it isn't, the editorial people will know it at once, and even if they run something—probably a shortened version of what you had in mind—they'll do it with written disclaimers or with personal disgust.

If you haven't advertised in the publication before, the space-salesman is the person to nail. He may insist that the editorial and advertising departments have nothing to do with each other. About 99 percent of the time, this is hogwash. Say, "I'd rather run my ad with you, but I need the editorial coverage, and that may put the ad elsewhere." Here is where guts becomes a factor. You have to decide whether, if he refuses, you'll run the ad. Obviously you can't put yourself out of business; if you're able to set up a combination editorial/advertising package with another publication, it probably is a better move even if that second publication isn't as dominant as the first one.

One benefit of editorial coverage is the reprint value. Take that news story or feature article, put "Reprinted from *Insurance Sentinel*" across the top, and use it as a direct mail piece. Reprints can be more powerful than anything you say about yourself.

Even if a publication invites you to submit a finished article, be careful. Don't give them a pompous piece of puffery. Remember the guideline—a story for a trade publication should be one that wouldn't annoy or disgust you if it were about a competitor.

Send pictures whenever possible; if graphs or artwork would clarify the story, submit them too. Years ago, written offers from suppliers to underwrite the cost of halftones or other artwork associated with a story were common. Avoid this today; it's a sign you think your position is weak.

The more you know about the advertising possibilities you can employ, the stronger your marketing decisions will be. Some advertisers coast for years with dead schedules in half-dead media. They ignore what might be beneficial to them in favor of the cronyism that stems from repeated ads in the same publication. Undoubtedly there's a benefit to cultivating a personal relationship with publications in your field, but be fair to your own marketing guidelines; too much advertising already is based on a backslap and a pair of hockey tickets for you to add to that sad avenue of unprofessionalism.

12

How to Write Advertising Copy that Sells

Samuel Clemens (Mark Twain) was once asked, "Can you teach people to write?"

He answered, "I can teach writers to write."

That maxim may be true of fiction, but I don't agree if Twain included advertising. It's my opinion that *anyone* can learn to write a creditable ad. The ad may not be clever, but if the writer adheres to Lewis's Three Laws of Mass Communications, he'll communicate on a level that should cause prospective buyers to respond better than they would to clever or cute writing that doesn't follow the Laws.

Preparing a Copy Sheet

Copy intended for a print ad or direct mail piece is typed, usually single-spaced, on one side of a sheet of paper. Double-spacing between segments indicates a new copy block in the ad.

Some copywriters double-space automatically, to make editing easier. Make your own decision and pray this is your only creative problem.

Copy to be read—radio commercials and the *audio* side of television commercials—is double-spaced.

For print advertising or a direct mail piece, type it as you want it to look. Don't type all capital letters and expect the typesetter to set the type in capitals and lower-case letters; he'll set it the way you've typed it.

Never handwrite an ad. Too many inaccuracies can be transmitted into the finished ad.

Be sure the name of the advertiser and the size of the ad appear, preferably in an upper corner, and also number the pages. If you have a method of dating or identifying each ad, this also helps, especially if you want to exhume an ad later on or if you have a series and want to be sure when you call the printer or newspaper that you're both talking about the same project.

Every word that will appear in an ad should be typed on the copy sheet. This is the ultimate record of what is printed or said, and it will be used by the typesetter. The layout artist may letter in some or even all the display type or headlines, but this may not go to the typesetter. Copy blocks can be identified by initials in the left margin ("Copy A," "Copy B") as additional insurance that the right piece of copy will appear in the right place.

Lettering the display type on your copywriter's rough layout doesn't free you from having to type it on the copy sheet. On occasion, a hurried copywriter will type, "Pick up coupon from previous ad," or "Insert standard signature, address, phone, and hours." These instructions may wind up in print themselves, if the typographer is literal minded and if no one else bothers to check the ad. So for extra insurance, type every word you want in print on the copy sheet.

Think Before You Write

The biggest single cause of failure to communicate— assuming some intellect is functioning—is the failure to consider the person receiving the message. The writer is thinking subjectively instead of objectively.

Consider a writer who is preparing an ad for a department store; he heads the ad, "Now On Sale!"

What has he accomplished here? What has he said? How does this headline help the store communicate with its buyers? "Our Entire Stock of Furniture, 30 Percent Off!" does communicate because it includes some specifics. Newspapers are full of dead advertising, and the Yellow Pages are a treasure house of noncommunicative phrases.

"Demonstration at your convenience." What motivators are included in this headline? Analyze the words, not just as you write them down, but as they come to mind. If they lack motivators, if they lack specifics, if they lack sense to a buyer, look elsewhere for selling inspiration.

Imagine that you run a trade school and have written a headline that reads "Learn to Earn." "Hey, George, that's pretty cute," says your assistant; "it rhymes." A rhyme is no substitute for a call to action. Will your phone ring because you said, "Learn to Earn"?

A communicator's job is to motivate, to move the readers out of their apathy. You want them to go through the mystic maze of positive reactions that terminate in their arms lifting the phone or their legs carrying them to your office. Always ask yourself: What motivates the people who can and will buy what I have to sell? What's their hot button? "Learn to Earn" sounds like a lot of work on both ends. Learning means study, and earning means labor. A better headline: "Will Your Income Jump 30% Ninety Days From Now?" You've reached the right person, and this type of incentive might motivate him.

A company that builds garages has an ad with this head: "Note These Features." If you weren't assuming an analytical posture, you might ask, "What's wrong with that?"

What's wrong is that you've forgotten that benefits are stronger than features. "Features" isn't a selling word, and "note" is too dispassionate and coldblooded to evoke an emotional response.

A psychological rule: *When emotion and intellect come into conflict, emotion always wins.* This is true not just some of the time or most of the time; it's always true. Emotion always wins the battle with intellect. A writer either prevents this conflict or finds an emotional word to replace the intellectual word.

Here's another rule: *Never introduce a nonselling factor that represents confusion.* Sometimes the introduction of extraneous elements initiates objections that wouldn't be there if the advertiser hadn't brought them up. For example, if a weight-reducing salon advertises, "No Embarrassment," the usual reaction would be, "Uh-oh—there *is* embarrassment."

Figure 12-1 Is this ad a violation of the Second Law (see Chapter 1)? Apparently so. Cleverness for the sake of cleverness is expensive, because ads that should carry solid marketing messages offer no reason to do business.

A shoe store headed its ad, "From a Private Collection." The writer didn't consider the overtone of "private collection"—someone's closet, from which you've taken these shoes. He didn't mean "private collection": he meant "designer collection," but that's not how the ad came off.

Also avoid using words that carry the wrong meaning to readers. A department store ran a half-page ad with only the copy shown in Figure 12-1.

What is "Goodwill" to people? Many must identify the word with Goodwill Industries, which deals in castoff and donated merchandise. The association is inevitable, and, lack of specifics aside, the ad suffers from this negative identification.

One more rule: Don't let smugness with your own product knowledge blind you. As an advertiser, ask yourself how many passes you have at someone within a single ad.

An individual reads through the paper or hears a commercial on the radio or sees your message on television. You have *one* shot at him, and that's all. If you're unclear, if you're not talking his language, flip goes that page, not because the reader hates you but because he rejects you—perhaps unconsciously—on the ground of competitive attention.

A car dealer's ad says, "Low Bank Financing." That isn't what the advertiser means. It's sloppy writing that keeps him from clarifying that he means low rates, not low bank.

Does all this seem too picky? If you think so, you're unconvinced that anything is wrong with the casual let's-run-something approach to ad writing. Ask yourself: Would I be this casual about the merchandise I'm selling in that ad? Would I be this unconcerned if all the dresses marked size eight turned out to be size twelve, or if the boxes were sloppily printed?

Comparative Advertising

Advertising is a fluid industry. Mass communication changes by the day, by the hour; what is gospel one day may be out of date a few days later.

Consumers are skeptics. They say, "Prove it" when we make a claim. "Don't just tell me it's better. Prove it." The old-timers still settle for the huff-and-puff "Ours Is Better" or "Our Prices Are Lower" pitch. But when you have a *nonproved comparative*, you have a *noncommunicative message* that doesn't motivate today's consumer. That consumer may be aware of you, but he isn't motivated by you.

Implicit in that realization is a problem within the core of big advertising. Those who measure the readership of ads measure awareness, not selling power. These two facets aren't parallel: We can be aware of a message but never respond to it.

The consumer says to us, "Prove it." How do we prove it?

Here's where we can begin to appreciate the value and growth of comparative advertising (advertising in which you compare what you're selling with your competitors). A few years ago, comparative ads reflected negatively on the person or company making the comparison. Five or ten years ago when comparative ads were a novelty, the huff-and-puff advertisers looked at them with sneers: "Is that the best you can do, attack someone else?" In one sense only is there any value in that criticism, because comparative ads have proliferated in some areas in which they shouldn't. Advertisers attack their competitors, and the public, unaware that the competition exists, begins to become aware of it. At this point I'll subject you to Lewis's Creative Danger Alert Number 1: *The public is never as aware of a competitive situation as are the people in it.*

Violating this Alert creates an awareness that may actually glorify the competition to prospective buyers who otherwise would be unaware of them. Another way of understanding the Alert is to realize that without a trigger of recognition by the recipient, the message is neutralized. Comparative advertising is most beneficial to advertisers who aren't in first place in their field. If they're the number one company, it's a mistake.

Comparative advertising succeeds best when the target is completely aware of the person or company under attack. When running for senator against a man who has held the office for the last 18 years, attack; if you're the incumbent senator, don't mention your opponent or debate with him.

You don't need Nielsen anymore.

Open a bottle of champagne. Send yourself some flowers. You don't need Nielsen anymore.

No more meetings that take two hours to say what could be said in one. No more fees that practically rival your net profits. No more Nielsen.

Because now you have National Scanning Services. A service that gives you the truth, the whole truth and nothing but the truth. For a fraction of what Nielsen costs.

First, let's talk about the truth. Nielsen uses averaging which obscures the immediate impact of every factor working on your business. But National Scanning Services gives you actual *sales* on a monthly or even *weekly* basis. So you always know what's going on, when. In other words, you always know the truth.

Next, let's talk about money. Nielsen can cost you as much as $500,000 or even more. But National Scanning Services only charges from $20,000 to $90,000. And you're getting a lot more truth for your money.

Now Nielsen is trying to muscle in on the truth by forcing you to take their new scanner service every time you buy the NFI. But, since you can only get it along with the NFI, it hardly can be called a bargain. And, since you're being *forced* to buy it, it can't even be called good manners. (Actually, you can't blame them. They don't have enough scanner markets to offer the service all by itself. In fact, they have fewer markets than we do. Which means, you're being forced to buy a more *limited* scanner service at four to ten times what it should cost.)

So, the next time you're in the market for the truth, come to National Scanning Services. You'll get more truth for less. And we'll even buy the flowers.

NATIONAL SCANNING SERVICES INC.
Scanners don't lie.

NabScan USA, INC. 165 West 46th Street, New York, N.Y. 10036. (212) 764-5800.
Contact: Ben Lipstein or Mel Appelbaum.

Figure 12-2 The name of the competitor under attack—Nielsen—is set in type far larger than the name of the company placing the ad—National Scanning Services, Inc. The technique has logic in it, since the readers of this ad—organizations who want figures on sales of various products carrying the universal products code—know the Nielsen name and probably don't know the newcomer's name.

Copy is strong, bordering on vicious: "Now Nielsen is trying to muscle in on the truth by forcing you to . . ." Who can fault a challenger for coming out swinging, trying to land a haymaker?

Berlitz
Eat Your Heart Out!

*We're Offering a Complete Language Course
In Just 30 Days for What You Charge for a Week!*

Learn a New Language at Home
...In Less Than 30 Days!

For Only $2.50 per Week
Under Easy Payment Plan

Italian...German...French...Spanish...English

The finest native teachers combined to produce what is without question the finest easy-to-learn language course ever offered!

In thirty days or less, at a fraction of what you'd pay at Berlitz, you can quickly learn Italian, French, English, Spanish or German...in your car or home. These cassettes are designed to help you achieve a high proficiency of fluency. You can be at home in any country where these languages are

MONEY BACK GUARANTEE!

spoken...able to understand and speak the language. And by regularly using the cassettes and supplementary texts, you can have a language fluency you would not believe.

To make it inexpensive, an easy purchase plan has been arranged. The entire set, which normally retails at $100 is offered now for $49.95...but you need only pay $10 down if you wish to pay the balance over a period of months. Credit cards are accepted as shown in the coupon.

You must be completely satisfied or return for full refund within 90 days!

Please rush me the following: @ $49.95, plus $1.50 to cover postage and handling charges. (N.Y. residents, add sales tax.)

Enclosed find $_____ in check or money order. No C.O.D.'s

I wish to use the following credit card: Show Account Number.

☐ Master Charge _____

☐ BankAmericard _____

☐ I wish to use your Easy Payment Plan, under which I pay $10 now and the balance over the next 6 months at 1½% interest per month on unpaid balance.

ENERGY INTERNATIONAL
P.O. Box N
2204 Morris Avenue,
Union, N.J. 07083

Check language desired:
French _____ German _____ English _____
Italian _____ Spanish _____

Please Print:

NAME _____

ADDRESS _____

CITY _____

STATE _____ ZIP _____

Figure 12-3 Like the National Scanning Services ad (figure 12-2), Energy International sets its own name in small type and its principal competitor's name in big type. A good comparative ad coattail-rides, in a sense, by linking the unknown contender to the known incumbent. A good rule: It's senseless for the giant, in turn, to compare itself with the relatively unknown pygmy.

In the early 1970s, when Volkswagen was the runaway best-selling compact car, almost every other compact car manufacturer attacked the little Beetle. These ads were, in fact, pioneer comparative ads. Some of these campaigns were immensely successful; the attack was aimed at a product well known to the recipient of the message. Volkswagen's fall brought Toyota into the number one spot, and the attacks shifted to Toyota.

When an advertising comparison assumes a foundation of information the consumer doesn't have, the message becomes incomprehensible. That's why I oppose comparative attacks on unknown quantities. Suppose one were to advertise, "TWA Has a Better On-Time Record than UTA." A consumer could make no comparison if he had never heard of that second airline. If Jaguar advertises that their car accelerates faster than the Morgan, Jaguar is attacking an automobile that 99 percent of the people never heard of.

A comparative ad by a small New York language school, Energy International, (Figure 12-3) works well:

Everyone has heard of Berlitz; no one has heard of Energy International (not a good name, I feel, for what they're selling). The ad doesn't attack Berlitz. Instead it glorifies EI's competing language course at Berlitz's expense. This is a near-perfect competitive ad.

The laundry list of benefits American Motors gave its buyers a couple of years ago (Figure 12-4) was also good comparative advertising. Instead of the nonsensical Car C and Car F, the ad directly compared the free post-sale services of the four major manufacturers; would that all the advertising (and design) of American Motors cars had been this powerful.

When a comparative ad degenerates into an attack, a disservice to all advertising results. The 1977 Bayer Aspirin attack (Figure 12-5) on Tylenol, now regarded as an advertising classic, is an example. Tylenol, which had become the best-selling pain reliever, had brought itself to the pinnacle by judicious, albeit borderline, comparative ads. Bayer, the former leader, counterattacked with the mien of an angry schoolteacher whose wild student had gone overboard. The murkiness of Bayer's own response may have damaged that adver-

PARTS FIXED OR REPLACED FREE					
	AMC	GM	FORD	VW	CHRYSLER
Engine/Drive train	YES	YES	YES	YES	YES
Spark plugs	YES	NO	NO	NO	NO
Points & Condenser	YES	NO	NO	NO	NO
Shock Absorbers	YES	NO	NO	NO	NO
Brake linings	YES	NO	NO	NO	NO
Clutch lining	YES	NO	NO	NO	NO
Wiper blades	YES	NO	NO	NO	NO
Light bulbs	YES	NO	NO	NO	NO
Hoses & Belts	YES	YES	NO	NO	NO
SERVICES PROVIDED FREE					
Wheel alignment	YES	NO	NO	NO	NO
Wheel balancing	YES	NO	NO	NO	NO
Align headlights	YES	NO	NO	NO	NO
Adjust carburetor	YES	NO	NO	NO	NO
Adjust distributor	YES	NO	NO	NO	NO
Adjust brakes	YES	NO	NO	NO	NO
Adjust clutch	YES	NO	NO	NO	NO
Adjust transmission bands	YES	NO	NO	NO	NO
Adjust & tighten belts	YES	NO	NO	NO	NO
Tighten nuts & bolts	YES	NO	NO	NO	YES
Free loaner car	YES	NO	NO	NO	NO
Trip Interruption Protection	YES	NO	NO	NO	NO

Figure 12-4 Many years ago Plymouth initiated—and then abandoned—strong comparative advertising against Chevrolet and Ford. A prospective car-buyer is implicitly comparing, and a comparison such as this one, from AMC, is strong competitive grist.

tiser, and Tylenol's position seemed little affected by the Bayer ad.

Today, comparative ads are an accepted way of proving superiority. Names are named; exhaustive and extensive tests are underwritten by one advertiser; those aspects of the test proving superiority become grist for a sales message, and those that don't are discarded. The direct, forceful comparison, once frowned on as impolite, has become a dynamic selling weapon in the Age of Skepticism.

The primary key to force-communication, a point I'd like you to write on your mirror, is: *Noncommunicative advertising dissipates impact.*

No, Mother, Tylenol is not found safer than aspirin!

To all concerned parents! If you've been confused by advertising for a Tylenol product that claims it works like children's aspirin but it's safer...and just as effective when used as directed—you should know this:

A U.S. Government Agency, the Food and Drug Administration, has issued a news release on the findings of a panel of experts appointed to study nonprescription pain and fever relievers. Concerning acetaminophen, the active ingredient in Tylenol products, the FDA states that "the experts found no basis for claims that this ingredient is safer than aspirin and urged labeling to warn against the danger of liver damage from overdoses."

These experts recommend the following warning for all acetaminophen products, including children's preparations: "Do not exceed recommended dosage because severe liver damage may occur."

Parents! Acetaminophen was not found to be safer than aspirin. And you can continue to feel secure if you have been giving your child Bayer Children's Aspirin all along.

Read and follow label instructions.

BAYER CHILDREN'S ASPIRIN

When you need a pain reliever and fever reducer for your child, get Bayer® Children's Aspirin.

Figure 12-5 When a giant strikes back, you know he's stung. Tylenol eroded Bayer sales; if Tylenol hadn't shaken up the market, Bayer undoubtedly would have ignored the challenge. In the mid-1980s, when Advil and Nuprin (descendants of the prescription pain-reliever Motrin) charged the hill, neither Tylenol nor Bayer reacted, suggesting that the effect on share-of-market wasn't profound.

Visualize your target walking past on the street; to get his attention, you beat on the window—with a sponge. The impact is dissipated. In advertising, this happens when the writer thinks not of communication but of word usage.

Writing What You Mean

A radio campaign used this messsage: "It's fun to shop at Armanetti Liquors." That's it—seven words. The writer of that spot could say, "Okay, the idea here is to get quick recall value." The owner of the liquor store might nod with some puzzlement and agree, but the serious student of communications would reply, "The advertiser isn't getting his money's worth."

I propose to you that by the time you get up tomorrow morning you can think of seven words that would also have the Armanetti name, a commercial that might actually move some merchandise or at least give a buyer a reason to walk through the door of Armanetti Liquors. For example, "Cold Duck—one buck—at Armanetti Liquors."

An advertiser heads his ad, "Seeing Is Believing." Is that really so terrible? To the true communicator, yes. One of the problems in mass communications is that a lot of people who really want to communicate are working for other people who haven't realized that the principles have changed in the 1980s. Instead of groping for trick phrases, a writer should ask, "What are we trying to sell? Let's name it. Let's describe its benefits. Let's see whether or not it conforms to some of the principles of effective mass communications." We might have an ad that could be attacked on the grounds of crudity or grammar but not on informational thrust. The message is more important than how we say it; that brings me to Lewis's Creative Alert Number Two:

Facts will outsell platitudes and generalizations every time.
And Creative Alert Number Three:

Good writing is lean.
Can you see why an ad headed "Now On Sale—Typewriters $199.95" is weaker than "Typewriters—$199.95"? Why words such as "very" have little weight? Why words such

as "quality" and "greatest" and the horrible, never-to-be used-again "etc." drain strength from copy?

A fourth key to force-communication is that puffery doesn't sell as well as fact. One sure way to avoid a weak, puffed-up ad is to imagine a head-to-head confrontation in which someone asks, "What makes your furniture better than the furniture in the store down the street?" You can't get away with nonsense statements such as, "Our furniture is better," "We give you a better deal," "The store where you get more," "The best deal in town," "Your number one place for furniture," or all the other old, tired cliches of unproved comparatives and superlatives that are nothing but puffery. You're forced to list specific advantages of doing business with you.

The Wild, Desperate Cry for Attention

A television commercial opens with a close-up of a wheelbarrow. The camera pulls back to show your friendly Ford dealer plopped into the wheelbarrow and being wheeled around his lot. "If it moves, we'll take it in trade!" he cries.

Promoting a motion picture called "A Bridge Too Far," movie impressario Joseph E. Levine used this headline to convince the public to see the film: "The Greatest Motion Picture of Our Time!" (The film bombed.)

Hundreds of advertisers (including the usually astute Toyota), unable to find a better selling weapon, give up and close their selling arguments in media with, "If you can find a better (whatever), buy it."

One might expect the little advertiser with the minuscule budget to lapse into a cry for attention rather than plotting a selling argument, but I, for one, awaken each day to greet with amazement the use of *nothing but* attention-getting devices or jumbles of words by advertisers who not only know how to sell but who have proved it.

In such cases—in which big advertisers are often as guilty as small ones—the advertiser ends his message too soon. He works for attention and quits. Sometimes he becomes the buffoon, sometimes he coasts on previous successes or a product that transcends his lackluster advertising; and sometimes he succeeds. The ratio for success, however, is too small to change anyone's mind about the overall failure rate in such advertising.

If such campaigns do succeed, how do they succeed? Do they bring serious buyers onto that Ford dealer's lot? Or do they simply result in a behavioristic recognition of the commercial as "that commercial" or the dealer as "that dealer who's pushed around in a wheelbarrow"?

Figure 12-6 When an advertiser violates the Second Law in print advertising, often it's by running an ad which makes sense on the radio but not in the newspaper. Here, the impression is one of totally undignified foolishness.

Another indication of imaginative sterility is the type of ad (Figure 12-6) exemplified by the air conditioning company that turns its message inside out. A cartoon man is swearing angrily, and the headline says, "This won't be necessary when you call us for service." Is this as powerful as a positive statement? The words "air conditioning" and "heating" don't even appear in the headline; the ad is nondescript and could represent a thousand businesses in its lack of individuality.

Sometimes novelty works so hard for its own sake that it actually produces revulsion. This can happen when someone forgets the Second Law and produces copy that's clever for the sake of cleverness instead of copy that's clever in order to sell a product.

While the following television script is the product of my own wild imagination and never was produced, it must call to mind many spots you've seen actually aired. Technically, nothing is wrong with the script. The spot has unity; the ideas progress logically; the product is shown in use and in a close-up.

What's wrong is the bad taste, almost palpable. We may have become so accustomed to bad taste it no longer has any significance *as* bad taste, but the question the writer—especially the knowledgeable and disciplined advertising writer—should ask himself or herself is whether there's a way of demonstrating product effectiveness just as dramatically but not as repulsively.

Read the script and you'll see what I mean (disclaimer: This is not an actual Alka-Seltzer script).

VIDEO°	AUDIO
MCU MAGNIFICENT TABLE SETTING: PULL BACK TO SHOW TWO MASKED ROBBERS—THEY EAT, THEN PUT TABLEWARE AND SILVER INTO BAGS	MUSIC: THEME UP AND UNDER FIRST ROBBER: Oh, man, I'm in trouble. (BELCHES) SECOND ROBBER: What's wrong?
ECU FIRST ROBBER	FIRST ROBBER: It's my stomach. Too much caviar and fine wine. My stomach's upset.
ECU SECOND ROBBER	SECOND ROBBER: You need Alka-Seltzer for fast relief.

°See Appendix 2, *Common Television Terms.*

WIDER SHOT: FIRST ROBBER GETS UP, GOES OUT THE WINDOW. SECOND ROBBER PUTS MORE ITEMS IN HIS BAG	FIRST ROBBER: Alka-Seltzer? Where would I get any this time of night?
	SECOND ROBBER: Try the drug store.
CLOCK WIPE TO: SECOND ROBBER FORCING HIS WAY INTO DRUGSTORE	MUSIC: UP
DISSOLVE TO: ROBBER AT COUNTER—HE TAKES A PACKAGE OF ALKA SELTZER	SFX: CROSS-FADE MUSIC WITH SIREN
ROBBER POURS SOME WATER AT SODA FOUNTAIN, DROPS IN TWO TABLETS	SFX: SODA-FOUNTAIN WATER RUNNING
	SFX: TABLETS PLOPPING
	SFX: SIRENS LOUDER, RUNNING FOOTSTEPS
ROBBER DRINKS ALKA-SELTZER	
	POLICEMAN: Hold it, Butch! It's the police!
CU COUNTER: EMPTY GLASS IS PUT ON COUNTER GLASS AND OTHER ITEMS ARE SMASHED BY BULLETS	SFX: RUNNING FEET SFX: PISTOL SHOTS
MCU ROBBER LYING ON THE FLOOR: POLICEMAN KNEELS BESIDE HIM	POLICEMAN: How do you feel, Butch? FIRST ROBBER: No more stomach cramps or heartburn for me.
ZOOM TO ECU ROBBER'S HAND: IT UNCLENCHES IN A DEATH SPASM, REVEALING ALKA-SELTZER FREEZE ON FINAL SCENE	JINGLE: Oh, what a relief—it is!

Meaningless Slogans and Logos

All of us have lapses. For the advertising writer, these lapses stem from boredom or laziness or smugness. Boredom comes from feeling you've said the same thing too many times; the message is stale; "Let's do something else for a change." Then, instead of forcing the new idea through the disciplined

Figure 12-7 Beware the play on words. "The bare facts . . ." suggests exactly the kind of cleverness-for-the-sake-of-cleverness pit into which this advertiser fell. The apple is especially unfortunate, since it suggests that this woman, whoever she is, will lead an unsuspecting male into trouble.

IF YOUR WORD PROCESSOR IS SO
POWERFUL AND "SMART", WHY DOES
IT REQUIRE EXTRA MEMORY AND
RUN UNDER JUST ONE VERSION
OF DOS?

QUIT BITCHIN'!

michael shrayer's

Electric Pencil PC

™

word processing system

... is the SMARTEST and most
POWERFUL word processor
ever developed for the
IBM PC/XT–because it runs
under DOS 1.0, 1.1 and 2.0,
WITHOUT MODIFICATION! It
also runs with as little as 48K all
the way up to 512K–on hard disk
too! ELECTRIC PENCIL PC is
the only word processing system
that takes advantage of EVERY
hardware feature of the
IBM PC/XT. Don't be fooled by
competitors who can't record
history, we have already done it!
Take a look at history for
yourself and ask for your dealer
demonstration disk today.
It's only $49.95. Call us
at (714) 946-5805.
Electric Pencil PC:

*The FIRST Best Seller will now
be the BEST Best Seller!*

DEALERS ONLY
Say "Michael told me to call"
and we'll send the Dealer Demo
FREE - Today!

The Thoughtware Company™

Order from your favorite distributor or order direct.   IJG, Inc., 1953 West 11th St., Upland, CA 91786 (714)946-5805

* IBM is a registered trademark of International Business Machines Corp.
** Electric Pencil PC is a trademark of IJG, Inc.

Figure 12-8 Attacking competitors is an acceptable and often superior advertising technique. Attacking the reader is usually suicidal. Adding vulgarity to
the mix is about as helpful as a boil on the neck. The advertiser calling itself
"The Thoughtware Company" didn't, in my opinion, give this idea enough
thought.

channels of effective mass communications, you subordinate the selling message to your own cleverness, a cleverness unrelated to the product. Even if you do generate interest from the reader or viewer, that interest is thinned by confusion.

Laziness is more common: A writer sits at a desk. His knowledge of what he's selling may be cursory and incomplete. He doesn't have the benefit of having sold whatever it is he's advertising on a head-to-head basis. Nor does he have any intention of ever having that benefit. Were he to walk into a showroom and let a salesman pitch him on the same automobiles at the same dealership for which he's writing, he'd have grist for a dozen ads. Instead he sits in a cubicle and concocts the copy in Figure 12-9. The typical reader must read this headline at least twice to get some message from it. Even then, it's vague, because it's not a direct promise of spending less, saving money, or reaping a specific benefit.

Smugness usually stems not from the writer but from an advertiser who decides to superimpose what he likes on the advertising campaign. This is the type of advertiser who, feeling that no one else is capable of doing it, tends to write his own ads. Into the ad go his children's pictures, logos that fail to enhance corporate image, and headlines and slogans that reflect ego instead of fact.

Giving yourself an honest and informed answer to one question will avoid the triple pitfalls of boredom, laziness, and smugness: What am I trying to sell?

A fourth lapse, not included in the master negative list because it isn't always negative, is *faddism.* A television show, a motion picture, or a public figure is responsible for a title or a saying, and immediately advertisers grab the phrase and use it.

While depending on fad words invariably weakens the dignity of the advertiser, there can be a strong temporary mnemonic value to this kind of coattail-riding. I personally hate this type of ad, but I can't deny its temporary impact on the marketplace. I do insist that it has an early burnout.

When Wendy's Restaurant's popularized "Where's the beef?" any number of local advertisers usurped the notion (See Figure 12-10). Burnout is visible even as the "campaign" starts.

Figure 12-9 The excuse for this ad is the definition of Bluebird, given at the right of the picture: "a sale that flies in out of nowhere." Few have ever heard this argot-definition. With hundreds of word processing programs fighting for a one-shot sale, thoughtful advertising projects benefits; meaningless slogans do not. (A competing example appears in Chapter 15.)

Figures 12-10a, 12-10b, 12-10c Old-timers remember a venerable hair-conditioning preparation called Vitalis. Its "Greasy Kid Stuff" campaign spawned countless followers, even including a competing hair preparation called, naturally, Greasy Kid Stuff.

Whenever a major advertiser captures the public imagination, smaller advertisers pick up the idea and use it. One example: "Close Encounters of the Third Kind" spawned "Clothes Encounter of the First Kind" (clothing store) and "Close Encounter of the Wurst Kind" (delicatessen).

Wendy's "Where's the Beef?" was a wildly successful mid-1980s campaign; but such campaigns are implicitly short-lived. These coattail-riders are neither inventive nor clever, and "Where's the Fish?" is particularly uninventive. Others: "Where's the Reef?" (a scuba-diving operation); "Where's the Beet?" (produce market); "Where's the Beat?" (discothèque). Someone suggested a campaign for an undertaker: "Where's the Grief?"

a

WHERE'S THE BEACH?

At Bahia Mar.
For just $19.84*

We're celebrating our 35th Anniversary with this special low weekend rate.

SPLIT-FOR-THE-BEACH WEEKEND Includes:

- Deluxe room (Friday, Saturday, Sunday arrival only)
- Welcome split of champagne
- Free parking
- Children under 18 free in parents' room
- All the excitement of Bahia Mar: home of Florida's most fabulous marina; heated outdoor pool; terrific restaurants & lounges; great shopping
- Perfect location: next to beach; close to Ft. Lauderdale sights

SPLIT-FOR-THE-BEACH MIDWEEK at $29.95*
Monday through Thursday arrival. Same great features as weekend package.

*per person, per night, double occupancy. Room tax additional. Not available to groups. Limited number of rooms. Subject to availability. Rates effective through December 21, 1984.

FOR RESERVATIONS CALL
RALPH TOLL-FREE AT
1-800-327-8154 OR
(305) 764-2233

Bahia Mar
HOTEL & YACHTING CENTER

801 Seabreeze Boulevard
Ft. Lauderdale, Florida 33316

Figure 12-10 (continued)

b

"WHERE'S THE FISH?"

IT'S HERE AT ANTHONY'S PIER 2

YES, MORE FRESH FISH THAN ANY RESTAURANT IN AMERICA TODAY AND THE BEEF, TOO. PRIME RIB SO BIG YOU'D THINK IT WAS FOR TWO PEOPLE.

ANTHONY'S PIER 2
ANAHEIM • NEWPORT BEACH

103 No. BAYSIDE DR.
"On the beautiful bay"
NEWPORT BEACH
640-5123
FREE Boat docking & parking

1640 S. HARBOR BLVD.
Near Katella, Opposite Disneyland
(Formerly Lancer's Restaurant)
ANAHEIM
774-0322   FREE PARKING

c

During Richard Nixon's presidency, when his "Let me make this perfectly clear" was a national cliché, a manufacturer of water conditioners ran an ad with a picture of a faucet, from which water was flowing. It said: "Let Us Make This Perfectly Clear."

Advertisers with dignity don't advertise this way. They ride above the waves of "in-talk," and only those advertisers with stunted imaginations or a belief in cleverness for the sake of cleverness risk their verbal surfboards in these treacherous breakers. Dealing in fads always weakens image. This type of ad has just one benefit: It can get attention where a stodgier ad fails, because it involves prior knowledge on the part of the reader or audience. But so what? An ad should sell something, not ride coattails. How much of a recognition factor is there for *you* instead of for Archie Bunker or E.T.? And, how about the buyers who don't know what you're talking about, who haven't seen the television show or the motion picture an expression comes from? To them, this unrecognized faddishness is as incomprehensible and as much a mystery as "Yes, We Have No Bananas."

All of us have seen high school yearbooks and charitable program books filled with ads such as, "Compliments of Mr. and Mrs. Al Smith." Some of the ads stemming from the triple pitfalls might as well be worded that way. These ads give representation without exploitation.

Here's the whole message, except for address, of Carolina Federal Savings & Loan (Figure 12-11):

We Help Make
Nice Things
Happen!

The writer of this ad didn't ask himself: *What am I trying to sell?* Those six words could just as easily be used for a bank—which means the competitive edge wasn't exploited— or for a store, or an ice cream parlor, or a restaurant, or, or, or. (The illustration used in this particular ad was a charcoal drawing of a squatting kettle labeled, "Instant Interest"—a term never explained.)

We Help Make Nice Things Happen!

Carolina Federal ◪
Savings and Loan Association
500 East Washington St./1925 Augusta St./2430 East North St. Ext. at Pelham
6050 White Horse Rd./(803) 271-2510

Figure 12-11 If you're looking for a place to put your money, what's the motivator here? A mistake many advertisers make, when they're afraid of 'factual superiority' as a copy-platform, is to use copy which doesn't relate specifically to them. "We Help Make Nice Things Happen!" is as apt for a restaurant, a hotel, or an airline as it is for a financial institution.

If You Make a Claim, Prove It

Something, somewhere, gave you the idea that yours is the best. What was it? I hope you share my disdain for unexplained comparatives and superlatives. I hope readers, listeners, and viewers do. The more widespread this disgust, the more likely that this cancer eating away at mass communications will be eliminated.

How easy it is! After making the claim, add the word "because" or the phrase, "Here's why: . . . " This will *force* you to replace flabby puffery with lean, powerful fact.

Figure 12-12   If you want your advertising dollars to do twice the work of an ad such as this one, substitute specifics for vague claims. Just *what* does this tiller do, besides till? What could be weaker as a claim of superiority than the cliche, "The World's Finest Garden Tiller"?

The World's Finest Garden Tiller, Does More Than Till!

7 HP Rocket

SPRING PRICES
Only on items
in stock

5 HP
Regular
$662.45
NOW $579.95

7 HP
Regular
$829.95
NOW $779.95

Ask about our "Easy Payment Plan"

BLAKELY'S
3141 N. Pleasantburg Drive
271-8700

An ad (Figure 12-12) by an Ariens Power Tiller dealer is, for the reader who really wants to know about this equipment, a frustration. Nowhere in the ad is the word "finest" explained. Worse, nowhere does this advertiser, who wouldn't have made the claim if he didn't have some selling ammunition to back it up, tell us what this does other than till.

The attempt to adapt an advertising message to the physical circumstances of its reception also can be deadly. This approach is old-fashioned—a hangover from Marshall McLuhan's vintage "medium-is-the-message" concept of television. Television is indeed the medium in which such advertising most often appears. Consider, for example, the Hertz Rent-a-Car commercial aired during a basketball all-star game:

(jingle) Hertz—the Superstar in Rent-a-Car. (spoken voice) You know it.

Is there any communication here other than corporate arrogance?

When a claim goes unproved, the competition has an edge, provided they can prove their claim. In some marketplaces the strange game of follow-the-leader causes dozens of advertisers to stumble all over each other. Here, for example, are only a few headlines from ads in one issue of a magazine exploiting income opportunities:

Make BIG MONEY with this LITTLE MACHINE! (Perma Products, N. Miami Beach)
A FULL 900% PROFIT FOR YOU . . . EACH AND EVERY TIME (Cameo Collection, New York City)
THIS CATALOG CAN HELP YOU EARN BIG MONEY!!! (Cook Bros., Inc., Chicago)
MAKE BIG MONEY FAST WITH THESE SUPER SELLERS (Johnson Smith Imports, Mt. Clemens, Michigan)
MILLION DOLLAR SUCCESS PLAN! (Defense Products, St. Louis)
EARN BIG MONEY!!! (Associated Consumers, Los Angeles)
$500 PER WEEK Average Earnings (Prudential Business Services, Los Angeles)
$50,000 YEARLY PLUS FREE CAR (Lekens Mfg., San Diego)
I'll Show You How To Make $50 to $250 Regularly in Spare Time Whenever You Want It! (Lucky Heart Cosmetics, Memphis)

UNIQUE OPPORTUNITY—MULTI-MILLION DOLLAR MAR-KET (C'est Moi, Portland, Maine)
Be A Millionaire! (Lee Des Combes Enterprises, La Jolla)
FREE MONEY! (Status Quo Corp., New York City)
BIG MONEY AHEAD FOR YOU (Howard Products Co., Dallas)
$1000 WEEKLY NOW POSSIBLE (Nichols Bronze Co., Sebring)
EA$Y WAY TO $UCCE$$ (Advertising Specialties, Spring-field, Missouri)
Exciting Income Potential . . . Part Time or Full Time (Success Motivation Cassette Tapes, Waco)
MAKE MONEY! (Tire Cosmotology, Inc., Dallas)
MILLIONS IN MAIL (Transworld, Toledo)
EARN $1000 MONTHLY (Unicorn, Colorado Springs)
UNUSUAL MONEYMAKING OPPORTUNITY FOR YOU (Research, Oklahoma City)
BIG MONEY . . . FAST . . . EASY! (National Press, Inc., North Chicago)

With the confusion generated by the sameness of these headlines, it's easy to have your ad stand out: It's the one that doesn't make a wild, unproved claim.

Who Needs a Logo?

Company logos are often given more attention than they deserve. Historically, logos served as identifiers. The illiterate buyer still could recognize the company's logo, and this recognition built a feeling of security. As far back as the thirteenth century, English bakers were compelled to put their individual marks on loaves of bread, so if a loaf were short in weight it could be identified. Certain marks came to be. regarded with confidence.

Today advertisers hire expensive designers to develop logos that may be visually pleasing but do little to sell a product. NBC spent $100,000 for a logo—the single letter "N"—that, after exposure, turned out to be identical to one developed casually and at almost no expense by Nebraska's public service television network.

Because the General Electric logo spells out the letters

"GE" most people would identify it, even though it couldn't play much of a part in a buying decision. But asked to draw the Ford logo, they'd probably put a light-bulb in the "O"; they couldn't remember the logos of United States Steel, Emba Mink, Burlington Mills, or hundreds of other major advertisers who spend millions promoting their logos—the one thing they sell that no one cares about.

In the electronic age brand-name recognition eliminates any need for logo recognition. The name is important, not the logo. Realizing this, Miller Brewing Company sued seven other brewers in an attempt to keep them from using the word "light" as part of their brand name, claiming exclusive rights because of prior use—Miller Lite Beer. The Supreme Court refused to honor Miller's complaint, stating, "A misspelled phonetic name for a commonly used word is not entitled to trademark protection." Still, interpretations are muddy: Domino sugar won a case against a pet food processor who picked up the Domino name, but Laura Secord Candy, whose "Turtles" are almost a generic name, lost a suit against the Barton Candy Corp. which brought out similar-looking "Creepies."

If the behemoths among advertisers are unable to make promotional capital of logo promotion, what chance has the small advertiser? An opinion: He can pay a competent artist $100 to $250 to design a modern, readable logo (far too many logos are incomprehensible), use it on his letterhead and in his ads as part of the company name, and promote that name, not that logo.

A fact is right if it relates favorably to the buying patterns or desires of the most people who can and will buy what you have to sell. Imagine that you sell inexpensive fashions. The salient facts are obvious. These garments cost less. They're designed from the latest Paris fashions. They're guaranteed to wear for three months without developing holes. Any fact that can motivate those to whom an ad is aimed are the right facts.

The technique for finding usable facts is simple. Follow three steps:

1. Assemble every positive fact you can list about whatever it is you're advertising.

2. Go over the list and mercilessly slash away pieces of puff that have slipped into the list of facts.
3. Use the rest.

One must be careful not to violate the Third Law of Mass Communications—$E^2 = 0$. This can happen when unselected facts are listed without viewpoint or direction. Some facts are more important than others; this is the selective process that builds winning headlines; and the more you know about your buyers the better you'll be at plucking out the facts that will motivate them.

Of primary importance in today's marketplace are facts offering a competitive edge. Whatever you sell, someone else is selling a similar product. His claims of superiority are there alongside yours, as illustrated by the direct selling and financial institution advertisements described in this chapter. If facts are listed dispassionately, and the competitor chooses facts enhancing his competitive position, you have far less chance to convert the skeptical buyer than he has. Your ad is generic. It explains why your product should be bought. His ad is competitive. It explains why the buyer should do business with him.

Obviously, too, in product introduction, what the product does is paramount. If no one ever has marketed an automatic remote-controlled lawnmower before, your advertising explains the absolute benefits; your competition is the conventional lawnmower, not another marketer of a similar product. But if you're one of three marketers of automatic remote-controlled lawnmowers, the very existence of three sources suggests public awareness. Then you sell against a dual competition: old-fashioned lawnmowers and other automatics. And on the day when no other lawnmowers are marketed except automatics, the competition once again has to be redefined.

Real pros can sometimes dismiss the opposition and make an all-encompassing claim. Suppose six brands of mouthwash exist that protect all day. If you're the first one to say, "Squirt! Fresh Breath from 7 a.m. to Midnight!" you have a huge competitive edge. The others can't generate power by saying, "Me, too!" You've usurped the unique selling proposition describing the benefit the buyers want, and the others have to scramble to catch up.

Key Words that Work

Traditionally, the word "you" has been the most important selling word. The most famous ad of all time, one that ran for 45 years, was for the Sherwin Cody School. It read: "Do You Make These Mistakes in English?" In the second most famous ad of all time, the "you" was changed to "I." The ad read: "They Laughed When I Sat Down at the Piano." (The ad was for a mail order course teaching recipients how to play musical instruments.)

"You" and "I" remain important advertising words, but unfortunately "I" has been corrupted into "we" as advertisers have concluded that the targets of their messages are deeply interested in their corporate progress. Safety lies in this path: Use "I" only in testimonials or as a surrogate for "you."

If you say, "We have this for you," you're safe; if you merely say, "We have this," the communication is intramural, and you've failed to reach the target.

The two most potent advertising words, many experts feel, are "free" and "new." Overuse and regulation of these words has robbed them of much of the impact they had a few years ago, but they're still winners and are usually safe.

Variations of "new," such as "now," "at last," "first time offered," "a breakthrough," and "never before" lack the powerful specificity of the original word but are beneficial as alternates. "Free" has a different problem: The Federal Trade Commission has restricted use of the word. If an item isn't really free—if something has to be bought in order to get it—then the offer must be described, and "free" is watered down to "free of extra charge" or "at no extra charge." This has led advertisers to clever alternatives. One is the use of coupons, stamps, and tokens good for products in combination with other components of the offer. The American coin-and-currency orientation puts a value on these enclosures, but obviously they can be made available only in print media or direct mail.

"Only" and "just" take the sting out of prices. A fur coat at $4,995 is expensive; at *only* $4,995, or *just* $4,995, it isn't so expensive.

Value also helps. "Made to Sell for $60" helps sell a

jacket priced at $35. But the word "value" itself has lost significance.

"Now you can" has power because it combines two key words and an action word.

"Public announcement," "an open letter to," or "a personal message to" have the benefit of suggesting inside information, private communication, and the possibility of becoming an insider.

Words suggesting obsolescence among competitors can help one's position within an industry. If a product can be regarded as an advance—it's faster, less expensive, more comprehensive, longer lasting, better looking, better equipped, safer, or more dependable—one is entitled to say, "successor to" or "The (whatever) That Makes All Others Obsolete."

Here are a few examples of flabby writing. These crossed my desk over a three-day period. What's happening on your desk?

Instead of "We're able to" use "We can."
Instead of "Great" or "Greatest," use anything.
Instead of "We were asked the question," use "They asked us."
Instead of "We are making," use "We make."
Instead of "None at all," use "None."
Instead of "Courageousness," use "Courage."
Instead of "In the month of February," use "In February."
Instead of "There are hundreds of styles that seem to never sell," use "Hundreds of styles never seem to sell."
Instead of "Levels of prices," use "Price levels."
Instead of "It was bought on May 25," use "We bought it May 25."
Instead of "All of a sudden," use "Suddenly."
Instead of "Nothing at all," use "Nothing."
Instead of "You may choose to order two ways," use "Order either of two ways."
Instead of "At this point in time," use "Right now."

Flabby writing never works. Sometimes an advertising writer will lapse into legalese—terminology that makes communication by generalizations. Words such as "factor" and "others" have no weight. This is part of a sentence that appeared in an ad: "Factors such as progress, education, and others. . . ." The weakness is obvious.

Look at the impossible self-description here: "It was made for the purpose intended." "This product has a wide variety of uses." Absolutely no impact. "In the world's finest art museums . . ." What is a "fine" museum? Can the nondescriptive word "finest" compete with the greater specificity of "most prestigious" or the truly specific "in the Metropolitan Museum and the Tate Gallery"?

"A product that is vital to your health" not only presents legal problems that can arise from false health claims, but draws no image at all. If it really is vital to health, prove it and describe how and why.

"Collectors will find this edition of exceptional value and interest to them" is loose, fatty writing, a dozen words, none of them specific. No image is created on which a buyer's greed can feast.

Every word counts. Along with a new ribbon for the word processor, get a slashing red pencil to cut out the layers of fat that can start to grow on even a carefully tended piece of lean copy.

How to Look Like a Giant Even Though You're a Pygmy

A lot of advertisers make the claim of being number one in their ads. "Sandusky's Number One Car Dealer"; "The Midwest's Number One Realtor"; "America's Most Respected Name in Tires"; "Palo Alto's Foremost Name in Insurance." The only reason these claims have any impact is that the public is trained to accept number one as being either the largest or the best. Yet public acceptance, the thin base on which many of these claims teeter, isn't measurable. And one would think it odd if the advertiser who claimed to be "This town's Number One Ford Dealer" weren't the largest Ford dealer in that town. So if you're going to advertise this, you'd better be the biggest. (Some techniques for size-intensification were listed in Chapter 9.)

Testimonials are another way to project a larger-than-actual size. Suppose you're a printer. There are scores of printers with shops larger than yours. You put together a mailing consisting of a thick bound book of 100 tiny—3-by-5 inch—pages. On each page is a testimonial from a satisfied buyer. The sheer bulk implies size, and the audacity of this power-house approach to printing sales may transfix prospective customers.

Another example: You own a moving and storage company, and you have two vans. Some of the giants have a dozen, which makes you a minor figure in local furniture moving. But you put together a campaign using testimonials from families you've moved. The ads are small—two columns by 6 inches appearing twice a week in the local newspaper. If you're highly promotional, you'll use the same people for radio spots, recording their own voices with copy prepared by you. Only one testimonial appears in any ad, but over a period of months, you can have what appears to be a bandwagon effect.

Or you use a celebrity, whether local or national. If what you sell isn't marketed to consumers, remember that celebrity testimonials aren't limited to consumer products; these people are for sale on any level.

If customers don't walk into the place of business, its easier to suggest larger-than-actual size. Mail order vendors know this well. Some of them have had legal problems stemming from false claims about size, integrity, or longevity. Still, any logical claim that isn't a lie should be exploited.

When claiming size, don't use a post office box as an address. This suggests pygmy-size, even if you're big. Only the giant companies can do this. Procter & Gamble and General Mills can use a post office box address; you shouldn't. If you have no way out, use "Lock Box" instead of "P. O. Box."

You may not want to use your home address. For a few dollars you can pick an address with some glamour. They're available. For example, New York's Fifth Avenue, Chicago's Michigan Avenue, and Los Angeles' Sunset Boulevard are known internationally as glamour addresses. For this reason those streets are peppered with office service companies willing to provide not only a mailing address but a phone number, for a moderate fee.

But what if you're headquartered in Scranton? Put both addresses on your letterhead, and indicate that correspondence should be sent to the mailing center in Scranton.

This may not work for everyone, nor is it a suggestion that one can get away with harmful deception. But neither is there any reason to collapse and say, "Okay, I'm small, everybody knows it, and there's nothing I can do about it."

Nothing you can do about it?

Sure there is.

13

A Look
Toward the Future

Visualize an ad in a publication, or a television commercial, in the year 2010.

Will it have a noticeably improved appearance over the way it looks in the late 1980s? Will the printed ad have startlingly accurate sharpness, and will the television spot surround the viewer with holographic realism? Will the atmosphere be charged with subliminal persuasions of which the target's mind isn't even aware, as he rushes out to buy?

An opinion: No.

Changes will be in marketing techniques, with technology running to catch up. Certainly all broadcast sound will have a stereophonic option; certainly newspapers will have to improve their reproduction. But are either of these as consequential as the ability to pinpoint a market by demographic homogeneity as well as geography?

Trends in marketing have never been easy to predict, and today they're harder than ever because many are tied to the vagaries of politics, many are tied to shifting technology, and many are over before most experts recognize their existence.

Let's explore those trends we *can* recognize.

Trends in Newspaper Advertising

July 1, 1984, was a landmark date in newspaper advertising. On that day, after a long midnight in which a buyer trying to mount a national newspaper-advertising campaign was confronted by 215 different page and column sizes, the Standard Advertising Unit system finally became a fact.

Publishers of almost all the metropolitan newspapers in the United States agreed that the normal print size of a full page is 13 inches wide and 21 inches deep, divided into six columns. On each page you have a choice of 55 ad sizes, from one inch to a full page; a "double-truck," or two-page spread, is a 56th size.

To old-timers, the biggest change was the retirement of the venerable "agate line." For generations ads had been figured by lines—14 to the column inch. One standard size, 100 lines, was just over seven inches deep. No standard ruler could measure lines, and printers often gave away agate line rulers as premiums. No more. Lines are out, and inches are in—forever, I hope.

A few newspapers, notably *U.S.A. Today*, have achieved great technical proficiency in color and black-and-white reproduction. A better paper finish is partly responsible; so are upgraded printing presses.

Trends in Magazine Advertising

The capability of offering multiple editions, to match the marketplace of any advertiser, has become standard. A look at the rate card of a magazine such as *Better Homes & Gardens* shows how many options an advertiser has.

Now we see the trend gathering steam within the ranks of business publications, and we know: When one introduces an advertiser benefit and succeeds, the others fall into line. By the end of the century, an advertiser should be able to eliminate waste in almost any publication.

Before the applause becomes too loud, I should point out that this sword has two edges. If we trim a piece of meat so closely that all marbling disappears, experimentation suffers. We tend to cut out of our advertising messages those individuals who aren't immediate buyers. Publications have to offer deep discounts to entice advertisers to buy "full-run" advertising. The computerized bookkeeping and scheduling systems become nightmares. Changes in readership patterns and availability of new buyer groups can elude us.

The impossible cost of printing papers has held back some of the improvements in reproduction, because many publications opt for cheaper, thinner paper instead of a coated stock which would permit fine screens. Some magazines have begun to shave the standard 7-by-10″ page ($6\frac{15}{16} \times 9\frac{7}{8}″$, for example). At this writing the prediction of paper availability suggests worse shortages until the end of the century, and tabloid publications already have reduced their dimensions or are considering such reductions.

In the mid-1980s the lead-time for magazine deadlines seems to be counter-evolving. Magazines are adding a day here and a week there, in defiance of what should be a technological speedup. This may be a temporary setback for advertisers who already complain about the long lead time for magazines and whose complaints often result in a media-shift to other outlets with shorter deadlines.

Certainly advertisers have every right to expect improvements; the same magazines which demand long lead times for insertions have incredibly efficient billing systems, often sending out invoices long before advertisers have their regular copies of the publication.

Opinion: This trend will reverse itself before 1990, because computerized scheduling and page makeup will obsolesce the midnight last-second pagination some publications still endure.

A better reason: *competition.*

Competition has become a troll under the bridge for magazine publishers—not only competition from other media but competition from other magazine publishers.

Nowhere is this more pronounced than in the world of personal computers, where magazines suddenly disappear after a brief and apparently successful flare of excitement.

Being well financed is no assurance of continued existence. Time, Inc., tried to compete with *TV Guide,* introducing a flashy new magazine called *TV-Cable Week* in 1983. By 1984 *TV-Cable Week* was only a memory to its few subscribers, a $47 million embarrassment to its publisher.

Cuisine, a highly respected upscale magazine owned by CBS, suddenly ceased publication in late 1984. The magazine was unable to achieve dominance in a field of epicurean magazines dominated by *Bon Appetit*. Success is relative: In some fields there's room for one giant and many pygmies but not for two giants, one of whom is a little smaller than the other.

Magalogs and Advertorials

A magalog is a catalog that masquerades as a magazine. The result is often a more attractive, more dynamic, more convincing product presentation.

Magalogs had been known to the vitamin/food supplement industries since the early 1980s. By the middle of the decade such marketing giants as Neiman-Marcus were using it. Magalogs, users claim (and I agree), have greater longevity and aren't regarded with the implicit distrust projected onto most unsolicited catalogs.

Advertorials are editorial sections with "articles" whose thrust, supposedly by authoritative editorial sources, glorifies the products or services of participating advertisers.

A typical advertorial arrangement is exemplified in Figure 13-3, part of a mailing to prospective advertisers in a special issue of a trade publication.

We have an old argument: Does the publication have the obligation to assure its readers that advertiser puffery isn't mistaken for editorial endorsement? An increasing number of magazines—and some newspapers, whose use of advertorials in the weekend real estate section is hoary—are saying that advertorials are a *service* to the readership because they present information about what's for sale in a readable manner.

As the argument rages, advertisers are drawn to the technique. But, like telemarketing, overuse and abuses will take the edge off advertorial sharpness.

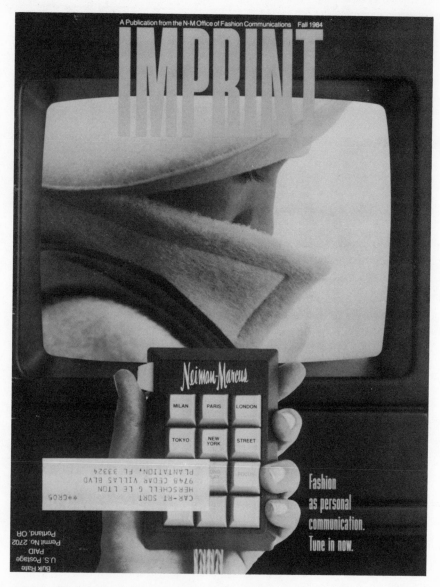

Figure 13-1 "Imprint" is the Neiman-Marcus magalog. This is the cover of a typical copy.

Figure 13-2 "Diet News" appears to be a magazine; this is the "Hotline Edition." It's a magalog which promotes Ever-Thin, a weight-reducing tablet.

A unique opportunity to communicate to your customers and prospects *twice*— FOR ONE LOW PRICE!

All year long, you tell your customers and prospects about your products and services. In ZIP TARGET MARKETING's August "Show In Print" issue, you can tell them about your company, too. Your marketing philosophy. . . reputation. . . competitive advantages. . . prime customers. . . background. . . staff. . . physical facilities. All in a brief "annual report" that will reach and influence ZIP TARGET MARKETING's responsive audience of over 30,000 direct marketing professionals, plus 2.8 pass-along readers per copy!

If you didn't take advantage of this once-a-year FREE advertorial in last year's "Show In Print" issue, you missed one of the most talked-about, best-read, informative issues of the year. . . one that drew *thousands of qualified reader inquiries and sales leads!*

A one-half page (or larger) ad in ZIP TARGET MARKETING 's August "Show In Print" issue qualifies you for a FREE half-page advertorial, including text and photos, to run in the same big issue. We regret that we cannot guarantee positioning of your free advertorial, but we will attempt to place your "report" as close to your ad as possible.

A SPECIAL OFFER TO OUR FULL-PAGE ADVERTISERS:

If you purchase a full-page ad in our "Show In Print" issue, you will have the opportunity to purchase a *full-page advertorial* at 25% of the full-page rate, with a guaranteed position adjacent to your ad. We're giving you an entire page to tell your story—at one-quarter of the full-page cost!

(Please note that advertorials do not count in computing ad frequency rates.)

Your ad and advertorial are a combination that will work together to build readership and response. You'll communicate to *all* the buying influences with a natural resource that ZIP TARGET MARKETING readers will retain and refer to throughout the year.

Figure 13-3 The magazine *Zip Target Marketing* solicited advertisers for its advertorial section with this mailing piece.

A Chance to Showcase Your Product *and* Demonstrate its Effectiveness to Over 80,000 Potential Buyers

This once-a-year reference—a virtual encyclopedia of the leading companies in the direct marketing and mailing industry—will be saved and referred to again and again by the prime decision-makers who turn to ZIP TARGET MARKETING for authoritative and useful information.

Your ad and advertorial will help these important buyers reach purchasing decisions for 1985 as they compare and shop the pages of this unique issue. And it will reinforce their interest before the National Postal Forum and DMA Annual Conference.

Just send us a case history about your company, its products or services. Remember, this material is to *inform* our readers who are anxious to know more about the firms who advertise in ZIP TARGET MARKETING.

If you have any questions regarding the preparation of your "Show In Print" advertorial, please feel free to call Mr. Jim McCanney at **(215) 238-5300.**

FULL-PAGE
Advertorial for 25% of Full-Page Rate, Adjacent to Your Ad

HALF-PAGE
Advertorial Free with Your Full-Page Ad
(Advertorial position not guaranteed.)

ISLAND HALF
with Surrounding Advertorial

HALF-PAGE
Advertorial with Half-Page Ad

(PLEASE NOTE: Clear identification of editorial-style ads will conform to the high standards established by the American Business Press.)

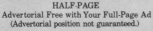

How to Prepare Your "Show In Print" Article for Publication

ISSUE and CLOSING DATES

"Show In Print" will appear in ZIP TARGET MARKETING's August, 1984 issue.

Advertorial Closing Date: **June 11**
Advertising Closing Date: **July 2**
Ad Material Due: **July 9**

WHAT TO WRITE

Your "Show In Print" article should lead with a short case history and may include information on the following: your product lines and services; how to use your products and services; the success of your products and services; a focus on a prime customer; how your company operates; your company history; new or projected developments or programs; distributors and/or branch offices. Include details to quantify the scope of your operation. Include a photograph of your equipment in use, if possible. You may also submit any appropriate diagrams or head shots of your chief executive officer.

Remember that it is in everyone's best interest to keep the article as interesting and readable as possible. ZIP TARGET MARKETING editors may change "Show In Print" articles to conform to the magazine's editorial style and reserve right of judgement for design and use of graphics.

AUTHOR IDENTIFICATION

Your "Show In Print" article should be by-lined with the author's title and corporate affiliation, as follows:

John J. Jones, Marketing Director, XYZ Corporation

All "Show In Print" articles will be clearly identified as *"Material Supplied by ZIP TARGET MARKETING Advertisers."*

SPECIFICATIONS

Finished manuscripts preferred. Press releases, annual reports, promotional or other material to support the advertorial on your company and its products or services will be accepted and converted to "advertorial."

Length of Copy:
½ page: Approx. 350 words
Full-page: Approx. 700 words

Photographs:
Black-and-white glossy photos preferred. *(NOTE: Number of photographs used in advertorial will vary depending upon size of article and layout considerations.)*

WHERE TO SEND MATERIAL

An issue such as this is going to take weeks to prepare. Send complete manuscript and/or materials *no later than June 11* to:

Jim McCanney
"Show In Print" Editor
ZIP TARGET MARKETING Magazine
401 North Broad Street
Philadelphia, PA 19108

☐ **YES,** I want to reserve space in ZIP TARGET MARKETING's August "Show In Print" issue.

☐ Full Page ☐ ⅔ Page ☐ Island Half
☐ ½ Horizontal ☐ ½ Vertical ☐ Other (specify) _____

☐ B & W ☐ Standard Color ☐ Matched Color ☐ 4 Color

☐ I want a FREE, half-page advertorial to accompany my ad of a ½-page or larger.

☐ I want a full-page advertorial, adjacent to my full-page ad, at 25% of the full-page rate.

☐ Manuscript and other materials covering basic facts about my company with _____ photos will be sent by June 11, 1984.
(Indicate No. of photos)

☐ Call me. I need more information immediately.

Name_____ Title_____

Company_____

Address_____ City/State/Zip_____

Telephone ( )_____ Signature_____

Figure 13-3   (continued)

Trends in Television and Radio

Paralleling the magalog and the advertorial is the "infomercial," which has had an apparently successful birth on cable television.

The infomercial is two to four minutes long. It combines a commercial sales message with information, that information being favorable toward the product advertised.

Marketers such as Kraft, Levi's, and Merrill Lynch have used infomercials. Immediate results have been strong.

More controversial is another expanding development: Unquestionably the major advertisers will add "bulk" to the commercial content of television with "split-30s" (splitting the time within 30-second commercials, to devote 15 seconds each to two different products sold by the advertiser).

Gillette Co., the leader in the split-30 movement, explained the philosophy behind doubling up: "Nobody wants to go to 15s, but the economics are such that for the two- to five-million-dollar advertised brands, it is the only way they can be on TV."

The comment itself proves that the old "medium is the message" thinking still lives. But the speciousness of the argument became more apparent as advertisers such as Alberto-Culver Co., Beecham Products, and Warner-Lambert embraced split-30s for products such as VO5, Aqua Fresh, and Rolaids—national brands whose budgets far exceed two to five million dollars.

What's wrong with the split-30 philosophy? The problem is discussed at length in Chapter 6: Television viewers sense more "bulk," because commercial length isn't the only determinant of viewer's fatigue.

No question about it: We can expect more commercials, because within any minute-limitation period, we'll see fewer and fewer 60s and more and more 30s and 10s. The 60-second commercial, once the "standard" length, now represents a thin two percent of network commercials and five percent of spot market commercials.

(On cable, this trend doesn't exist. In fact, program-length infomercials bring the average commercial length way, way up.)

Recall has become a real problem for television advertisers. In 1965 18 percent of all respondents could remember a commercial message five minutes after it aired. By 1974 five-minute recall had dropped to 12 percent. By 1984 it was seven percent—and this was *before* split-30s were given an open sesame.

Some advertisers say, not without logic, "See? If recall drops, we need better mileage from our TV dollars, and the split-30s will help us by giving us twice the apparent exposure." Sure—but how much lower will split-30s push the recall factor?

(A disclaimer: Recall is an uncertain yardstick of a commercial's effectiveness.)

In 1975, TV stations might have been more united in rejecting split-30s. But in the mid-1980s, television stations had learned to run scared. Cable had begun to erode their share of audience, and share of commercial dollars had to follow.

Cable has also been pulling dollars out of magazine and outdoor advertising. From revenues of $514 million in 1984, cable is expected to generate $5.7 billion in advertising by 1994. Although, as of this writing, cable honors the restrictions against cigarette advertising, no such restriction inhibits alcoholic beverage advertising.

What can happen, as cable saps dollars away from other media, is a relaxing of many self-imposed rules which exclude advertisers whose dollars gradually become logical. After all, what's the difference between hard liquor and wine and beer, except for the percentage of alcohol?

As taboos vanish, once-forbidden products lose their stigma. It wasn't that long ago that commercials for brassieres and hemorrhoid ointments had difficulty getting station clearance; now contraceptives appear regularly.

But the giants still stumble. Prudential Insurance Company violated the Second Great Law ("In this Age of Skepticism, cleverness for the sake of cleverness may well be a liability rather than an asset") with an expensive commercial showing people dying and going to heaven.

No question about it: The commercials *were* clever. But Prudential dropped them in favor of commercials showing

Figure 13-4 A trade ad such as this one would have been incomprehensible to advertisers of the year 1975. By 1995 we can expect a host of cable time-brokers.

people *recovering* from life-threatening situations because their research, they admitted wryly, showed "people like the new ones better."

Radio, always more flexible than television, already offers tremendous audience segmentation.

What many of the stations reaching small, specific interest groups—"narrowcasting" to them—lack has been range. Special-interest broadcasting is usually on low-power stations with limited coverage.

Power increases are the order of the day. Some stations have leased satellite transponders, giving them the potential of nationwide coverage.

For general-interest stations, morning drive time continues to be the most listened-to and most expensive. Most of the big stations within metropolitan areas are indistinguishable from each other, offering weather, news, trafficopter reports, and a multitude of commercials. Universally, music is down and talk is up, in percentage of air time.

Fighting for fragments of rating points leads to reliance

on expensive cash-jackpot promotions and outrageous on-the-air personalities. Civilization doesn't advance through these tactics, but a wily station can increase its audience share.

And audience share becomes significant as the number of television stations mushrooms. Suddenly, after years of quiescence, would-be telecasters are bombarding the Federal Communications Commission with requests for construction permits.

Most of these permits are for UHF (ultra-high frequency) channels—14 to 83—because the VHF (very high frequency) channels, 2 to 13, are long since spoken for. In mid-1984 535 VHF and 358 UHF commercial stations were on the air in the United States. If all the new permits resulted in stations going on the air, by mid-1986 the number would be 562 VHF, 610 UHF. Audience-fragmentation is one inevitable result; lower cost for commercials is another. Greater availability of ethnic and special-interest programming is a third.

Trends in Direct Marketing

Electronic direct marketing hasn't developed as its promoters had hoped. This doesn't mean that by the end of the century, examining and ordering merchandise and services through the television set won't be commonplace. It does mean that direct marketers can't avoid this reality:

Technology constantly adds power to the means of communication but is no substitute for communication.

An example of this is Knight-Ridder's *Viewtron,* launched with a lavish promotional campaign in the Miami area. Initial projections were for a minimum of 5,000 subscribers by the end of 1983; by the the end of 1984, subscribers, according to trade sources, numbered fewer than 2,000.

Viewtron's prices, at introduction, were formidable: $600 as a "discounted" price for a special keyboard, plus a $12 monthly fee, plus a $1 per-hour charge for access, in addition to usage fees. Later, prices were reduced (drastically), but the image had already been set: an elitist toy.

The need for Viewtron and other television-based direct marketing techniques obviously had been poorly established. The same circumstances may attend Comp-U-Store, a subsidiary of Comp-U-Card International, which assembled a core of 10,000 subscribers over the five-year period 1979–1984.

Technology for the sake of technology is no longer a novelty; any medium launched in the skeptical 1985–2000 period has to position itself as a perceived value to (a) advertisers and (b) consumers.

Thus, we have MCI Mail, an overnight computer message-delivery service. We also have GTE Telemail, General Electric's Quik-Comm, ITT's Dialcom, H&R Block's Compuserve, the Reader's Digest's Source Telecomputing, and others in various stages of embryo as this book goes to press. How many of them will survive, even to the day when you read these words? Unless backed by an almost fanatical belief in future acceptance, survival depends on establishing a communications niche in which both advertiser and target-individual see *value*.

The 800 number, a staple of direct marketing, has a trend of its own: the *vanity number*.

This is a number using letters instead of numbers to aid memory retention. Some examples:

Holiday Inns—800-Holiday
American Express—800-The Card
Dean Witter Reynolds—800-The Dean
National Car Rental—800-Car Rent
Flowers—800-Flowers
Chicago Chamber of Commerce—800-Hot Town

The trend has begun to spread to local numbers. Any seven-letter word seems to be more memorable than a string of numbers. So a mortgage company petitions for and gets a local number spelling F-R-E-E-D-O-M in one city and J-U-S-T-I-C-E in another.

The paradox is that a business with a vanity number has to advertise the number itself, to gain consumer retention. The number becomes the end as well as the means!

Trends in the Marketplace

A 1984 Gallup Poll verified what many marketers could
have stated flatly without research: Brand loyalty continues to
drop.

More than 40 percent of all shoppers have *no* brand loyalty, switching back and forth from brand to brand witin a
product category, depending on price and whim.

Private label sales are skyrocketing—up 50 percent in a
single six-year period. Products, like the media on which
they're advertised, will have to position themselves as specialty items for a particular segment of the marketplace in
order to survive. Thus, by the end of the century we will surely
have not only a toothpaste for adults, a toothpaste for denture
wearers, a toothpaste for smokers, and a toothpaste for children, but also toothpastes for ethnic, economic, and physical
situations.

Will marketing be more closely regulated, or less? Apparently less, at least for the rest of the 1980s. The once-tough
Federal Trade Commission now defines "misleading advertising" in terms far more benevolent to the advertiser than was
true in the 1970s. Those who want detailed information can
get it from the FTC's Public Reference Branch, Washington,
D.C. 20580; but in brief:

The FTC no longer regards misleading advertising as a
serious threat to the public. A little cheating, the Commission
feels, is better than a meddling bureaucracy. Of course out-
right fraud will be prosecuted, but half-truths and mild cheating will depend on lawsuits by competitors and consumers to
implement any controls.

Will this work? For lawyers, yes. For advertisers who
mourn the denigration of the marketplace, and for consumers
whose skepticism will become a little more profound, perhaps
not. We may be in an administrative backlash reacting against
the overregulation of the previous decade.

Early in this new ball game, BMW was suing Ford over
the advertising claim that the Ford Thunderbird "outhandled"
the BMW 633CSi; General Motors petitioned the FTC to ease
any restrictions on that company's advertising, so it could com-

pete in this new wide-open marketplace in which comparative advertising deals in opinion as much as fact.

What may exacerbate a circumstance which otherwise might be only mildly annoying is the unmistakable trend of putting responsibility for advertising in the hands of untrained know-it-alls. From 1972 to 1985, the number of advertising agencies increased from about 7,000 to about 11,000, despite the many consolidations and mergers that dotted this period.

Many of the new agencies are "house agencies," extensions of the advertiser. For the knowledgeable advertiser who does most of his own creative work anyway, a house agency is supremely logical: He can save the 15 percent agency commission and save liaison time as well. But in an unpoliced advertising arena, this advertiser has no governor on the throttle, a fine breeding ground for wild and borderline advertising claims.

What else? International toll-free 800-code phone numbers open worldwide borders to the lines of marketing. Successful experiments in enhanced television-picture quality have (under laboratory circumstances) doubled the standard U.S. screen from its coarse 525 lines to a superfine movie-quality 1,050 lines. Every facet of marketing is speeding up—except the delivery of the U.S. mails.

14

Problem Solving: Try It for Yourself

Any businessman develops an instinct that goes into gear when he plans his promotions. If nothing else, he knows what's safe and what isn't. Many are lost when confronted with change. What reflexively came to mind in the men's clothing business leaves a blank in the women's clothing business. The instincts work only in a familiar atmosphere.

Here is a list of 15 business problems. Put yourself in the entrepreneur's shoes and decide what would be a logical approach to advertising in each case.

Obviously, there's no single answer to any marketing program, and a suggestion that the use of consumer magazines might be more valid than a suggestion to use trade publications or broadcast is only a matter of opinion. My proposed solutions follow each problem.

Problem 1

A furniture store located in a city of 250,000 wants to project some excitement into a sale. This is a single store, not a chain, and it's not the largest store in town.

Where would you advertise and what would you say?

Solutions

Put better than half the budget into newspapers, remembering that a sale of this sort requires a listing of items. Use radio as an underscore. Direct mail to existing customer lists is a must.

One way to bring people into the store is to have one-of-a-kind and hot-list specials, not listed in prior announcements but as the sale progresses. Separate specials can be reserved for the direct mail program to existing customers. Give yourself a bonus if you included a coupon in the newspaper ad; the coupon can be good for a discount on any specially tagged item.

If you suggest television, this isn't an error. A reason to omit television, though, is because generating excitement, the key to successful advertising, requires multiple exposures, and you won't get that, dollar for dollar, on television.

Problem 2

An auto rental company has lower rates than Hertz or Avis but not as low as Dollar or Thrifty. With offices in most cities, the company has no airport booth; the customer has to make a phone call and then be picked up by the company's local van and driven to the office, somewhere near the airport.

Where would you advertise and what would you say?

Solutions

Give yourself a top score if you thought of the in-flight airline magazines. Perhaps you demurred because the competitors also advertise there, and Dollar, who has your prices beat, would have its own ad; but it is still the best medium because you reach the most people who can and will buy what you have to sell. Having a message that overcomes the less-expensive competition should be as logical for you as it is for Hertz. Did you think of putting a display unit inside the air terminal? This is a point-of-purchase impulse-grabber. Use visitors' magazines such as "Where" and "Key." You can also take a small space ad in the *Wall Street Journal* and try the daily papers. Broadcast is out because using it would be a violation of the First Law. Building up your unknown name is the key to this campaign, and you also need on-the-spot, impulsive decision making.

Compare your prices with higher ones, not lower ones ("Call us instead of Hertz or Avis and buy yourself a steak dinner every day with the difference you'll save—at least ten dollars a day"). Avoid going head-to-head with cheaper competition. Without specifics, though, you'll get only overflow calls, since you show no apparent benefit over those car rental companies with airport booths.

If you choose direct mail, to whom will you direct it? You may know who veteran travelers are, but you don't know *when* they're traveling. If the direct mail includes a "V.I.P." preferred rate-and-service card, though, it might work.

Problem 3

A company dealing in business incentives, such as trips to the Bahamas for their clients' good customers, Christmas gift programs, and packaged-sales incentive programs, wants to build its business among new clients, most of whom, the company assumes, never heard of them—and some of whom have no idea what a business incentive is.

Where would you advertise and what would you say?

Solutions

Put half the budget into direct mail, which can be directed to specific types of businesses. An ad program can be scheduled in publications such as *Potentials in Marketing* and *Premium Incentive Business* (for this category, check the business publication edition of Standard Rate & Data Service). Any remaining dollars can be saved for the *Wall Street Journal* and the business section of metropolitan newspapers in October and November, the best months for grabbing a share of the Christmas gift business.

Offer an item—a vacation trip, a piece of leather luggage, a two-inch television set—that a company might not think of or be able to get easily without you. Be specific. That's what makes the phone ring. You might offer a free something or other, or a discount on a sample, for an inquiry on the respondent's company letterhead.

If you opted against direct mail on the grounds that every competitor also uses direct mail, you may have a point, but then, where else would you go? If you suggested consumer media, you're wasting 50 impressions for every one hitting a prospective buyer.

Problem 4

A hotel or resort wants to increase its business. It operates at about 60 percent of capacity, which isn't bad, but big blocks of rooms are empty for two or three months at a time.

Where would you advertise and what would you say?

Solutions

The best place to advertise is in travel or meetings-and-conventions' publications. The key is the empty blocks of rooms, which provide a logical pitch for business to fill those months on some sort of deal. You also might consider due-bill advertising or a trade with any medium (rooms in exchange for space or broadcast time). Trade-outs are a mixed bag; a lot of the advertising space is a waste, but on the other hand, many of the due bills (be sure to put a date on them) aren't used. Direct mail is a possibility: Meeting planners are prime candidates, since they use blocks of rooms at specific, prearranged times, and you can offer discounts during specific months. Volume users, such as travel agents or big local corporations, are also logical direct mail recipients.

For a theme, ask yourself: What's different about your hotel or resort? Is the bed turned down at night? Are shoes shined, continental fashion? Do you offer free transportation to the airport? Is there preregistration for groups so they need only pick up their keys? Is there a special weekend package including meals? Avoid generalities such as "One of America's Premier Resorts," which means nothing and motivates no one. You also might offer a discount "take-a-look" package for those who make legitimate inquiries on company letterheads.

Ads in hotel publications, red books, and the Yellow Pages may help, but you won't find the fastest solution to empty rooms in these long-range methods.

Problem 5

A 100-bed nursing home is about to open. Occupancy must be better than average, since a 75 percent occupancy rate is needed to break even. The home is in a good suburban section of a major metropolitan area.

Where would you advertise and what would you say?

Solutions

Send a piece of direct mail to those who recommend nursing homes; hospital personnel and doctors are excellent. Using the Yellow Pages is a must, since decisions of this type are often made based on a comparison of what's available among local facilities. Small-space ads in local newspapers, especially those in the higher-income sections and suburbs, will keep the name current. Outdoor advertising makes sense, too, especially since this is a new nursing home in need of name recognition.

Make a big hoopla over the opening. Possible clients might be invited to visit. There should be a planned opening, designed to show off the facilities. Any sales promotion to the public-at-large must emphasize what is unique about the home. The first announcement should have a "now accepting reservations" snob appeal.

Broadcasting advertising is fine, if you find the right time of day, probably late evening, when decisions of this type are made.

Problem 6

A respected company in the office-equipment field has just developed a photocopy machine. While the machine is as good as any, the company is not known, as is Xerox, IBM, or Savin, as a manufacturer of photocopy machines. Where would you advertise and what you would say?

Solutions

Use a multimedia campaign, planning ads for *Business Week* and commercial purchasing publications to coincide with the arrival of a direct mail package to businesses, associations, and institutions. If there's a dealer organization for other items in the line, prime the dealers to mount their own direct mail campaign at the same time, and give them cooperative advertising money for space ads in the business sections of local newspapers. Television spots on sports programs will work if you say something startling, but if you're after inquiries, they won't work without the direct mail backup.

A free trial that doesn't look like an obligation is standard direct mail fare, and it works if specifics are mentioned, e.g., "Use it in your office from May 10 to 14. The man who brings it in and picks it up won't be a salesman." Is there a unique selling proposition? "Faster" means nothing, but clarity of image reproduced means something, especially if this machine isn't a monster that will dominate the office.

Time, Newsweek, and *U.S. News* ads are good, but they alone won't work. Radio, during morning drive time, might pick up some business, as might evening drive-time advertising when a businessman might be seething over the performance of his existing copy machine.

Problem 7

An automobile dealer wants to increase his share of the market. There's nothing unusual about his dealership. He handles a medium-priced car, and local competition is heavy. He belongs to the dealer association which advertises as a unit in the metropolitan area. The dealer has no price advantage over his competition.

Where would you advertise and what would you say?

Solutions

A car dealer must be in the newspapers on weekends, preferably in the automobile section with both display and classified ads. This is where people who are about to buy will look. Some dealers have built an image using broadcast, and this works provided the newspapers aren't shorted. Direct mail is a medium used with increasing effectiveness among car dealers.

In ads list specific makes and models of cars by years. Tell specifically what that car is worth. Use the classified section only for used cars. In display ads, again, specificity helps, e.g., "You can lease this car for $185 a month, but you can buy it for $188 a month. For only $3 a month more, you own it!" or "If you drive one of these cars, you don't need one dime of cash as a down payment. Drive in—and drive a new car home." Back this up with a list of cars that qualify as a down payment, going all the way back for five or six model-years if possible. Look for that elusive unique selling proposition. For example, can you give a service certificate with a used car, guaranteeing condition?

If you chose the showy "Madman Muntz" approach typical of many car dealerships, you should consider: It's dangerous and may kill your competitive image with serious buyers unless carefully engineered.

Problem 8

An employment agency wants to increase both the number of applicants who use it and the number of clients to whom it supplies personnel. The agency handles general office help and junior executives.

Where would you advertise and what would you say?

Solutions

If you failed to include the Sunday "Help Wanted" ads, you're out of the ball game. This is the one place you have to cover, regardless of what else you do, to get applicants. Getting clients is a different story. A radio hotline of immediate job availabilities is a fine idea. If you're building a personality, a series of television spots, with the head of the agency on-camera discussing openings, might work. Direct mail to business offices is effective if it suggests you have a screening technique they lack. Prescreened and prechecked referrals are inducements to harried business persons who need a reason to turn to employment agencies rather than running their own ads.

Don't overpitch. If you come on too strong, listing so many benefits you seem to be pleading for jobseekers, applicants feel *they* control *you*. Strive for verisimilitude—the appearance of truth in job descriptions. Offer free booklets and free aptitude tests in display ads or broadcast spots. Privacy and no waiting are big inducements to those who may have lost their dignity in other employment agencies.

All media will work, including local community publications, but the message must match the reader of that message.

Problem 9

A shoe company sells its men's line directly to the customer. Its representatives get no salary; they receive a commission on sales. Most of the salesmen are 55-65 years old and work part time. Work shoes outsell dress shoes two to one. The company wants to recruit more salespersons and will send a complete sales kit to every legitimate inquiry.

Where would you advertise and what would you say?

Solutions

Direct mail to retirement lists should be dynamite. For space advertising Standard Rate & Data lists a number of publications that reach direct salespeople—publications such as *Spare Time*, *Selling Direct*, and *Opportunity*. Magazine remnants in such publications as *Parade* or *TV Guide* would be excellent. The low cost-per-thousand of remnants makes this fertile recruitment territory. Newspaper classified ads are a waste of time. You can't compete with "help wanted" ads which offer a guaranteed salary.

Pitch the ads to persons seeking an easy income; emphasize that experience is unimportant, and avoid the word "sales." Headlines such as this should work: "In the time you take to read this ad, you could make $10" or "Enjoy An Easy Second Income." You might try this approach: "I want two men and two women who can repeat thirty words eight times a day during a two-hour period to make $120 a week." It's hokey, but it brings leads. Ads should be motivational without suggesting hard selling or cold calls.

Broadcast won't work for recruitment. You have to tell too much to get people to respond. You're trying to get people to work for straight commission and not quit after they sell to their relatives. Using the words "Free Shoes for Yourself" as a theme might work if the competition hasn't overworked this. Any ad promising an easy way to make good money, or suggesting uses of that money—a new car, a vacation—represents sound thinking.

Problem 10

A realtor wants to get more business. He sells single-family houses. Where would you advertise and what would you say?

Solutions

An absolute must is newspaper classified, because this is where live buyers look. Sunday is the best day, although there's increasing action on Friday and Saturday. Direct mail to personnel managers and executive recruiters might bring referrals. Any kind of advertising inside airline terminals will reach prospects, especially if the "sell-piece" is pocket-sized. Fixed-position ads (car cards on buses, for example) also might work, as will any medium reaching people about to move. A special congratulatory mailer to persons listed in the papers as having been promoted might bring a small amount of business. Radio is a fine idea, since scattershot is indicated when one doesn't really know who the buyers are.

A theme such as "House-Hunting? We'll Be Your Legs!" or any variation of this will work. In direct mail be even more specific. Send a checklist to help the prospect describe what he wants (how many bedrooms, location, how many baths, general price range). Include a postage-free return envelope. Copy approach to personnel managers and executive recruiters must prove you'll handle everything; all they need do is turn a warm body over to you, and you'll find the right house for it.

The Yellow Pages are a long-range necessity, but you won't get fast action. People want to know about a house, not about a realtor. Television helps, if the format is right. You can't keep showing the same house, and no one wants to look at a real estate man's face. This medium is better for a developer who has more romance to sell.

Problem 11

The manufacturer of a combination burglar-and-fire-alarm system for homes wants to market the product through department stores. The price of his unit is competitive, but the name isn't a well-known brand.

Where would you advertise and what would you say?

Solutions

Department stores respond to a television schedule. Consider putting heavy dollars into television, using open-ended spots with the local store names tagged on at the end. Prepare ads that dealers can use in newspapers and give the dealers a cooperative-advertising allowance for running these ads with their names dropped in. Let the stores send direct mail but prepare a dealer insert they can enclose with their monthly statements; also create counter displays the stores might or might not use (but certainly won't use if you don't supply them).

Sell a little fear and guilt, two great motivators that are naturals for this type of product. For example, "Will tonight be the first night in years you can turn off the lights and sleep without fear?" That the same unit eliminates the two big fears—fire *and* theft—gives this product an edge over the smoke detectors. One advantage of television is that it puts the viewer inside a dramatic situation. Show innocent children sleeping, confident parents turning off the lights, and a prowler deciding which house to crack. You aren't selling detectors; you're selling a state of mind.

If you considered direct mail or magazines, you forgot this is a retail promotion. If an ad shows the gadgetry at the expense of describing the benefits, you're selling equipment, which can work if your product is the most sophisticated. But many people fear equipment they don't understand. They want a simple way to have protection, especially if they're buying it across the counter at a store. If you included some sort of advertising pamphlet for the store personnel themselves, you're smarter than almost anybody.

Problem 12

A beauty salon in a quiet neighborhood finds that failure to promote itself has caused a slow decline in business. Some normally overbooked appointment times are available, an alarming sign. The shop is well equipped and in a good neighborhood.

Where would you advertise and what you would say?

Solutions

Community newspapers are the best bet. Only the Vidal Sassoons of this world draw their trade from an entire metropolitan area; the typical beauty salon has a local clientele. Direct mail to simple-to-obtain neighborhood lists works well, depending on what the mailer says. Sometimes radio pulls; it might be worth an experiment if you can make an advantageous time-buy, which you usually can during the 9 A.M. to 3 P.M. period.

If you have open appointments when most women want them—Friday afternoon and Saturday morning—run a "Don't Despair" ad, altruistically pointing out that your additional capacity makes it possible for you to accommodate a few more appointments even in these prime hours. For direct mail or space advertising, some weekly specials ought to get that phone ringing; these are best in combination with something else ("Manicure $2 When You Have Your Hair Styled"), so you don't get a reputation for being a discounter.

If you thought to promote the operators rather than the specials, this isn't all that bad an idea, although it has been worked to death. Women have seen enough of "Mr. Kenneth" and "Mr. Dominic" to be jaded by names alone. Advertising a clinic that offers free grooming advice is okay, but you'll have an enormous organizational problem on your hands, and what if nobody comes? If you advertise the newest hairstyle, with photos, be sure styles aren't a turnoff to local matrons who are the core of your business (unless you want the hip, jet-set, way-out image).

Problem 13

As the communications expert for a retirement community in Florida, you know two facts: (1) Retirees come from all over the East and Midwest, especially the colder areas, and (2) in Florida, there are many competitors trying to divert buyers to other communities. Your place is near Delray Beach, which has many such developments. The usual facilities and amenities are available, and the development is based on modestly priced duplex-condominium townhouses. Current residents are satisfied and speak well of the development.

Where would you advertise and what would you say?

Solutions

Use *Modern Maturity* and *50 Plus*, of course, although these publications have been milked heavily. Publications in the *Army Times* group are valid, because armed services personnel are often early retirees who leave the service with a chunk of cash.

Direct mail should be strong, since there are plenty of lists among the geriatric groups. Consider mailing to clubs, professional associations, and unions. Using radio and television within the development's geographic area will work, not only to stave off competitors but also to draw eligible locals who surely are the best impulse buyers. And use outdoor advertising: For low-cost name retention, image, and a feeling of security among prospective buyers, nothing can beat it.

The advantage of buying over renting is a logical theme if you can present sound advantages for this age group. Another inquiry-getter, especially among those unfamiliar with similar facilities in competing developments, is a list of buyer benefits, ranging from free carpeting to membership in an ongrounds club. Testimonials work well, especially when they're numerous. In direct mail, assuming you already have a core of buyers, a list of names from the same geographic area to which you're mailing is potent ("These Buffalonians won't freeze next winter . . . ").

Some of these units can be moved through ads in local daily newspapers, but you won't be reaching the logical buyers at the lowest possible cost. These aren't homes; they're retirement condominiums, and 80 percent of newspaper readers in a community won't be interested.

Problem 14

A local bank, in a community of 75,000, wants to increase the amount of deposits in savings accounts. The bank is the solid number two bank in the town, which has three banks and two savings-and-loan institutions. In the past, the bank has run mostly ineffective ads showing the percentage of interest various savings plans draw.

Where would you advertise and what you would say?

Solutions

All local media should be used, including television, if possible. A bank is a city-wide institution, and being number two calls for aggressive use of media. Direct mail is iffy, since we're dealing within a local area which can be reached at less cost through print and electronic media. A few outdoor signs will work if the theme is strong, since outdoor advertising can reinforce both print and broadcast campaigns as a memory-jogger.

Number two is in a classic position to attack number one. What is your unique selling proposition? Can you legally say, "Highest Interest of *Any* Bank in Town"? If not, you're almost as sound with "parity" advertising: "No Other Bank Pays Higher Interest." Hours are good for a bank to advertise. "Open 63 Hours A Week" or "More Banking Hours Than Any Other Bank in Town." If you have no advantage, give away free maps of the city; offer teen-agers free checking. But be aggressive.

Although a bank needs a listing in the Yellow Pages, this medium presents a problem—namely, you must wean away depositors from the other banks, and you can do this only by showing a comparative advantage. If your media mix includes heavy use of local newspapers, you're safe. But strength comes from a powerful attack mounted in all local media so everyone in town knows what your benefits are. Word ads with care, because bank advertising is regulated. But don't let stuffiness creep in—come out swinging.

Problem 15

An art-supply store has opened in a city of a half-million residents. The store is slowly getting its share of business from art students, commercial artists, and dilettante artists, but faster growth is needed. The store doesn't want to expand into other lines, but wants to concentrate on paints, pastels, transfer type, canvas, layout pads, and other items within the arts and crafts line.

Where would you advertise and what would you say?

Solutions

Community newspapers are usually artier than metropolitan newspapers. A city of a half-million population undoubtedly has several such papers. If there's a college newspaper, it should be a prime medium. Handbills on campus can be a profitable means of advertising. Broadcast probably involves too much waste—remember the First Law.

Put coupons in almost every ad until buying patterns are set. This is especially helpful in attracting nonartists who might take a shot at a paint-by-numbers kit and get hooked. Bright, nontechnical ads with weekly specials will bring some store traffic. Hit hard at the holidays with unusual, offbeat gift ideas.

Did you consider direct mail? To whom? If you thought this through and agreed to inexpensively printed lists of availabilities, mailed to advertisers, ad agency art directors, teachers, and a gradually building list of buyer names, it might work. But mass mailings? No. There are better ways to reach the nonbuyers in a marketplace of this type. One-minute-or-shorter television spots showing how easy it is to paint are a good speculative idea, provided the store doesn't depend on this approach as its only advertising.

Logic and Clear Thinking

Can any advertising problem be solved by logic? I think so!

Too many advertisers, even veterans, look for tricky solutions to problems that can be solved by clear thinking. To keep your own critical and creative faculties sharp, every day invent one advertising problem and determine a solution. By the time you've hit number 365, you'll be more expert than a lot of the bored professionals who, because they forget that the purpose of running ads is to sell something, draw attention to themselves instead of to the product they sell.

Constantly reconsider your situation. Is your advertising program aimed at solving a marketing problem, or are you just filling up space and air time because you want exposure and think the medium is the message? An organized approach to marketing not only moves you into the ranks of the experts, but it ultimately has to save some money, since every ad you run will have as its goal an attempt to influence someone—a logical buyer—to do something you want him or her to do.

15

Examples of Good and Bad Advertising

What's the difference between a good ad and a bad ad?

By this time you should have more than a subjective opinion. You should, in fact, have an objective opinion based on the solid criteria of mass communications—and, I hope, the Three Great Laws.

Few people can be so dispassionate that they can judge an ad on any basis except their own experiential background. To a chef a good ad has appetizing food in it. To an accountant a good ad is formally balanced, neat and not flashy, with a logical beginning, middle, and end to its sales argument. To a car buff, a good ad has a sleek automobile somewhere in the illustration. To the typical student, a good ad is "different" from other ads.

But to someone who has dedicated himself or herself to writing ads that work and placing those ads where they'll pull, there can be only one definition of a good ad:

> A good ad is an ad that reaches, at the lowest possible cost, the most people who can and will buy what you have to sell. It emphasizes logically the most important point, and it isn't clever for the sake of cleverness.

When you examine any ad—especially your own—evaluate it on a "vertical" basis: Did it reach the target group? And you don't reach them just by running your ad in a publication they read. You don't just announce your availability to do business. You reach them by telling them something that motivates them to buy.

Coming up are 25 ads. Look at each one. Reread it. Then

decide whether it's a good or bad example. Obviously, in a book, print ads are the logical type of communication to examine, but the same rules work for broadcast.

In the mix are consumer and trade ads. Don't forget: Put yourself inside the target-reader's brain.

Figure 15-1: Data Base Research Corporation

Let's start with an easy one. Think this ad is good? Go to the foot of the class. It has two immediately obvious problems.

First, it's a flagrant violation of the Second Law. It tries to be clever for the sake of cleverness. Second, it's old-fashioned hucksterism: It's a software *jungle*, so these fellows have jungle camouflage on their faces, get it?

Read the first sentence of body copy. If you can find anything there to cause you to want to read on, I propose there's something wrong with you. The first big subhead says, "What counts is performance." I suggest they read that to whoever wrote the copy and did the layout.

Bad ad.

Figure 15-2: Chase Manhattan Bank

Bank ads are usually flat, but this one hits dead-center in its target.

A dialogue/headline can be tricky, because it can veer away from the message. This question and answer states exactly (and clearly) what the bank has to offer, competitively: fast action on a loan.

The first sentence, "Chase marine loans come about faster," almost kills it, not only because it's a weak comparative but because the phrase "come about" is a cutesy-pie play on a nautical term. But even this weakness can't deliver a mortal blow to an elegant idea.

Good ad.

Figure 15-3: Gold Plus Plan

About 60 percent of the ad is the singer and not quite two bars of music. The music doesn't seem to match the lyrics.

Figure 15-1

"I need about $85,000 for the new boat."
"You want it Monday or Tuesday?"

Chase marine loans come about faster. Because we're experienced in marine financing.

We make it possible to purchase the boat you want whether it's large or small, new or used, power or sail. And if this is your maiden voyage, we'll even arrange the Coast Guard documentation as well.

Because Chase is world class all the way. We cater to a very special kind of customer, accustomed to fast, flexible and, above all, very personal service. In fact, we can lend you up to $350,000 or more. You'll also find our rates are competitive. We have about the best down payment terms on luxury yachts you'll find. We offer fixed or variable rate financing, all on a simple interest basis. And, right now, if you choose variable rate, not only will you get the current lower priced interest rate, but your monthly payment will remain conveniently fixed.

See what we mean by smooth sailing. Phone Chase today. If you qualify, one of our vice presidents will personally see to it that you get the yacht financing that's right for you.

CHASE®

Chase Manhattan of Florida

Gables International Plaza
2655 Le Jeune Road–Suite 701
Coral Gables, Florida 33134

Fill in this coupon for a marine loan application and more information on all the financing available to you at Chase.

Arvida Financial Plaza
Suite 300–Town Center
5550 Glades Road West
Boca Raton, Florida 33431

Name _____

Street _____

City _____ State _____ Zip _____

Home Phone _____ Business Phone _____

FBJ-5-21

Chase. For the credit you deserve.
Phone in Coral Gables: 443-2217   In Boca Raton: 368-2580

A Chase marine loan is secured by the vessel. Chase Manhattan Financial Services, Inc. © 1984 The Chase Manhattan Corporation.

Figure 15-2

Page 2   SOUTH FLORIDA BUSINESS JOURNAL   August 20, 1984

It costs you forty-five cents for a nickel candy bar,
And a dollar's worth of gas won't even start your car.
Yeah, we got problems here in the land of the free,
But there's no place I'd rather be in times like these.

Barbara Mandrell

It's Times Like These That Everyone Needs The Gold Plus Plan

Because they're doing something to help. The Gold Plus Plan is one of the leading health care plans in the country.

And it includes office visits, prescriptions, eye exams, prescription eye glasses, specialty services, hospitalization and more.

The Gold Plus Plan offers better benefits with the best quality care, while still controlling the cost for both of you. With health care costs rising three times as fast as inflation every employer and employee must seek better alternatives.

That's why the business sector is turning to the Gold Plus Plan as a desirable cost-containing alternative for their employee health care plans.

Find out more about how you can offer the Gold Plus Plan. You'll be really glad you did.

Gold Plus Plan®
FOR GROUPS
To find out more call toll-free **1-800-462-2273**

Figure 15-3

And what are these lyrics about? "Free" and "these" are presented as rhyming; the message is something of a downer.

What I don't get is the relationship between those lyrics and what they're selling. Yeah, yeah, I see the words "cost-containing alternative"; what'll you bet Barbara Mandrell doesn't understand those words? The payoff, "Find out more about how you can offer the Gold Plus Plan. You'll be really glad you did," could hardly be weaker.

Bad ad.

Figure 15-4: The Gallery Restaurant

What'll you bet the owner of the restaurant wrote this ad himself?

The message is: "$2 off each dinner." Every night? During certain hours? As a standard policy, which could mean every price is marked up two dollars to cover a permanent discount? What?

Hauling Leonardo da Vinci and the Mona Lisa into the ad is about as "left-field" a move as anyone could make. It's attention-getting, but will it cause anyone to want to go to this restaurant? Think of how many other ways the two dollars discount could have some wallop in it. And think, too, of the specifics left out—such as the word "only" after "tonight."

Bad ad.

Figure 15-4

Figure 15-5: Humana Care Plus

By the time you realize the mumbo-jumbo is a put-on, you've quit reading.

What's wrong here is that Humana has taken an idea which would have worked in a radio commercial—an announcer begins to drone on, and then a second voice cuts cleanly over the first—and used it in print, where the separation between *their* approach and *our* approach isn't clarified until the reader has drawn a final conclusion about our presentation.

Humana has a solid message to transmit. What is it? Reading this ad, you're hard pressed to find it: "We own and operate hospitals nationwise. So we can control our health care costs." It's buried in the text, and few will read that far.

Bad ad.

Figure 15-6: Ingels Inc.

Much as I dislike the notion of celebrities for sale, I'm fascinated by this ad.

A reader, seeing the ad in *Adweek* or *Advertising Age*, can't resist looking at least part way through the list. He may not get all the way to the last name—Marty Ingels' Mother," not a bad way to cap off the ad (and not a violation of the Second Law, because it slices any negative edge off reader-reaction), but even random sampling brings up recognizable names at every turn.

If you're considering buying the use of a celebrity name and see this ad, the impact has to be formidable.

Regrettably, a good ad.

Figure 15-7: Computer Design Inc.

This ad says, "Computer Design does not advertise prices."

I wonder why they're proud of this. How can anyone buy a computer without knowing the cost? Yes, I understand what they're saying: They won't be drawn into the brutal price-cutting arena in which most computer stores wallow. But what, then, is the unique selling proposition of this vendor?

Instead of mumbo-jumbo, we give you an affordable health care plan.

If you're concerned about sky-rocketing health care costs (and who isn't?), talk to us at Humana. The first thing you'll notice is that we never resort to insurance mumbo-jumbo.

We have no reason to. We own and operate hospitals nationwide. So we can control our health care costs. And pass the savings along to you. With guaranteed rates for more than one year. That's the biggest advantage of Humana Care Plus.

We offer a wide range of flexible plans. So whether you're a company of five employees, or well over 1000, there's one just right for you.

Even individuals can sign up through their companies.

We'll never give you double-talk when explaining our benefits, either.

When you have Humana Care Plus, you are assured quality health care at Humana Care Plus participating hospitals.

And you can keep your own doctor. That's important to us because it's important to you.

So why put up with insurance gobbledegook? When Humana Care Plus offers lower rates. Excellent coverage. And greater flexibility.

In a language you'll understand.

If you're an employer, call (305) 776-1722, and we'll send you detailed information.

The health care plans from the health care professionals.

Humana Care Plus participating hospitals: Humana Hospital-Bennett, Humana Hospital-Biscayne, Humana Hospital-Cypress, Humana Hospital-Palm Beaches, Humana Hospital-South Broward.

Figure 15-5

ASK Joan Collins

• and Robert Mitchum • and Orson Welles • and Lauren Bacall • and Ricardo Montalban • and George Peppard • and Morgan Fairchild • and Mr. T • and Heather Lockleer • and Chevy Chase • and James Brolin • and Jimmy Stewart • and Barbara Eden • and Buddy Ebsen • and Mohammed Ali • and Sarah Purcell • and Eddie Albert • and Lloyd Bridges • and Ernest Borgnine and Shirley Jones • and Dick Van Patten • and Marcus Allen • and Phyllis Diller • and Rodney Dangerfield • and Burgess Meredith • and Juliet Prowse • and Jill St. John • and Julius Irving • and Lindsay Wagner • and Rita Moreno • and Mickey Rooney • and Jack Palance • and Jennifer O'Neill • and Diane Von Furstenberg • and Leonard Nimoy • and Scott Carpenter • and Elke Sommer • and Mel Tillis • and Doc Severinsen • and Audrey Landers • and Tony Randall • and Mclean Stevenson • and Joyce Brothers • and Arnold Schwarzenegger • and James Whitmore • and Mary Ann Mobley • and Howard Cosell • and Melvin Belli • and Ester Rolle • and Jayne Meadows • and Robert Conrad • and Don Knotts • and Toni Tennille • and Martin Mull • and Carl Reiner • and Ruth Buzzi • and David Steinberg • and Hope Lange • and Herschel Walker • and Tina Louise • and Ava Gabor • and The Smothers Brothers • and Rick Monday • and Helen Reddy • and Alan Carr

• and Steve Allen • and Jo Anne Foxx • and Red Skelton • and Billy Carter • and Paul Williams • and Newton • and Peter Price • and E.G. Marshall • and Gary Burghoff • and Milton Berle • and Tony Martin • and Jerry Dennis • and Cesar Newman • and Ginger • and Trini Lopez • and • and Macdonald Carey • and Henry Youngman and Rosey Grier • and and Roddy McDowell • Richard Roundtree • and Avery Schreiber • and Nipsey Russell • and Bobby Riggs • and Rudy

The list goes on forever: Top celebrities placed by Ingels Inc. in a successful commercial project.

Are you considering a Personality for something? Why not let us run all your interference. We'll deliver you an instant picture of the *entire celebrity field*. You make your choices, we bring in your star. And you pay us NOTHING EXTRA. Try us. We're good.

INGELS, INC.   (213) 852-0300

• and Roger Miller Worley • and Redd • and Joey Heatherton Billie Jean King • and Sid Ceasar • and Wayne Lawford • and Vincent • and Dorothy Lamour and Barry Sullivan • Dan Haggerty • and Lee Lewis • and Sandy Romero • and Barry Rogers • and June Allyson Aldo Ray • and Lexie Nye • and George Plimpton • and Roger Williams • Linda Day George • and Bobby Morse • and John Newcombe • and Arte Johnson • and Martin Milner • and Vallee • and Arthur Hill

• and George Jessell • and Kaye Ballard • and Morey Amsterdam • and Kevin McCarthy • and Cyd Charisse • and Bert Parks • and Gordon MacRae • and Rex Reed • and Buddy Greco • and Meadowlark Lemon • and Scatman Crothers • and Jackie Vernon • and Ed Byrnes • and John Cappalletti • and Buster Crabbe • and Tracy Austin • and Sheila MacRae • and Dorothy Malone • and Paul Burke • and Julia Meade • and Ann Miller • and Xavier Cugat • and Andrew Sisters • and Dennis Day • and Gisele MacKenzie • and Mickey Dolen • and Chubby Checker • and Ted Bessell • and Fats Domino • and Roger Miller • and Cliff Gorman • and Barnstable Twins • and Lyle Waggoner • and Martin Landau • and Don Adams • and Marty Allen • and Shaun Cassidy • and Steve Lawrence • and Eydie Gorme • and Della Reese • and Ron Palillo • and Rossano Brazzi • and Kevin Dobson • and James Earl Jones • and Merl Haggard • and Red Aurabauch • and Marty Ingels Mother•

Figure 15-6

Figure 15-7

222

Deep in the ad, they coattail-ride; it's a price pitch after all: "Show us your best deal (we may ask you to prove it in writing) and we'll match it." Aha! Parity advertising, not offering to *beat* the price of someone who *will* quote that price, but just to equal it. If the paragraph with this copy were the whole ad, it would be much improved.

Bad ad.

Figure 15-8: *Golle & Holmes*

Here's another "huckster" ad. The word is "Pass." So we show a hockey player passing the puck. We might have shown a football player throwing a pass or a bridge player with no cards higher than a nine, but those aren't as exciting, are they?

This ad ran in *Financial Planning*, and believe it or not, they're talking about passing a professional examination. What if they hadn't used this illustration but had, instead, used a rubber stamp "Pass" on a picture of 100 people with only four of them set off to one side?

Here's a case where the subhead would have been better off without the main head.

Bad ad.

Figure 15-9: *U.S. Postal Service*

It's almost embarrassing to admit the U.S. postal service has created a dynamic, readable ad.

The headline is a powerful grabber: A man identified as the Processing Section Supervisor of Pacific Gas & Electric (somehow more credible than the president of that company) makes a flat, no-ifs-or-buts statement about saving money with Zip+4—and the amount saved seems to be enormous.

An interesting device: Much of the selling copy is inside the coupon, which somehow makes it less pitch and more fact.

Good ad.

Figure 15-10: *Investacorp, Inc.*

Visualize this scenario: Someone asks you a riddle. While

PASS.

96% of our clients passed Series 7. The first time.

We're Golle & Holmes Financial Learning. We wrote the book on self-study courses for the Series 7 exam. PASSTRAK™ for Series 7 is a condensed version of our proven Securities Basic Study Course (SBSC). Vital statistics: SBSC is used by eight of the top ten NYSE brokerage firms. 96% of our SBSC students passed Series 7 the first time. PASSTRAK is a lean, concise version of SBSC.

Stack the odds in your favor with PASSTRAK. You'll learn what you need to know to pass Series 7. The first time.

For complete information on PASSTRAK, call Dick Dwinal at Golle & Holmes today, 1-800-328-8322, Ext. 370; or, in NYC, 1-212-608-6444.

We teach the best.

Golle & Holmes
Financial Learning

© 1984 Golle & Holmes Financial Learning

Figure 15-8

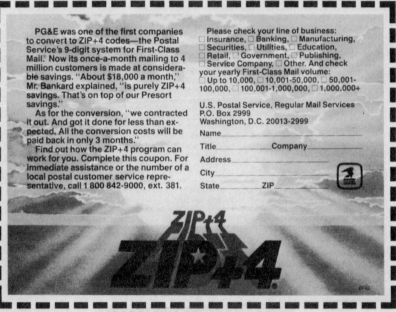

"ZIP+4 codes will save Pacific Gas & Electric Company $200,000 this year."

MAIL THIS COUPON TO SEE HOW YOUR COMPANY CAN SAVE, TOO.

PG&E was one of the first companies to convert to ZIP+4 codes—the Postal Service's 9-digit system for First-Class Mail. Now its once-a-month mailing to 4 million customers is made at considerable savings. "About $18,000 a month," Mr. Bankard explained, "is purely ZIP+4 savings. That's on top of our Presort savings."

As for the conversion, "we contracted it out. And got it done for less than expected. All the conversion costs will be paid back in only 3 months."

Find out how the ZIP+4 program can work for you. Complete this coupon. For immediate assistance or the number of a local postal customer service representative, call 1 800 842-9000, ext. 381.

Please check your line of business:
☐ Insurance, ☐ Banking, ☐ Manufacturing, ☐ Securities, ☐ Utilities, ☐ Education, ☐ Retail, ☐ Government, ☐ Publishing, ☐ Service Company, ☐ Other. And check your yearly First-Class Mail volume:
☐ Up to 10,000, ☐ 10,001-50,000, ☐ 50,001-100,000, ☐ 100,001-1,000,000, ☐ 1,000,000+

U.S. Postal Service, Regular Mail Services
P.O. Box 2999
Washington, D.C. 20013-2999

Name_____

Title_____Company_____

Address_____

City_____

State_____ZIP_____

ADDRESSING TOMORROW TODAY.

© USPS 1984

Figure 15-9

How Can 88% Be More Than 95%?

Some companies promise magical pay-outs...but when the magic is performed by slight of hand and trick mirrors, their unfortunate representatives often discover that the magic is gone.

We pay out 88% of the entire commission allowance on mutual funds, public partnerships and private placement programs. We pay out 80% on stocks, options and bonds after the clearing costs. We don't charge set-up fees or monthly assessments.

We provide the full range of financial products and services, the finest sales aids and backup, full administrative support and superior compliance and due diligence...all available throughout our fifty-state network.

If you are interested in opening an Investacorp O.S.J., phone Scott Sherwood at 800-327-7900 (in Florida, 800-432-0193). We put the magic back.

INVESTACORP, INC.
6839 Main Street, Miami Lakes, FL 33014

Specialists in Servicing the Financial Professional

Figure 15-10

you're puzzling over the answer, he drops dead—and you never do get the answer.

That's the case here. The headline throws down the gauntlet: "How Can 88% Be More Than 95%?" Okay, I give up. How *can* 88% be more than 95%?

The text doesn't give us a clue. In fact, because the word "sleight" in "sleight of hand" is spelled "slight," we're more fogged up than ever. This company pays out 88%. Period. Mystery still at large. 95%? I learned in school it's 7% more than 88%, and I still think my teacher was right.

Bad ad.

Figure 15-11: Chemical Bank

Except for the reverse heading, this ad has almost no production. There's no trickiness in it.

"How to . . . " is always a grabber in a headline. It usually works because whatever follows has to include reader-involvement. In this case, the word "Capitalize" isn't the best because the word itself has multiple meanings.

Read the first paragraph of body copy: straightforward, no-nonsense, absolutely clear. The sales message develops its explanatory aspects without ever losing the reader. Despite the questionable word "Capitalize" . . .

Good ad.

Figure 15-12: Executive Presentation Systems Corporation

This ad, in a trade magazine, is for a company which markets color charts and graphs.

What better way to emphasize the value of charts and graphs when making a presentation than a group of blindfolded decision makers?

Obviously, blindfolded they can't "see" his point. The body copy reemphasizes the argument with statistical evidence and logical support.

Good ad.

HOW TO CAPITALIZE ON THE EQUITY IN YOUR HOME WITHOUT SELLING IT.

If you own a house anywhere in New York, New Jersey or Connecticut, you may borrow from $15,000 to $100,000 from Chemical Bank.

PRESENTING CHEMICAL BANK'S HOME EQUITY CREDITLINE

This is no ordinary home equity loan. It's a revolving line of credit that gives you instant access to the equity you've built up in your home. And you only have to apply once.

If you qualify, you'll have a flexible credit line that offers you control of your financial needs. You'll be able to access the amount of money you need, anytime you need it, just by writing a check ($500 minimum).

You can use the money any way you like and extend your payments out over a 15-year period. And should you choose to pay it off early, there's no pre-payment penalty.

MAXIMUM FLEXIBILITY FOR A MINIMUM OF INTEREST

You may borrow up to 75% of the current value of your home (less the balance of your first mortgage), at a very competitive rate. In fact, for pre-ferred customers, this variable rate is just 1½% above the prime rate as reported by the New York Times. And you pay this interest only on the money you actually borrow.

To capitalize on this idea, simply call one of our second mortgage specialists and find out more about Chemical's Home Equity Creditline. You can reach them at any one of these numbers: (212) 245-8510, (516) 933-0982, or (914) 694-9789 (Mon.-Fri., 9-5). Or just fill out the coupon below.

Please send me more information and an application.

Name_____

Address_____

City_____

State_____Zip_____

Mail to: Chemical Bank
           300 Jericho Quadrangle
           Jericho, NY 11753
           Attn: Home Equity
                 Department
                              NHIS-11/84

CHEMICAL BANK
MEMBER FDIC

© 1984 Chemical Bank.   Equal Opportunity Lender

Figure 15-11

"And, in conclusion, I'm sure you can all see my point."

That's the problem. Without the aid of visuals to illustrate your point, the people you need to persuade *don't* see.

The fact is, visuals help people comprehend and retain *over five times* as much information as they can from verbal presentations alone.

Support graphics give you the edge you need. They let you turn complicated data into easy to digest material, understood at a glance. Decisions critical to your future are easier to make. The total picture is quickly in focus.

Now, with The Executive Presentation System™, the power of color graphics can be yours at the touch of a button. EPS is a computerized desktop system—giving you total control and confidentiality. Easy to operate, EPS quickly and cost-effectively produces full color charts and graphs on transparencies, slides and prints. With eye-opening impact to make you more effective in today's business environment.

See for yourself. Send today for your free brochure. See how color graphics can make your efforts more productive. After all, seeing *is* believing.

FREE. Executive Presentation Systems Brochure.
Mail to: Executive Presentation Systems, Department FP-1,
5854A Peachtree Corners East, Norcross, GA 30092. (404) 447-8401

Name

Title

Firm

Address

City   State   Zip

Phone

Executive Presentation Systems Corporation™
AN INTELLIGENT SYSTEMS COMPANY

Figure 15-12

Figure 15-13

Figure 15-13: Jacques-Miller

Who he?

This man says he's sold on Jacques-Miller, and that should tell me something. What it doesn't tell me is who he is.

Is he the president of General Motors? Chairman of Citibank? The local minister? Jacques-Miller's father? Confusion is compounded because the body copy is written from a "we" point of view, which suggests he's a principal of the company.

If the man is a professional model, this is a lousy idea. If he truly is someone of consequence, identify him and the ad will have some verisimilitude—which it can't without that ID.

Bad ad.

Figure 15-14: Olympus

This is as close to perfect as an ad can be. Why? Because the powerful first headline sentence is followed by a doubly powerful second sentence, which retrospectively adds even more power to the first sentence.

The body copy is loaded with specifics. Here's one ad that doesn't crow about product superiority and never offers any proof.

Another proof implicit in this ad: It proves an advertiser doesn't have to spend a ton of money overproducing an ad to make it effective. Obviously, this is a . . .

Good ad.

Figure 15-15: Miller Displays

Oops! Somebody never learned the Second Law.

This advertiser has staged a scene which makes him look foolish. This can happen when one falls in love with an idea and doesn't know how to illustrate the idea so someone else can understand it.

The result is the impression that the advertiser is the one who doesn't "have all his oars in the water." He misspells the word "preceded," but this isn't the most grievous error: Looking foolish is.

Bad ad.

There is only one other 35mm program camera that is made as well as this one.

And that camera costs four times as much and can't do half the things that the new Olympus OM-2S Program camera can.

Go to your dealer. Ask to see the world's most expensive program camera and the new Olympus OM-2S Program.

Ask which one accepts over 300 lenses and system components for possibilities impossible to outgrow.

Ask which one automatically fine-tunes exposure *during* exposure, with and without flash, for pictures other programs can't capture.

Ask which one brings true spot metering to manual mode for creative control you've never before known.

As you'll see, while no other program camera offers any of these advantages, the new Olympus OM-2S Program offers them all.

Which is astounding in a camera that's over a quarter lighter, and smaller than the most expensive program camera in the world.

And roughly a quarter of its cost.

For details, see your Olympus dealer. Or write Olympus, Dept. 25, Woodbury, NY 11797. In Canada: W. Carsen Co. Ltd., Toronto.

OLYMPUS
There is no longer a choice.

Figure 15-14

Figure 15-15

Figure 15-16: Leading Edge Products, Inc.

This is one of the best comparative ads I've seen, and it's especially good when we realize that it comes from the murky world of computer software.

Leading Edge tells a story—how the U.S. Department of Agriculture came to make its decision about which word processing program to use. The story has to be true, because a government agency is involved. What verisimilitude!

The ad names specific competitors and, without damning them, quietly makes the point of superiority. We believe every word.

Good ad.

Figure 15-17: The Paddington Corp.

What this fellow seems to be saying in a color bleed page parallels the ill-fated "Drink Schlitz or I'll kill you!" campaign. I get the impression that if we try to hurry him, he'll beat us about the head and shoulders with his cane.

I must admit, I don't get it. The name of the scotch is unusual enough to be mnemonic in itself. Copy such as "So it captures your attention. And then rewards your interest" doesn't seem to have been written about this whiskey.

I think, too, that ten minutes' cogitation would have resulted in a better slogan than "It's worth a lot of time." This ad isn't terrible, but think how much better it would have been with a comprehensible copy-platform.

Bad ad.

Figure 15-18: Eastern Air Lines

All right, let's think of the key benefit of a frequent flyer program. Free travel, right?

But if that travel is from Cape Canaveral to Edwards Air Force Base, by way of a month in space, we might have the right stuff but not a benefit we'd want.

No one yet has climbed out of a space capsule saying, "Gee, I didn't have to do a thing to get that fascinating ride."

A BUREAUCRAT'S GUIDE TO WORD PROCESSING

Now, if it were you or I and we wanted a word processing program for our IBM-type PC, we'd probably stop off at our local computer store and simply diddle with a few.

You and I, however, are not the U.S. Department of Agriculture.

(Nor any of its permutations of subsystems like the Economic Research Service, National Resources Economics Division, Data Services Center, etc., etc.)

So when the USDA told ERS to tell NRED and DSC to look into a truckload of w.p. programs for all their PCs, the last thing they wanted was simple diddling. Their dedicated Wangs and Lexitrons were far too few to handle their needs, their IBM® PCs weren't compatible with them anyway, and nobody really, quantifiably, knew from word processing with a personal computer.

Definitely not a diddling-mode condition.

As they put it in The Exchange, an internally distributed publication of the Department of Agriculture: "A needs assessment showed that, in the long-term, a word processing system is needed that can increase word processing capability and also be compatible with ERS' Long Range Information Management goals."

Well. "Needs assessment" led swiftly to "procurement action," which galloped into an "objective review" of the eight top-rated PC programs on the market (as compiled by The Ratings Book published by Software Digest), along with Wordstar® and Display Write 2, because they had some around.

Thus armed with the names, the final evaluators (a team of secretaries from NRED who would be the primary users of the PC software) became armed with each of the programs, along with checklists to record such things as ease of use, advanced features, and similarity to their existing dedicated equipment.

The first to be eliminated from the prospect list were Office Writer™ and Samna™, since they're copy-protected and couldn't be transferred to hard disks.

Next, IBM's Display Write 2: because it's "not compatible with other software used in ERS (like Lotus 1-2-3," dBASE II® etc.)" and it's "full of confusing menu options and cryptic error messages." Au revoir IBM.

Then, three more, for a variety of reasons.

Which left the following:
Volkswriter® Deluxe™
MultiMate™
Leading Edge™

Volkswriter Deluxe? "Too complicated and confusing." Not "easy to learn or use."

MultiMate? Not bad. It actually tied the winner in a few categories.

The winner being the one that won 82% of the votes in the Ease of Use/Ease of Learning categories. The one about which they said, "The ability to store deleted text and automatic document backup features were both highly desirable." The one they thought they'd quickly "be able to use . . . for their day-to-day word processing tasks."

The whole process took some three months of work by people in DSC to support the NRED in its work with the ERS and DSC to make the world a better place for the USDA.

But the results were well worth the wait. Because at last they've solved their word-processing problems . . . "With Leading Edge!"

THESE ARE THE PACKAGES THE COMMITTEE EVALUATED:

THESE WERE THE FINALISTS:

THIS WAS THE WINNER: LEADING EDGE™ LEADING EDGE WORD PROCESSING

LEADING EDGE PRODUCTS, INC. LEADING EDGE SOFTWARE DIVISION. 21 HIGHLAND CIRCLE, NEEDHAM MA 02194 TEL 800-343-1436 (617) 449-4655 HELP HOTLINE 800-523-HELP

IBM is a registered trademark of International Business Machines

Circle number 4 on inquiry card

Figure 15-16

Figure 15-17

Imagine how far they could have gone with a Frequent Traveler Bonus Program like ours.

If you fly a lot on business, join Eastern's Frequent Traveler Bonus Program. Even the shortest trip earns you 1,000 bonus miles toward free travel to over 90 cities in the U.S., 17 cities in Europe, 16 Caribbean islands, South America, Mexico and more. So join now. And land in the most exciting places in the world.

EASTERN
We earn our wings every day

© 1984 Eastern Air Lines, Inc.

Figure 15-18

It's a mismatch with any frequent flyer program because we don't sense that we're getting something for nothing.

We all understand what Eastern has done here: used the picture they felt would get the most attention. Photographs of Disney World and Rio are old-hat. But this one is skewed from the benefit point. Regrettably, it's a . . .

Bad ad.

Figure 15-19: Bi-Tech Enterprises Inc.

If you see a single redeeming feature in this ad, you must be the person who wrote it.

The word "Bi" has many connotations, and this may have been in the mind of the writer. The ridiculous illustration isn't the only weakness. Read the headlines and try to turn it into user-benefit.

In my opinion this ad is the poorest of all the examples in this section, and it proves that anyone can write an ad, albeit not necessarily with any success.

Bad ad.

Figure 15-20: Borden, Inc.

Great copy appears to be simple.

So it is here, even including the very word "simple." The copy-platform is that the cheesecake is sinfully good and simple to make, with Eagle Brand condensed milk.

The first paragraph is a classic: "Don't tell anyone. But this sinfully delicious, creamy rich cheesecake is a snap to make!"

To prove it, the ad includes the entire recipe. Even with the big, mouth-watering photograph and the recipe, the ad doesn't appear cluttered.

Good ad.

Figure 15-21: Southern Floridabanc Savings Assocation

Huh?

If this ad were for United Van Lines the headline would make sense. For a savings & loan, it's peculiar.

Figure 15-19

Figure 15-20

Now we're your coast-to-coast Moving Company.

And we're celebrating our expansion with our best rates ever on 6-month CD's and Gold Coast Super N.O.W. accounts.

With the opening of our new branches in Sarasota and Lehigh Acres, we've reached a very special milestone in Moving Company history: we've now got Florida covered with great rates and services, from the east coast to the west.

To celebrate, we're offering very special, limited-time rates on two of our most popular accounts: our 6-month certificate of deposit and our high interest, Gold Coast Super N.O.W. checking account.

Naturally, we have to limit an offer like this. So come in soon. And come out with a coast-to-coast smile on your face.

Rates subject to change without notice. Federal regulations require a substantial penalty for early withdrawal of time accounts.

Southern Florida's highest yielding 6-month certificate of deposit!

YIELD:

11.96%

RATE:

11.30%

$1,000 minimum deposit.

Maximum interest on checking with our Gold Coast Super N.O.W. account!

9.5%

$2,500 minimum deposit.

Southern Floridabanc Savings Association

The Moving Company

MAIN OFFICE: **RIVIERA BEACH,** 1217 E. Blue Heron Blvd., 845-1000
BOCA RATON, 160 W. Camino Real, 368-0905
PALM BEACH GARDENS, 1963 PGA Blvd., (Just west of U.S. 1), 845-1000

Figure 15-21

241

The copy in the ad says the institution has "reached a very special milestone in Moving Company history." That milestone—covering one state "with great rates and services, from the east coast to the west," is thin even for the in-group of which the reader isn't part.

Only the officers of the s&l care about covering the state—and nowhere do we have evidence that the organization has more than three offices. The important message is high-yielding certificates of deposit, and why this advertiser wastes communications dollars with "moving company" double-entendres is beyond me.

Bad ad.

Figure 15-22: Ford Motor Company

Suppose you're visiting a car dealer. "Why is your car better than Chevy, Plymouth, or Renault?" you ask.

"Because at Ford, quality is job 1."

Wouldn't you look elsewhere for your car?

I know Ford has used this theme incessantly. But think to yourself: Can this ad, without a single specific in it (in fact, Ford doesn't even give us an example to chew on), compete with any automobile ad which does offer specifics? If a local dealer ran this ad, would it fill his showroom?

Bad ad.

Figure 15-23: Renault

While we're knocking automobile ads, figure this one out.

Renault says it's a "remarkable" car because—get this— it comes "from a country that designed the Concorde." If this were a college course in logic, the argument would rate a solid "D." (Incidentally, England also qualifies, because the Concorde was a joint French-English project. Now we can include not only Peugeot, Simca, and Citroen but Jaguar, Triumph, and Sunbeam.

Deep in the ad, too technically presented, are specifics of Renault superiority. But the whole ad is just a group of words strung together, and the final line—"Where great engineering lives in great design"—is ultimate proof.

Bad ad.

Quality is Job 1

"To eliminate squeaks and rattles, you have to pinpoint them first."

JOE SEIDEL
Product Design Engineer

At Ford Motor Company, we go to extraordinary lengths to get rid of squeaks and rattles.

From the prototype stage onwards, we run test models on a brutal "rolling road" shaker machine, while an engineer like Joe Seidel pinpoints the source of the noise with a sensitive stethoscope. The engineers then propose a remedy which, if it proves successful, is applied to every similar model on the assembly line.

There's a new spirit at Ford Motor Company. And everyone is involved—from the man in the corner office to the people on the assembly line.

This dedication to quality is already paying off. Overall, a 25% improvement in quality since 1980, as reported by new car owners.

At Ford Motor Company, Quality is Job 1.

Ford
Mercury
Lincoln
Ford Trucks

Figure 15-22

WHEN THERE IS A CAR FROM A COUNTRY THAT DESIGNED THE CONCORDE...

...a car designed by the first people to fly so far into the future... why drive an ordinary car? When you can drive the remarkable Renault 18i.

It begins with a philosophy of design that makes Renault Europe's leading builder of cars: a truly fine automobile is not a collection of parts; it is a series of interdependent systems based on total system design.

Example: Renault designed the 18i long travel suspension as part of a system that includes chassis design, bio-mechanically tuned seating, front and rear anti-sway bars and rack and pinion steering.

Example: The 18i total system design matches a lightweight front wheel drive system to a 1.6 litre engine and a Bosch L-Jetronic fuel injection system. The result is surprisingly responsive performance with remarkable fuel efficiency.*

37 HWY* EST   **26** EST MPG

*Compare these 1981 EPA estimates with estimated mpg for other cars. Your actual mileage depends on speed, trip length and weather. Actual highway mileage will probably be lower.

And now every Renault is covered by American Motors' exclusive Buyer Protection Plan, the only plan with a full 12-month/12,000-mile warranty.

Knowing these facts, there's no excuse for you to drive an ordinary car when you could drive the Renault 18i.

Available at more than 1300 Renault and American Motors Dealers in sedan and Sportswagon models.

◊RENAULT
American Motors ◢◢

Where great engineering lives in great design

Figure 15-23

Figure 15-24: Metropolitan Transportation Authority

This little ad (⅓ page) ran in *Frequent Flyer* magazine.

What a perfect match! Anyone who has had the experience of trying to get a cab when it's raining in New York City will understand, appreciate, and identify with this ad.

Using a cartoon makes the ad more appealing than a photograph would have made it; it can't turn sour.

Copy in the ad is 100% specific. Price, length of time, hours the train runs, and the phone number for more information—all are presented forthrightly. No one was showing off in print.

Good ad.

Figure 15-24

Figure 15-25: MBSI

I don't get it.

This ad is hard to read, because the original has red type over a red-brown background and also reverses type from a light-colored background. Still, straining, I can read it—but I don't get it.

What on earth does a violin-maker have to do with business software? The picture takes up half the ad, and I begrudge this space-allocation because the type is set so small it's hard to see.

We have the explanatory line, of course. It's the second line of body copy: "There are no inexperienced master violin makers. And so it is with software."

I submit, that's about as weak a copy-platform as anyone ever worked hard to noncreate. The picture is at odds with the sales message, and the message itself—there is no substitute for experience—is a cliché in the first place.

Bad ad.

Conclusion

If you're in constant disagreement about the effectiveness of these sample ads, ask yourself two questions:

1. Are you in awe of major advertisers and feel their approach is unassailable *because* they're major advertisers?
2. Are you admiring cleverness instead of salesmanship?

If you have to choose between being clever and being a communicator, I hope you don't hesitate for one second. Cleverness is an asset to the individual who has it; if you're clever, God gave you a leg up, and you have a better chance of being bright than the dull clod in the next seat.

But never let boredom with the limitations of the advertising media drive you to cleverness for the sake of cleverness. Invariably, when you do that, some less-clever advertiser will just present the beneficial facts and outadvertise you.

The overriding purpose of this book is to take the mystery

REALWORLD EXPERIENCE

THERE IS NO SUBSTITUTE

RealWorld™ Business Software For Most Popular Microcomputers

ACCOUNTS RECEIVABLE□ORDER ENTRY□INVENTORY CONTROL
SALES ANALYSIS□ACCOUNTS PAYABLE□GENERAL LEDGER□PAYROLL

Whatever the product or service, it takes experience to produce quality and lasting value.

There are no inexperienced master violin makers. And so it is with software.

The staff at RealWorld Corporation have been creating packaged software products for nearly ten years. During that time, over 40,000 users have kept us in touch with reality.

We don't sell "disposable software". We haven't tried for the fanciest packaging. We won't promise our products will "walk off your shelves" without some help from you.

But we will say this: become a RealWorld Software reseller. If you don't agree we're providing top quality and lasting value, or if you're not satisfied for any reason, we'll refund your money. (Subject to details in our reseller agreements.)

Self running demos and dealer training kits are now available.

For more information, call the 800 number of our office nearest you.

mbsi™ *A Division of RealWorld Corporation*

DOVER ROAD, CHICHESTER, NH 03263

603/798-5700 TOLL FREE: 800-255-1115

California: 800-441-1777 Western U. S.: 800-321-1777

Figure 15-25

out of advertising so anyone can understand it and handle it effectively without overpaying. Effective advertising is no more difficult than selling something to a skeptical stranger who lets you know he's considering several of your competitors as well as you. Would have you have a "muscle-girl" hold your product or show him a picture of a violin-maker—or make a silly joke, or dare him to understand what your benefits are? Or would you *specify* the benefits of doing business with you?

Keep your dignity and let your advertising target keep his. Tell him what he wants to know, without puffery and without making nervous jokes. It's the road to communications heaven.

APPENDIX 1

Common Advertising Terms

Ben Day   A patterned screen used to give texture to the background.

B.R.E.   Business reply envelope.

E.T.   Electrical transcription. This is a radio term that originally referred to 16-inch, 33 rpm records, but now embraces almost any type of recording. Most spots today are recorded on reel-to-reel tape and transferred to cassettes, which permit split-second cuing.

F.S.I.   Free-standing insert, a preprinted section delivered by the advertiser to a newspaper, which includes it on a specific day.

Halftone   Photograph reproduced in printing by use of a screen/dot pattern. A newspaper will have a coarse halftone screen of about 65 lines per square inch; most magazines printed on machine-finish paper take a 133-line screen; fine enamel papers can handle up to 200-line screens.

Handsche; I.P.I.; Pantone; P.M.S.   Names of the leading standard color charts that enable any printer to match, exactly, by number, the color requested.

Kilohertz   The replacement name for kilocycles. Refers to the frequency of A.M. radio stations. The longest waves are 530 kilohertz; the shortest A.M. waves, highest on the dial, are 1,600. F.M. broadcasts on "megahertz," shorter waves from 88 to 108.

Letterpress, offset   Printing processes. Most advertising work today is offset.

Line   An obsolete reference to the depth of an ad. There are 14 lines to an inch, although this has nothing to do with how many actual lines of type are set. A 56-line ad is four inches deep; a 100-line ad is a little longer than seven inches.

Mergenthaler   Inventor of the linotype, which is seldom used to set type today. The Mergenthaler Company is one of a number of competitors in modern computer-typesetting.

Merge-Purge   Electronic cross-checking of mailing lists to prevent duplications.

Pica   Horizontal type measurement, $\frac{1}{6}$ of an inch.

Point   A term used to describe type size. There are 72 points to an inch. Thus, if you want type $\frac{1}{2}$-inch high, you would ask for 36-point type; if you want 9 lines of type to an inch, set "solid," you would ask for 8-point type ($8 \times 9 = 72$).

R.O.P., R.O.S.   Run-of-paper or Run-of-station. The medium runs your ad anywhere it likes; in exchange, you pay less.

Rate card   Description of charges for space by publications or for time by the electronic media. Most broadcast stations and magazines have only one rate card, which means that ads cost the same whether or not an advertising agency places them. Most newspapers have two rate cards, a local or retail rate card, and a national or general rate card. The national rate card is 25 to 35 percent higher than the local rate, for reasons that are discussed in this book.

Reverse   A block of type that is, literally, reversed from the normal black type on a white background. The background is black; the type, white. It is also possible in color ads to have a color reverse, in which the background is a color and the type is reversed out in white.

SDRS   Sandard Rate and Data Service, which publishes rate schedules for most media in the U.S., and some in Canada.

SMSA   Standard Metropolitan Statistical Area—the agreed perimeter and population of each city, with suburbs.

Tintblock   A light color or a gray tone, usually used to give some life to an area of a page or as a background for types or pictures.

Unmod   Unmodulated sound-track for a television commercial. This means there is no sound on the track. Because the sound runs 26 frames ahead of the picture, film television spots should have 36 frames— 1½ seconds—of unmod before the sound starts. (A list of television terms is in Appendix 2.)

525-line screen The U.S. standard for television. In other words, a television picture is made up of 525 lines. Britain has a 625-line system, which gives a substantially better picture quality. There is also an 800-line screen, but it tends to break up on the slightest provocation.

APPENDIX 2

Common Television Terms

COOKIE	Cucaloris—a sheet of metal or cardboard with irregular cut-outs. Placed in front of a light aimed at the background, it changes a solid tone into patterns and shapes.
CU	Close-up.
DISS	Dissolve.
ECU	Extreme close-up.
FREEZE	Single frame of scene held without motion.
LIMBO	"Featureless" background.
LS	Long shot.
MCU	Medium close-up.
MLS	Medium long shot.
MS	Medium shot.
PAN	Move camera laterally.
SFX	Sound effect.
SUPER	Superimposition—a caption superimposed over a scene.
SYNC	Synchronous sound
TILT	Move camera vertically.
TRUCK	Move camera dolly parallel to the set.
VO	Voice over.
ZOOM	Adjust camera lens to give closer or wider view (zoom in, zoom out).
2-SHOT	Shot including two people.

APPENDIX 3

Samples of Advertising Agency Forms and Control Materials

You're free to copy any of the forms on the following pages, substituting your own name, address, and phone number. A suggestion: Every communication with media should have your address and phone number on it.

communicomp inc.

Box 15725, Plantation, Florida 33318

(305) 473-2044

ORDER **No.**

☐ IF CHECKED HERE, THIS IS
    AN INSERTION ORDER

☐ IF CHECKED HERE, THIS IS
    A SPACE CONTRACT

DATE

⌐ TO PUBLISHER OF   ⌐ REPRESENTATIVE

PLEASE PUBLISH ADVERTISING OF
FOR

——— SPACE ———   ——— TIMES ———   ——— DATES OF INSERTION ———

CLOSING:

POSITION

COPY	CUTS	KEY	

ADDITIONAL INSTRUCTIONS   SIZE

Please do not back up coupon with another coupon ←

RATE   CIRCULATION   ON SALE

LESS AGENCY COMMISSION ON GROSS	LESS CASH DISCOUNT ON NET	LEFT HAND COUPON	RIGHT HAND COUPON

SPECIAL INSTRUCTIONS:

PLEASE
ACKNOWLEDGE

After publication, please send
one complete copy of this issue
and two tear sheets of this ad
to us.

order issued by

Headline, Key Word, or Identification:

This is an insertion order. The information on it does more than tell the publication or broadcast station what you want; it prevents misunderstandings. If you have misinformation about rates, ad sizes, or when an issue closes, the publication should spot the error and notify you. I say "should" because sometimes when an ad arrives right at deadline, the medium will rush the ad into production, ignoring the insertion order—and permalizing any mistakes on it.

COPY   COPY   COPY

client:

date: file:

description:

communicomp

Box 15725. Plantation. Florida 33318

(305) 473-2044

This is a copy sheet. It has an implicit advantage over a plain piece of paper: At a glance one can identify the content. If you write on a word processor or computer, use the "file" category for code letters or numbers that will enable you to recall the copy without a lengthy search.

MEDIA SCHEDULE

Client:

Date:

communicomp
Box 15725, Plantation, Florida 33318
(305) 473-2044

Publication	Issue Size	Cost	Remarks

approved: _____

This is a media schedule sheet. When planning a campaign, whether for a year or for a week, a form like this makes it possible to see on a single page what you're running and what it costs. If someone else has final budget approval, a signature on the "approved" line will save arguments—and maybe jobs.

Client:

Date:

Contact:

Billing information:

communicomp

Box 15725, Plantation. Florida 33318

(305) 473-2044

THIS IS: __ Creative
__ Production
__ Media

JOB IS DUE:

Describe work to be done:

Is background information attached? (If not, please give background information below.)

This is a work order. The purpose of this form is to give yourself assurance, as the job starts, that all necessary materials and information are on hand. The same work order form can be used for creative, production, or media.

communicomp

job no._____

client:_____

Box 15725, Plantation, Florida 33318
(305) 473-2044

_____individual job basis

_____monthly

_____other (_____)

date	type of expense	by (init.)	billable?	remarks

scheduled billing date _____

actual billing date _____

On the project cost sheet, enter activity on the particular job. If someone phones and says, "Add a background to the photograph," note who called to say it and when the call came in. This is your record of activity—when you ordered type or art, and from whom; who said and did what; and what your own total costs were. You can identify costs that otherwise might be buried forever. The blank line at mid-upper right is for the title of the job.

Budget-Stretcher Checklist

This article, "Ten Ways to Stretch Your Advertising Budget," by Robert W. Bly, is reprinted with permission; it originally appeared in *Business Marketing* Magazine.

I reprint it here because it's a good final checklist of ways to save money without sacrificing the integrity of your message.

Ten Ways to Stretch Your Advertising Budget

by Robert W. Bly

Most business-to-business advertisers have smaller ad budgets than their counterparts in consumer marketing. Here are 10 ways to get more out of your advertising dollars—without detracting from the quality and quantity of your ads and promotions. In some cases, these ideas can even *enhance* the effectiveness of your marketing efforts.

ONE *Use your ads for more than just space advertising.* Ads are expensive to produce and expensive to run. But there are ways of getting your advertising message in your prospect's hands at a fraction of the cost of space advertising.

The least expensive is to order an ample supply of reprints and distribute them to customers and prospects every chance you get. When you send literature in response to an inquiry, include a copy of the ad in the package. This reminds a prospect of the reason he responded in the first place and reinforces the original message.

Distribute ads internally to other departments—engineering, production, sales, customer service, and R&D—to keep them up to date on your latest marketing and promotional efforts. Make sure your salespeople receive an extra supply of reprints and are encouraged to include a reprint when they write to or visit their customers.

Turn the ad into a product data sheet by adding technical specifications and additional product information to the back of the ad reprint. This eliminates the expense of creating a new layout from scratch. And it makes good advertising sense, because the reader gets double exposure to your advertising message.

Ad reprints can be used as inexpensive direct mail pieces. You can mail the reprints along with a reply card and a sales letter. Unlike the ad, which is "cast in concrete," the letter is easily and inexpensively tailored to specific markets and customer groups.

If you've created a series of ads on the same product or product line, publish bound reprints of the ads as a product brochure. This tactic increases prospect exposure to the series and is less expensive than producing a brand new brochure.

If your ads provide valuable information of a general nature, you can offer reprints as free educational material to companies in your industry. Or, if the ad presents a striking visual, you can offer reprints that are suitable for framing.

Reuse your ads again and again. You will save money—and increase frequency—in the process.

TWO *If something works, stick with it.* Too many industrial marketers scrap their old ads and create new ones because they're bored with their current campaign.

That's a waste. You shouldn't create new ads or promotions if your existing ones are still accurate and effective. You should run your ads for as long as your customers read and react to them.

How long can ads continue to get results? The Ludlow Corp. ran an ad for its erosion-preventing Soil Saver mesh 41 times in the same journal. After 11 years it pulled more inquiries per issue than when it was first published in 1966.

If a concept still has selling power but the ad contains dated information, update the existing ad—don't throw it out and start from scratch. This approach isn't fun for the ad manager or the agency, but it does save money.

THREE *Don't over-present yourself.* A strange thing happens to industrial advertisers when they get a little extra money in the ad budget: they see fancy four-color brochures, gold-embossed mailers, and fat annual reports produced by Fortune 500 firms. Then they say, "This stuff sure looks great—why don't we do some brochures like this?"

That's a mistake. The look, tone, and image of your promotions should be dictated by your product and your market—not by what other companies in other businesses put out.

Producing literature that's too fancy for its purpose and its audience is a waste of money. And it can even *hurt* sales—your prospects will look at your overdone literature and wonder whether you really understand your market and its needs.

FOUR *Use "modular" product literature.* One common advertising problem is how to promote a single product to many small, diverse markets. Each market has different needs and will buy the product for different reasons. But on your budget, you can't afford to create a separate brochure for each of these tiny market segments.

The solution is "modular literature." This means creating a basic brochure layout that has sections capable of being tailored to meet specific market needs.

After all, most sections of the brochure—technical specifications, service, company background, product operation, product features—will be the same regardless of the audience. Only a few sections, such as benefits of the product to the user and typical applications, need to be tailored to specific readers.

In a modular layout, standard sections remain the same, but new copy can be typeset and stripped in for each market-specific section of the brochure. This way, you can create many different market-specific pieces of literature on the same product using the same basic layout, mechanicals, artwork, and plates.

Significant savings in time and money will result.

FIVE *Use article reprints as supplementary litera-*
ture. Ad managers are constantly bombarded by requests for "incidental" pieces of product literature. Engineers want data sheets explaining some minor technical feature in great detail. Reps selling to small, specialized markets want special literature geared to their particular audience. And each company salesperson wants support literature that fits his or her individual sales pitch. But the ad budget can only handle the major pieces of product literature. Not enough time or money exists to satisfy everybody's requests for custom literature.

The solution is to use article reprints as supplementary sales literature. Rather than spend a bundle producing highly technical or application-specific pieces, have your sales and technical staff write articles on these special topics. Then, place the articles with the appropriate journals.

Article reprints can be used as inexpensive literature and carry more credibility than self-produced promotional pieces. You don't pay for typesetting or production of the article. Best of all, the article is free advertising for your firm.

SIX *Explore inexpensive alternatives for generating leads.*
Many smaller firms judge ad effectiveness solely by the number of leads generated. They are not concerned with building image or recognition; they simply count bingo-card inquiries.

If that describes your approach to advertising, perhaps you shouldn't be advertising in the first place. Not that lead-generation isn't a legitimate use of space advertising. But if leads are all you're after, there are cheaper ways to get them.

New-product releases lead the list as the most economical method of generating leads. Once, for less than $100, I wrote, printed, and distributed a new-product release to a hundred trade journals. Within six months, the release had been picked up by 35 magazines and generated 2,500 bingo-card inquiries.

Your second-best inquiry-generator is the direct-action postcard pack. You can write and typeset your own postcard for less than $200. And running the card in a trade journal's post-card pack generally costs from $800 to $1,200. But that same $800 to $1,200 would probably buy only a sixth or a third of a page in the magazine.

I've seen a single postcard mailing pull nearly 500 inquiries, and you'd have a hard time doing that with the average one-third-page ad.

SEVEN Don't "overbook" outside creative
talent. Hire freelancers and consultants whose credentials—and fees—fit the job and the budget.

Top advertising photographers, for example, get $1,000 a day or more. This may be worth the fee for a corporate ad running in *Forbes* or *Business Week*. But it's overkill for the employee newsletter or a publicity shot. Many competent photographers can shoot a good black-and-white publicity photo for $200 or even less.

When you hire consultants, writers, artists, or photographers, you should look for someone whose level of expertise and cost fits the task at hand.

EIGHT *Do it yourself.* Routine tasks, such as
mailing publicity releases, duplicating slides, or retyping media schedules can be done cheaper in-house than outside. Save the expensive agency or consultant for tasks that really require their expertise.

Even if you don't have an in-house advertising department, consider hiring a full-time administrative assistant to handle the detail work involved in managing your company's advertising. This is a more economical solution than farming administrative work out to the agency or doing it yourself.

NINE *Get the most of existing art, photography,*
and copy. Photos, illustrations, layouts, and even copy created for one promotion can often be lifted and reused in other pieces to significantly reduce creative costs. For example, copy created for a corporate image ad can be used as the introduction to the annual report.

Also, you can save rough layouts, thumbnail sketches, headlines, and concepts rejected for one project and use them in future ads, mailings, and promotions.

TEN *Pay vendors on time.* You'll save money by tak-
ing advantage of discounts and avoiding late changes when you pay vendor invoices on time. And, you'll gain goodwill that can result in better service and fairer prices on future projects. ∎

Index